The New Northern Irish Politics?

Also by Jonathan Tonge

Northern Ireland: Conflict and Change
Sinn Fein and the SDLP: From Alienation to Participation
  (with Gerard Murray)
Peace or War? Understanding the Peace Process in Ireland (edited with
  Chris Gilligan)

The New Northern Irish Politics?

Jonathan Tonge

Published 2005 by
PALGRAVE MACMILLAN
Houndmills, Basingstoke, Hampshire RG21 6XS and
175 Fifth Avenue, New York, N.Y. 10010
Companies and representatives throughout the world

PALGRAVE MACMILLAN is the global academic imprint of the Palgrave Macmillan division of St. Martin's Press LLC and of Palgrave Macmillan Ltd. Macmillan® is a registered trademark in the United States, United Kingdom and other countries. Palgrave is a registered trademark in the European Union and other countries.

ISBN 0–333–94832–7 hardback
ISBN 0–333–94833–5 paperback

This book is printed on paper suitable for recycling and made from fully managed and sustained forest sources.

A catalogue record for this book is available from the British Library.

A catalog record for this book is available from the Library of Congress.

10   9   8   7   6   5   4   3   2   1
14 13 12 11 10 09 08 07 06 05

Printed in China

For Connell

Contents

List of Tables and Figures   viii

Acknowledgements   xi

List of Abbreviations   xiii

Introduction   1

1 **The Conflict**   9

2 **The Solution? The Logic of the Good Friday Agreement**   31

3 **Unionism New and Old**   59

4 **The Diminishing Centre Ground: Whither the
Third Tradition**   82

5 **New 'Green' Politics: Growing Electoral Dominance
by Sinn Fein**   102

6 **The Big Tent at Stormont: The Northern Ireland Assembly**   123

7 **Never the Sum of its Parts? The Executive**   149

8 **Cross-Border and Confederal Dimensions**   163

9 **Civil Society and the Problem of Sectarianism**   188

10 **A New Policing Service?**   219

11 **The International Context**   237

Conclusion   255

Bibliography   266

Index   279

List of Tables and Figures

Tables

2.1	The Good Friday Agreement referendums, 1998	35
2.2	The application of consociational principles in the Good Friday Agreement	39
2.3	Perceived implications of the Good Friday Agreement among party members in terms of it being a step towards a united Ireland	42
2.4	Attitudes towards the idea that the best solution for Northern Ireland would be power sharing with cross-border bodies	42
2.5	Constitutional preferences in Northern Ireland	49
3.1	Self-ascribed national identity of UUC members	64
3.2	UUP–DUP electoral rivalry, 1997–2004	66
3.3	Support for the Good Friday Agreement by Orange Order Members of the Ulster Unionist Council	71
3.4	OLS regression of the ballot on Orange Order voting rights, by Orange Order membership and leadership contest vote, 2000	72
3.5	Logistic regression of Trimble–Smyth voting in the Ulster Unionist Party leadership election, 2000	73
3.6	UUC members' views on dual majority voting and power sharing with cross-border bodies	75
3.7	Potential UUC vote transfers to other unionist parties, according to yes or no votes for the 1998 Good Friday Agreement	78
3.8	UUC members' attitudes to political integration into the United Kingdom, by GFA vote in the 1998 referendum	79
3.9	Summary of policy positions in the UUC and DUP	80
4.1	Alliance members' national identity by religious affilation	87

4.2   Alliance visions and the Good Friday Agreement   88
4.3   Alliance Party electoral support, 1973–2003   89
4.4   Descriptive statistics (means and percentages) for the
      explanatory variables in the Alliance and UUC
      comparison   95
4.5   Significance of age in respect of the Alliance Party's
      possible redesignation as unionist   96
5.1   SDLP members' perceptions of the party   104
5.2   Party label correlations among SDLP members   105
5.3   Scalar attitudinal indicators among SDLP members   107
5.4   SDLP members' views on the best solution for
      Northern Ireland's constitutional future   110
5.5   Share of nationalist electoral votes, 1982–2004   112
6.1   Composition of the Northern Ireland Assembly,
      1998–2003   125
6.2   Stages of the legislative process in the Northern
      Ireland Assembly   135
6.3   Northern Ireland Assembly committees prior to
      suspension in 2002   137
6.4   Protestants' views on whether the Northern Ireland
      Assembly and executive did a good job in the
      day-to-day running of Northern Ireland   141
6.5   Protestants' views on the Northern Ireland Assembly
      being suspended for a number of years   142
6.6   Party members' views on whether a devolved Northern
      Ireland Assembly would improve local services   144
8.1   Priorities of the British–Irish Council   170
8.2   Attitudes towards cross-border cooperation between
      Northern Ireland and the Irish Republic, by area
      of cooperation   173
8.3   EU Structural Fund programmes 2000–4   179
9.1   Paramilitary violence, January 1998 to July 2002   191
9.2   Sectoral representation in the Civic Forum   203
10.1 Public views on whether reform of the police in
      Northern Ireland had gone far enough, by religious
      denomination   228
10.2 Views of the members of the main pro-GFA
      parties on the Patten recommendations for police
      reforms   229

10.3   Perceptions of the treatment of Protestants and
       Catholics by the RUC/PSNI   230
10.4   An implementation deficit? The Patten Report and
       implementation of its proposals, 1999–2001   232

Figures

3.1   Voting by age in the Ulster Unionist Party leadership
       contest, 2000   69
4.1   Relative positions of party memberships along the
       nationalist–unionist dimension   98

Acknowledgements

A large number of debts have been incurred in the production of this book. The European Studies Research Institute at the University of Salford has always been conducive to research, and has provided considerable financial support. In 2003 a generous scholarship from St John's College, University of Oxford, facilitated completion of the book. Steven Kennedy at Palgrave Macmillan has been unfailing in his patience and support. I am also grateful to an anonymous reviewer for very helpful comments on a draft of this book. The Economic and Social Research Council provided generous support via three projects: R000222668, New Nationalism in Northern Ireland; L327253058, The Role of 'Extra Constitutional' Parties in the Northern Ireland Assembly (with Professor James McAuley); and R000223414, Third Traditions in Northern Ireland.

At Salford, particular thanks are due to Dr Jocelyn Evans. Dr Sharam Taromsari, Dr Catherine McGlynn, Andy Mycock, Jennie Coates and Dermot Zafar all provided useful ideas, as did Professor James McAuley (Huddersfield) and Dr Gerard Murray (Edinburgh). Paul Bew (Queen's) provided consistent help in facilitating visits to Belfast by Salford staff and students. Dr Peter Shirlow (Ulster) is always a source of fresh insights. I am indebted to the ever helpful Yvonne Murphy and Kris Brown at the Linenhall Library in Belfast.

On a personal note, special thanks are due to Maria, not least for her patience; to my son Connell, to whom this book is dedicated; and to his mum Anita and my parents.

Thanks are also due to a large number of people from political parties who agreed to be interviewed or assisted the project in other ways. The list here is far from exhaustive, but includes Tim Attwood, Eoin O'Broin, Sean Brady, Betty Campbell, Gerry Cosgrove, Sean Crowe, Pat Doherty, Dawn Doyle, Jayne Dunlop, Tom Ekin, Stephen Farry, Paul Ferguson, Lyn Fleming, David Ford, Michelle Gildernew, Raymond Glover, Peter Henderson, Eddie Kinner, Tom Holland, Bob Houston, Bobby Lavery, Hazel Legge, Allan Leonard, Alex Maskey,

Michael McDonnacha, Mitchel McLaughlin, Joan O'Connor, Rita O'Hare, George Patten, Brid Rodgers, Robbie Smyth, Eileen Ward, Dennis Watson and Jim Wells.

Many might disagree with the arguments in this book; responsibility for its contents is entirely my own.

JONATHAN TONGE

The author and publishers are grateful to the Political Studies Association/Blackwell Publishing for permission to reproduce copyright material from *Political Studies* as Tables 4.1, 4.2 and 4.4, and Figure 4.1. Every effort has been made to contact all copyright-holders, but if any have been inadvertently omitted the publishers will be pleased to make the necessary arrangement at the earliest opportunity.

List of Abbreviations

ANC	African National Congress
CIRA	Continuity IRA
DUP	Democratic Unionist Party
EPCU	European Policy Coordination Unit
ETA	Euzkadi ta Azkatasuna
EU	European Union
GFA	Good Friday Agreement
IFI	International Fund for Ireland
INLA	Irish National Liberation Army
IPLO	Irish People's Liberation Organization
IRA	Irish Republican Army
LSP	Local Strategy Partnership
NILP	Northern Ireland Labour Party
NIWC	Northern Ireland Women's Coalition
NORAID	Irish Northern Aid Committee
NSMC	North-South Ministerial Council
PIRA	Provisional Irish Republican Army
PLO	Palestine Liberation Organization
PNV	Partido Nacionalista Vasco
PSNI	Police Service of Northern Ireland
PUP	Progressive Unionist Party
RIRA	Real IRA
RUC	Royal Ulster Constabulary
SDLP	Social Democratic and Labour Party
SEUPB	Special European Union Programmes Body
UDA	Ulster Defence Association
UUC	Ulster Unionist Council
UUP	Ulster Unionist Party
UVF	Ulster Volunteer Force

Introduction

The Northern Ireland peace process has transformed a violent conflict into a cold peace. The subsiding of 'war' into (armed) peace, has created scope for a thawing of historical ethnic rivalries. Yet the political process accompanying the peace process has been beset by difficulties. Political antagonism between (Protestant) unionists, defending Northern Ireland's place in the United Kingdom, and (Catholic) nationalists, anxious to maximize the Irish dimension to political arrangements, remains acute. The 1998 Good Friday Agreement was designed to manage such tensions within a peace framework of devolved and all-island institutions. It was a deal aimed at ending nearly 30 years of conflict by allowing representatives of Northern Ireland's competitive ethnic blocs to share power on a permanent basis for the first time. Until 1998, 26 years of direct rule from Westminster had accompanied armed conflict, a 'war' partly precipitated by the nature of devolved, one-party unionist rule from 1921 until 1972.

However political progress was impaired by divisions within unionism over whether such a deal was an appropriate means of defending the Union of Great Britain and Northern Ireland and preserving the Britishness of Northern Ireland in terms of culture and institutions. The erosion of unionist confidence in the Good Friday Agreement contrasted with the support of the overwhelming majority of nationalists, who saw the deal as an advance in terms of equality and change in Northern Ireland.

Recent years have seen a transformation of the situation in Northern Ireland as economic progress is evident and political violence, although not extinct, has diminished substantially in terms of the number of deaths and injuries. The majoritarian dominance of the Unionist Party, evident during the first 50 years of the province, has long vanished and discrimination against nationalists has effectively been eradicated. Yet sectarianism remains, with physical separation of the Protestant and Catholic communities in many parts of the province. The political process has not consolidated the fortunes of the moderate representatives of nationalism and unionism: the Social Democratic and Labour

1

Party (SDLP) and Ulster Unionist Party (UUP) respectively. Instead they have been eclipsed by the so-called extremes of Sinn Fein, which is still linked to the Provisional IRA, and the Democratic Unionist Party (DUP), led by the Reverend Ian Paisley, a leader who has long fused politics and religion. The political institutions established under the Good Friday Agreement have endured an on–off existence. Blame for their repeated collapse reflected the lack of consensus in Northern Ireland. Unionists blamed continued republican paramilitary activity; republicans remained unconvinced of the willingness of unionists to share power with their historical opponents.

The manner in which armed peace has been juxtaposed with political progress and reversals has raised a number of issues and debates. Central to these is whether consociation – a form of government pioneered particularly in the Netherlands and Belgium, that seeks to hold together divided societies by accommodation at the elite level – is the most appropriate means of addressing the conflict in Northern Ireland. Most commentators agree that the Good Friday Agreement was consociational, being an accommodation between political elites based on power sharing between ethnic rivals, proportionality in government, mutual rights of veto and community autonomy (cf. O'Leary, 1999; McGarry, 2001; Wolff, 2002b). One dissenter, a critic of consociation as a normative and analytical tool, argues that consociation principles have always been a movable feast (Dixon, 2003). Critics of consociation question whether acceptance of ethnic division can ever create the necessary conditions for its eradication (for example Taylor, 2001). The application of consociational ideas to Northern Ireland has been associated by detractors with increased segregation and sectarianism.

Theoretical discussions on consociation have led to debates on the practical application of such ideas. Why has the design of the Northern Ireland Assembly been problematic? Can consociational ideas be successfully applied in Northern Ireland when a key external actor, the Irish government, is involved in an interlinked set of institutions? Can consociation be described as successful when there is a clear division within as well as between ethnic blocs? What lessons can be applied to Northern Ireland from attempts at conflict resolution elsewhere?

The next broad area of debate concerns the main ideologies that have shaped politics on the island. Does the apparent transformation of Irish republicanism constitute a repudiation of long-held principles (see for example Ryan, 1994), the inevitable denouement given the circumstances in which the Provisional IRA was born (McIntyre,

1995) or merely tactical adjustment to the prevailing political context (Todd, 1999)? Similarly, are the divisions within Ulster unionism merely debates on the most appropriate response to a constitutionally sound but emotionally difficult Good Friday Agreement? Alternatively, do the rivalries between and within unionist parties reflect a broader contest between pluralist unionism, embracing historical opponents and a cultural unionism that is less enamoured with any proposed dilution of the Britishness of Northern Ireland (see for example Porter, 1996)?

Is there anything new in Northern Ireland politics?

The political setbacks since the Good Friday Agreement have raised the question of whether much is new politically in Northern Ireland. Despite the seemingly glacial politics, there *have* been major changes, and an imperfect and uneasy new Northern Irish politics has emerged. Most republicans have moved from violence to constitutional politics, thus facilitating change. Having earlier pledged to destroy the northern province, in 1999 republicans entered the partitionist Northern Ireland Assembly at Stormont. Despite campaigning for a 32-county united Ireland, Sinn Fein ministers presided over the important ministries of education and health in a province that had been denounced for years as an entity that could not be reformed. The Provisional IRA ended its war, having earlier insisted that it would continue its armed struggle until the end of Britain's colonial rule over Northern Ireland. The government of the Irish Republic, having opposed the division of Ireland since its enactment, withdrew its constitutional claim to Northern Ireland after voters overwhelmingly supported its renunciation. The Good Friday Agreement made clear that Northern Ireland would remain part of the United Kingdom for as long as this was the desire of a majority of its citizens.

A new Northern Irish politics thus emerged from the demise of traditional, territorial republicanism, the central tenets of which were the political indivisibility of the island and the illegality of Britain's colonial claim to the north, held against the wish of the majority of the Irish people for unity. Nationalist politics were no longer abstentionist. The SDLP had of course engaged politically for much of the post-1970 period, but nationalist participation was now nearly universal, due to Sinn Fein's changed approach. The new republican approach was paradoxical. For Sinn Fein, it meant majority support among nationalists and substantial electoral gains. However it begged the question of whether governing Northern Ireland in any way enhanced the prospect of a united, independent Ireland, a scenario that seemed as distant as ever and no longer a constitutional imperative, or even a political project, of any Irish government. The revisionist republican project, insofar as it existed, was based on the electoral growth of Sinn Fein and the possibility of it holding governmental positions as a coalition partner in both a revived Northern Ireland executive and the government of the Irish Republic. Optimists believed that this scenario might afford republicans some power to shift major policy areas to an all-island basis in a manner palpably absent from the Good Friday Agreement.

Despite their constitutional victory, many unionists appear to be uncertain about how to develop a new politics. Whilst a section of unionism appears to be willing to move towards a civic, cooperative form of politics, a rival wing is less convinced of unionism's political triumph. These sceptics seem to be unwilling to believe that the mainstream republican war is over, whatever the evidence to the contrary, citing alleged residual paramilitary activity such as a Provisional IRA spy ring at Stormont. They dislike the painful non-constitutional aspects of the Good Friday Agreement and are unhappy about the perceived diminution of cultural and societal aspects of their Britishness. Combined with reluctance among republicans to surrender publicly, these uncertainties have destabilized the political institutions established under the agreement. The post-conflict new Northern Irish politics have been based on a chilly peace, marked by instability, reluctance among many unionists to deal with the IRA/Sinn Fein, and only grudging accommodation.

The elite accommodation of 1998 was brokered as the prospect finally appeared ripe for a consociational settlement in Northern Ireland. With the internal threat from most republicans having subsided and the external demands by the Irish government ended, the deal sought a measure of loyalty to political structures in Northern Ireland, with these linked to the two nations – Britain and Ireland – that commanded the overarching loyalty of the majority of citizens of Northern Ireland. The consociational deal was criticized even by those who voted yes in the referendum of May 1998; for such critics the accommodation of elites in a deal that managed, rather than eradicated, difference tended to freeze the sectarian fault line. For consociationists, the recognition of competitive ethnic blocs and differing national identities was a realistic starting point for a deal that provided a framework for the peaceful and cooperative management of difference.

The arguments of this book

This book addresses the debates sketched above. It begins with a brief historical outline of the nature of the political problems in Northern Ireland. It suggests that, despite unionists' loss of confidence in the deal, the Good Friday Agreement was in many respects a unionist triumph. Given that the micro-agenda of the agreement involved awkward internal reforms for unionists, in addition to paramilitary prisoner releases, it was a difficult deal to sell, but in constitutional terms the embedding of the 'principle of consent' was palpably a unionist triumph. Articles 2 and 3 of the Republic's constitution were traded and the position of Northern Ireland, for so long seen by the Irish government (and a fair slice of world opinion) as illegitimate, was legitimized.

Chapter 2 expresses scepticism of the claim that the referendums on the Good Friday Agreement, held north and south of the border in 1998, amounted to a genuine exercise in Irish self-determination. The agreement acknowledged that a united Ireland was the aspiration of the majority of the people of Ireland, but did little to remove the barriers to fulfilment of that wish. Indicative referenda on a range of constitutional options, which would have leant towards a genuine exercise in codetermination, were not risked, even though support for the agreement might still have been strong.

Chapters 3 to 5 examine the extent to which a new politics has emerged within Northern Ireland's party system and assess the growth of support for the centrifugal forces of the DUP and Sinn Fein. Parties seen as stoutly defending their ethnic bloc can prosper in a consociational bloc system in which two parties contest votes within each bloc. However to blame consociation for bloc politics, or sectarian contests, is naïve. Bloc politics in Northern Ireland have existed under a variety of political forms, and the idea that consociation has led to the triumph of political extremes is misplaced. The growth of support for Sinn Fein is the party's reward for moderation and disavowal of violence. Sinn Fein's approach is that of a rational actor, with the party well placed to dominate nationalist politics within an ethnic bloc system. This electoralism should not necessarily be conflated with traditional republicanism. The Sinn Fein leadership has been obliged to deny the inevitability of aspects of the Good Friday Agreement and to concentrate on the aspects of the deal most tempting to the movement: prisoner releases, equality and change.

The DUP opposed the agreement, but nonetheless participated in government with Sinn Fein. Chapter 3, on unionist politics, draws on survey evidence from the UUP to identify distinctive strands of unionism. Rational civic unionists wish to shift unionism towards a more pluralist and inclusive form, but are hampered by the party's structural complexities and the uncompromising unionism of the DUP. Anti-agreement unionism is far from homogeneous. Within its ranks can be found administrative integrationists, demanding the full integration of Northern Ireland in the United Kingdom. There are electoral integrationists, who wish to see mainland political parties contest elections in Northern Ireland. There are 'direct rulers', content to see continued rule from Westminster for several more years. Many anti-agreement unionists, in contrast, strongly desire devolution, but reject the terms of the GFA.

Meanwhile the traditional political centre, as represented by the Alliance party, continues to wither, with consolidation of the bloc system exacerbating its problems. The Alliance's rejection of unionist and nationalist visions has been compromised by its willingness to prop up ailing pro-agreement unionism in order temporarily to rescue the agreement, a move that is unpopular with its members, as survey evidence in this book suggests.

Chapters 6 to 8 examine the performance of the political institutions established under the Good Friday Agreement. Characterized by instability from the outset, each of the bodies has encountered difficulty with embedding complex, devolved, binational and confederal political relationships. Chapter 6 offers a sanguine view of the Northern Ireland Assembly from 1999 to 2002 as a modestly successful legislative and scrutinizing vehicle, with coherent committee structures. With committee arenas of cross-community cooperation evident in local councils, the extension of workable, cooperative relationships to the Assembly level was a viable proposition. The executive, which is discussed in Chapter 7, offered a less happy model, being beset by the problems – aside from the 'normal' devolution issue of the Barnett formula – of political grandstanding, lack of collective responsibility, rotation of ministers, dubious allocation of portfolios and lack of linkage to strand two of the Good Friday Agreement.

Strands two and three of the agreement are explored in Chapter 8, which argues that the north–south and confederal aspects of the agreement are somewhat anodyne and inconsequential. The all-island dimension, arising from the prolonged struggle to create Irish unity, is modest and ringfenced. It is the European Union, not the minimalist binationalism of strand two, that has enabled the main north–south activities. Symbolism, rather than substantive movement towards all-island economic and political activity, has been the norm, a problem heightened by continued political wrangling. The aspiration for Irish unity might be better reflected in structures that mark a shift towards binational, joint authority if the Good Friday Agreement, renegotiated or otherwise, is not revived.

Chapter 9 assesses the role, or more accurately the lack of it, of civil society in shaping the political process. The chapter is mildly sceptical of the claim that sectarianism has increased as a consequence of the consociational agreement. Nonetheless it does argue that a depoliticization of society has occurred, as the stress on identity and culture have been at the expense of the old contesting politics of national sovereignty, self-determination and independence. As the constitutional question arising from those contests has diminished, the focus has shifted to the problem of sectarianism. The chapter defends the consociationist view that a deal between rival ethnic blocs does not legitimize sectarianism, although on different grounds than one might expect from consociationists. One of the themes of this book is that those who speak of 'sectarian politics' tend to assume, erroneously, that the pursuit of republicanism (or certain forms of unionism) is sectarian rather than ideological. Social transformationists argue that consociational deals cannot remove sectarianism from society, and that what is required instead is local, grassroots, transformative action. This view is critically dissected, firstly on the traditional consociational ground that societal transformation can accompany an overarching consociational deal, and secondly on the ground that consociationists and social transformationists ignore the border as a symbol and consolidation of division. A transformationist approach might incorporate a withering of the border by the formation of all-island social, political and economic commonalities.

Chapter 10 investigates the substantial changes to policing, which are indicative of how Northern Ireland has been reformed, although reformism has of course been only one aspect of the republican project. Nationalist hostility to the police is subsiding, a process that will accelerate when Sinn Fein completes its political journey and backs a six-county police force. Chapter 11 argues that a comparative approach involving exogenous influences is vital to the study of Northern Ireland, but that endogenous factors, centred on the reshaping of republicanism, are largely responsible for the creation of the new Northern Irish politics. The book's conclusion is that the demise of traditional republicanism has left a political void that could be filled, irrespective of the ultimate fate of the Good Friday Agreement, with a growing binationalism and diminution of the north–south border, this partly taking place within broader EU and transnational contexts.

1
The Conflict

Part of the problem with formulating a solution for the difficulties of Northern Ireland is the extent to which the history of Ireland is itself contested. This chapter offers a whirlwind historical tour to familiarize the reader with the basis of the conflict.

The first, loose, system of 'government' was via tribal Gaelic chiefs, followed by Christianity in the fifth century. Although the Gaels are generally seen as the 'native' Irish, having arrived in the fifth century, they were also 'invaders of Ireland' (Boyce, 1991, p. 26), although it has been claimed that the invasion was largely peaceful (Cronin, 2001). Unionist-leaning authors assert that the arrival of the Gaels was preceded by the settlement of various Scottish tribes in Ulster (Adamson, 1974; Wilson, 1989). Even if the 'we were here first' arguments cannot be resolved, it can be asserted that Ireland has never been entirely united, Gaelic and free.

The origins of political problems can be traced back as far as the loose establishment of British colonial rule in Ireland in the twelfth century. This was followed in the early seventeenth century by the arrival of Protestant settlers, mainly from Scotland, in the north-eastern part of Ireland. Divisions between Scottish Protestants and Irish Catholics became apparent after the plantation of Ulster by the Scots from 1609. Post-plantation, the next four centuries of politics in Ireland concerned the fermenting and attempted management of division, in what has often been seen as a zero-sum game between, broadly, Protestant British unionists and Catholic Irish nationalists, with these two traditions coexisting uneasily in the north-east corner of the island.

The struggle for Irish independence from Britain began as early as 1641 and was continued in the 1798 rebellion. That uprising was led by Wolfe Tone, who came from a Church of Ireland background, had Catholic links and was a Deist. At this stage the link between Irish nationalism and Roman Catholicism was far from automatic. In parts of the country, however, the uprising did have a sectarian flavour, with, for example, Protestants being killed by the rebels at Wexford (Jackson, 1999, p. 18). Britain's attempt to consolidate its rule throughout Ireland via the 1800 Act of Union bought time for colonial rule.

The forces of Irish nationalism grew during the nineteenth century, fuelled by famine and contests over the ownership of land. Concurrently, economic development in Ulster highlighted the sense of difference felt by northern Protestants. Anxious to placate constitutional Irish nationalists, the Liberal government attempted to give Ireland semi-autonomy within the British Empire by means of its Home Rule Bill of 1886. Protestants in the north-east corner of Ireland were enraged by what they saw as a threat to their political, religious, economic and cultural liberty. Formed in 1905, the Ulster Unionist Council united the political and religious forces of unionism, effectively fusing a political organization, the Unionist Party, with a religious movement, the Orange Order. Backed by the vast numerical and military strength of the 'paramilitary' Ulster Volunteer Force, Ulster unionism was a virulent force that could not easily be absorbed into any semi-independent Ireland. Unionism's strength defeated the Home Rule Bills of 1886, 1893 and 1912.

Hitherto weaker than Ulster unionism, Irish nationalism had also grown in virulence as a result of the response of the British government to the 1916 Easter Rising against British rule. Although the rebellion was weak and largely confined to Dublin, the subsequent execution of several of its leaders gave the rebels a hitherto unknown sympathy. The partition of Ireland emerged as an unsatisfactory but pragmatic option to acknowledge the competing strengths of unionism and nationalism.

It is here that history is again contested. For unionists, partition – although initially not desired, given that unionists favoured the *status quo* – was justified. According to this view, the six-county country of Northern Ireland had democratic legitimacy as its creation reflected the balance of political forces. Unionists won 69 per cent of the votes in the six counties that were to form Northern Ireland under the 1920 Government of Ireland Act. Nationalists had a fundamentally different reading of the legitimacy of partition. Campaigning for an independent, united Ireland, Sinn Fein won 73 of the 105 parliamentary seats in the 1918 Westminster election, the last occasion on which the people of the island voted as a single unit. A further six seats were gained by Home Rule nationalists. For republicans, partition gave veto rights over a democratic election to a national minority, Irish unionists. In response Sinn Fein established *Dail Eireann* and refused to recognize continued British rule, which continued via the parliaments in Dublin and Belfast. As IRA activity soared, the British government conceded greater independence to the 26-county southern state via the 1921 Anglo-Irish Treaty. However the island remained partitioned, with a unionist-dominated, devolved parliament governing the north and the Irish governing the south, which remained within the British Empire.

Sinn Fein and the IRA split over whether to accept the Anglo-Irish Treaty, leading to one of the bloodiest episodes of Irish history: the civil war of 1922–23. The defeat of the antitreaty forces was perhaps inevitable, given the military and political resources available to the forces of the new Irish Free State. To these were added the moral resources of the Catholic Church, which threatened excommunication to those republicans who wished to prolong the war. Although hostility to the 26-county Irish Free State was maintained by diehard republicans, even the antitreaty forces, led by Eamon de Valera, had taken the constitutional route by 1927, with de Valera's Fianna Fail entering *Dail Eireann* as an opposition party and then forming a government after the 1932 Irish election. De Valera adjusted the workings of the treaty to establish greater independence for the 26 counties, the transition to a republic being completed by (pro-treaty) Fine Gael in 1949. However the Irish government could do little about partition, other than to ensure that the 1937 constitution formally refused recognition of Northern Ireland as a legitimate political entity by refering to the pending 'reintegration of the national territory'. Armed campaigns to force the withdrawal of the British government's claim to Northern Ireland were continued by militant republicans on a small, sporadic scale, the border campaign of 1956–62 causing 18 deaths but producing no political dividends. As part of a cyclical pattern, to be repeated at the end of the twentieth century, formerly militant republicans adopted parliamentary strategies, denouncing and abandoning those who continued to pursue Irish unity by violent means.

From civil rights to insurrection

Although Northern Ireland was always an insecure province, it appeared for several decades that the 1920 Government of Ireland Act and the 1921 Anglo-Irish Treaty might have brought fairly peaceful closure to the Irish question. Although a cold war existed between north and south, with politics frozen, there seemed that little could be done to alter the *status quo*. Northern nationalists, trapped within what quickly developed into a unionist-dominated enclave, did not like Northern Ireland and loathed the discrimination they endured. The extent of that discrimination is contested, as highlighted by the pioneering work of Rose (1971) and the later partial exoneration of the unionist government (Wilson, 1989). However the fact that discrimination did exist can scarcely be disputed (Farrell, 1980). Despite seeing themselves as second-class citizens, nationalists were not sufficiently motivated by border concerns to offer much support to the IRA's campaign of the 1950s. The very modest unionist reformist agenda of the 1960s, developed by the prime minister, Terrence O'Neill, raised nationalist hopes of better treatment. Reformism opened divisions within unionism, yet to heal, over the most appropriate means of securing the union. To some degree the debate within unionism took on a class form, as enlightened patricians treated nationalists with kindness in an attempt to entice them into the structures of the state. Other unionists continued to view nationalists as the enemy within, aided in ideological terms by an irredentist southern state.

Increasingly willing participants in the province, but not in its unionist form, nationalists began to agitate for civil rights during the late 1960s. The Northern Ireland Civil Rights Association (NICRA), a broad body straddling the social classes, provided an umbrella organization for the movement. It had a mainly middle-class leadership, although the idea that the middle classes directed the civil rights campaign has been refuted (Dixon, 2001). Although some liberal unionists joined in the early stages, the movement struggled to attract Protestant support. Many unionists took the jaundiced view of a later leader of the Ulster Unionist Party, David Trimble, that the civil rights campaign was 'really just the Republican movement in another guise' (Coogan, 1995, p. 63).

In reality NICRA was a disparate and often uneasy coalition of nationalists, republicans and socialists, sometimes with little in common other than a desire to confront a discriminatory unionist regime. Its 'members' (the term exaggerates the extent of organization as NICRA acted as little more than a somewhat ineffective umbrella) included communists, socialists, non-aligned radicals, working-class non-ideological Catholic 'defenders' (later to join the ranks of the

Provisional IRA), middle-class moderate Catholics (later to form the Social Democratic Labour Party, SDLP), veteran Republican IRA sympathizers, trade unionists and a sprinkling of liberal unionists. Indeed the civil rights movement was a more disparate coalition than the combination of sectarian orange and relatively moderate elements who comprised the unionist regime at Stormont. Unionist rule contained a range of discriminatory practices ranging from the petty to the malevolent and veering from veiled to blatant. Farrell (1983) highlights the insecure nature of the state, in which a large number of Protestants were employed in the police force to ward off a supposed threat from nationalists. The perception of threat was perhaps greater than the reality; the IRA's border campaign of the 1950s attracted little interest and fizzled out amid internal acrimony and disillusionment. Nationalists did not like the border and partition, but they were insufficiently aroused to take to arms to bring about its abolition.

Bew *et al.* (1996) acknowledge the clear existence of discrimination, but indicate that the unionist government presiding over such practices was not a monolith. Discrimination arose partly from the adoption of populist positions by sections of the unionist leadership, stances that sometimes created internal tensions. Discrimination against the nationalist population was practised in the public sector and condoned in some parts of private industry (Whyte, 1983). Motivations varied from contempt for Catholics to more political reasons associated with the alleged republican threat to the state (Darby, 1976). Nationalist self-exclusion, particularly through abstention from Stormont, is claimed to be a contributory factor, although it is difficult to see what benefits would have accrued to participation, given Unionist majoritarianism (Buckland, 1981).

O'Neill's reformist agenda was not hugely dissimilar from that espoused by NICRA. The Northern Ireland prime minister shared its desire to reform the local electoral franchise, which disproportionately disenfranchised Catholics through the requirement that voters should be rate-paying home-owners. O'Neill was also desirous of ending the gerrymandering of electoral boundaries and advocated the suspension of its least subtle exponent, Derry City Corporation. O'Neill's attempted restructuring of unionism lacked solid support among the working class. His patrician appeal to Protestants that they should treat Catholics well 'in order that they will live like Protestants' was offensive to the minority community and failed to assuage uncertainty among unionists (*Belfast Telegraph*, 10 May 1969). O'Neill's project was also based on economic modernization, but he operated in a polity in which the division of spoils had always taken importance over the aggregate story.

The rising figure of Ian Paisley, leader of his own inventions – the Free Presbyterian Church, the Protestant Unionist Party and, from 1971, the Democratic Unionist Party – held political appeal for doubters among the loyalist working class and religious appeal for rural evangelicals (Bruce, 1986). Ideological divisions were apparent within the unionist regime from the outset; however these divisions were kept in check by a combination of the voting system (which discouraged minor parties), unity of purpose, a lack of class-based challenges and the void in nationalist politics. As civil disobedience replaced sullen abstention as the means of nationalist political participation, unionism imploded.

The main response to the civil rights movement from the unionist government was to deploy the Royal Ulster Constabulary and its reserves, the B Specials, to prevent marches taking place along illegal routes. With the police force unsupported by most nationalists, demands for civil rights developed into civil strife in 1968 and 1969. The political limits of O'Neillism were highlighted by the security-based response. O'Neill had no plans to change Northern Ireland's security forces, although in 1969, when the British government was obliged to send in troops, the B Specials were disbanded. The Hunt Report on the disturbances of 1969 suggested that the Northern Ireland police force should be disarmed, a recommendation that was first ignored and then abandoned when the IRA was reborn (Hunt Report, 1969). When sending in troops to quell disturbances, the British government was aware that a quick fix to Northern Ireland's problems was unlikely. Indeed Prime Minister Harold Wilson, who was privately critical of the unionist government, believed an army presence would be required for at least seven years (Pimlott, 1992).

The paramilitary campaigns

The series of security-based responses were unaccompanied by serious political thinking. In this vacuum the Provisional IRA, which had amounted to a mere handful of 'dissident' republican ultras upon its formation in January 1970, began to flourish. A combination of structural and episodic forces gave rise to the birth of the Provisional

IRA. The organization was committed to the defence of northern nationalists, but insisted that its primary loyalty was to the provisional Irish government of 1919. How the Provisional IRA is defined depends on the level of analysis. Among its 'foot soldiers', particularly in urban areas, the events of 1969 to 1972 dominated. In this respect Anthony McIntyre (a former member of the Provisional IRA) is justified in asserting that the organization was rooted in northern defenderism, rather than being a lineal descendant of the earlier IRAs, which saw all legitimacy as flowing from the 1919 *Dail Eireann* (McIntyre, 2001).

McIntryre's argument does explain the motivation of many who joined the Provisional IRA in its formative years. Nonetheless, among the leadership of the Provisionals, which included figures such as Ruairi O'Bradaigh and Sean McStiofain, there was faithful adherence to the ideals of 1916–19. The first utterance of the Provisional IRA was 'We declare our allegiance to the thirty-two county Irish Republic, proclaimed at Easter 1916, established by the first Dail Eireann in 1919, overthrown by force of arms in 1922 and suppressed to this day by the existing British-imposed six-county and twenty-six-county partition states' (*Irish News*, 29 December 1969). This does not invalidate McIntyre's analysis, given that the same statement lamented the 'failure to provide the maximum defence possible' for nationalists, but it can be argued that there was a duality of purpose to the Provisional IRA (MacStiofain, 1975, p. 143).

Given the adherence to traditional republicanism, the claim that the Provisional IRA began as a 'force for the self-protection of the Catholic population' is a partial presentation (Cronin, 2001, p. 234). The Provisionals were unsuccessful in their protective role, a self-ascribed duty that nonetheless had useful recruitment and propaganda qualities. Their offensive role, designed to end British sovereignty over Northern Ireland, also failed, although it yielded advances for nationalists within the province that constitutional nationalism might not have obtained. The split in the IRA that led to the formation of the Provisionals, occurred after the leader of what became known as the Official IRA, Cathal Goulding, made two proposals to the IRA's 'General Army Convention' in 1969, a grand term given the moribund nature of the organization. Goulding argued for the establishment of a broad 'National Liberation Front' that would bring the IRA into alliances with other left-wing groups, including the Irish Communist Party. He also wished to end republican abstention from *Dail Eireann*, Stormont and Westminster (Horgan and Taylor, 1997b). The latter proposal would have meant the end of traditional republicanism and it was primarily for this reason that the Provisional IRA was formed. The plight of northern nationalists was acknowledged as a contributory factor, but the end of abstentionism, breaches of the IRA constitution and the shift towards 'communist' politics were cited by the Provisional IRA as justifications for the republican schism in 1969–70.

Although the split has been seen as one of southern Official IRA versus northern Provisional IRA, the leadership of the latter included a number of southerners. Furthermore, those northerners who were seen as 'Catholic defenders' were often veteran republicans, (for example Billy McKee) who maintained a lifelong allegiance to the republic established in 1918–19. New recruits were informed that 'the Army [IRA] is the direct representative of the 1918 Dail Eireann parliament ... the legal and lawful government of the Irish Republic' (Coogan, 1995, p. 208). The Provisionals therefore had a historical reason for their existence, based on the orthodox republican fundamentalism and militarism of Padraig Pearse, in which, according to one critic, 'the people and their governments counted for nothing' after 1918 (Laffan, 1999, p. 458). For the initial leaders of the Provisional IRA the events of 1968–69 were a vindication of their view that the northern state could never be viable. They sought to translate nationalist disaffection with the unionist regime into a push to deal with the 'unfinished business' of 1916–22.

From the summer of 1969 until April 1970, Northern Ireland was relatively calm and the Provisional IRA recruited few members in its formative months, but then a combination of sectarian rioting and a catalogue of poor judgements about responsive actions by the British Army (encouraged by the ailing Stormont government) fuelled IRA recruitment. These actions, taken amid a deteriorating political and security situation, included the 1970 Falls curfew, the introduction of internment in 1971 and the nadir, Bloody Sunday, in January 1972.

The commitment of the Provisional IRA to armed force and the security blunders by the British Army and RUC led to a devastating paramilitary campaign of violence. This whirlwind of loyalist violence was mainly retaliatory, but also contained offensive elements and was overwhelmingly sectarian. The IRA claimed that its purpose was to 'shoot at the uniform', although in the mid 1970s, a number of its own volunteers wondered whether the organization had descended into a sectarian war (Bean and Hayes, 2001). A breakdown of killings by republicans indicates that uniformed enemies were their main targets, but not so decisively as to eradicate the anxiety of those who wished the war to be conducted only within that parameter. The combined British Army, Royal Ulster Constabulary (RUC) and Ulster Defence Regiment deaths amounted to 1008 between 1969 and 1999, or just 27 per cent of the 3744 killings during this period.

The Provisional IRA was an uneasy coalition of volunteers, fusing dedicated republicans, Catholic sectarians, romantic nationalists, virulent anticommunists, outright militarists, socialists and communists within its ranks. Some of its left-wing volunteers joined remnants of the Official IRA to form the Irish National Liberation Army (INLA), an ostensibly left-wing version of the IRA, but one that appeared equally keen to participate in actions that were seen by opponents as largely sectarian. A consequence of the split of 1970 was the perpetuation of a series of deadly republican feuds, particularly between Provisionals and Officials, for much of the 1970s. These quietened in the 1980s, when the IRA and INLA began to tolerate each other and conducted similar operations. In 1992 the IRA moved decisively against a republican offshoot, the misleadingly titled Irish People's Liberation Organization (IPLO), another organization offering leftist rhetoric but dealing mainly in criminality and gangsterism.

The Provisional IRA's offensive, which began in the summer of 1970 and gathered momentum early in 1971, appeared to pay dividends. With the unionist government suspended from March 1972 and the British government prepared to negotiate with the Provisional IRA by the summer of 1972, there was belief among some republicans in the imminence of victory. For republicans, the British government's desire to retain control over Northern Ireland had not been seriously tested since partition. There was little sign of a strong commitment to other colonies; rather there was much global evidence of withdrawal. Yet the introduction of direct British rule represented military and political setbacks for the Provisionals. It provided, albeit slowly, greater coherence to the counterinsurgency strategy of the British Army, unfettered by the political posturing of unionists. For many moderate nationalists the move also removed the immediate source of resentment, the unionist regime. Whilst disaffection with the British government and its security apparatus easily replaced this resentment amongst many working-class nationalists, the relative unity of purpose among the nationalist population, as seen in its desire to overthrow the unionist government, was no longer in place. As noted earlier, although the civil rights campaign contained disparate elements it engendered a sense of community solidarity. After the collapse of the Stormont government, however, particularly with the rise of a moderate Catholic middle class, the nationalist community was an imagined community, a varied and heterogeneous people. Although nationalists aspired to Irish unity, the strength of their desire varied enormously. While this was not reducible merely to social class, it did reflect differences between those who had not done too badly from the province and those who continued to endure poor living standards. Formed in 1970, the Social Democratic and Labour Party (SDLP) offered a political outlet for mainly middle-class nationalists who preferred constitutional politics. The party also offered a platform for those who preferred labourist politics, even if the party soon essentially became a vehicle of Catholic nationalism. Those who could see no future in the province had the option of joining the Provisional IRA.

Loyalist paramilitaries operated under a variety of names. Surprisingly the Ulster Defence Association (UDA), a mass organization of 40 000 members in the 1970s, remained legal until 1992, despite the fact that its paramilitary wing, the Ulster Freedom Fighters (UFF), busied itself with sectarian killings throughout the conflict, mainly Catholics chosen at random. This strategy was designed to deter the working-class nationalist community, which was seen as a homogeneous entity, from offering support to the IRA. A similar pattern of assassination was followed by the Ulster Volunteer Force (UVF), a numerically pale imitation of the mass movement of the same name much earlier in the twentieth century, but nonetheless capable of instilling fear into Catholics through its activities. Loyalist violence emphasized to the British government and nationalists the potential price of withdrawal from Northern Ireland, stressing that movement towards a united, independent Ireland would lead to civil war. Although loyalist paramilitarism often lacked the discipline usually displayed by the Provisional IRA, periodically lapsing into drug dealing or feuding, its proponents believed that it was decisive in winning the 'war' in its final stages. Loyalist paramilitaries refined their targets in the late 1980s and early 1990s, targeting Sinn Fein and IRA members in addition to randomly selected Catholics. During the 1980s in particular, there was collusion between branches of the security forces and loyalist paramilitaries, as detailed in the Stevens Report of 2003 (see Chapter 10).

As early as 1977 the IRA recognized that immediate British withdrawal was not on the agenda. The movement had already shown interest in direct discussions with loyalist groups on the possibility of marrying some loyalists' desire for an independent Northern Ireland with the republican belief in the need for a federal Ireland. However talks between an independent loyalist, Desmond Boal, and a former IRA chief of staff, Sean MacBride, acting at the behest of loyalist and republican paramilitaries respectively, failed to bridge the differences. At the 1977 Bodenstown commemoration speech, Jimmy Drumm, a leading figure in the republican movement, emphasized that the belief in an imminent British withdrawal had been an illusion. This illusion had not merely been promoted by the leadership, but had also been harboured by ordinary volunteers. Drumm's speech heralded a new approach, based on more subtle military means and designed to maintain a long war. The new approach was a necessary riposte to the military pressure placed on the IRA by Secretary of State Roy Mason, who was more interested in squeezing the IRA 'like a tube of toothpaste' than in fostering political initiatives (quoted in Urban, 1992, p. 11).

As the IRA reorganized from loose brigades into smaller, more secretive cell structures its internal security tightened. However it was to be another four years before the impetus for a long war properly developed. Electoralism began to permeate the movement, largely by accident rather than design. Following the death of ten republicans on prison hunger strike in 1981, Sinn Fein gathered political strength after a prolonged struggle for the restoration of its political status, which had been withdrawn in 1975. The dying hunger striker, Bobby Sands, stood successfully as the Anti H Block candidate in a Westminster by-election in May 1981, when nationalists of various shades rallied to the cause and Sands was unopposed by other nationalists or republicans. After Sands' death his election agent, Owen Carron, won the subsequent by-election.

One year later Sinn Fein began to contest elections and won 40 per cent of the nationalist vote. The extent of support for Sinn Fein indicated that the desire for armed struggle to achieve unity was not the preserve of a tiny minority. A vote for Sinn Fein during that period was interpreted as endorsement of the IRA's paramilitary campaign. Indeed Sinn Fein's 1982 *ard fheis* made clear that support for the IRA by Sinn Fein electoral candidates was a necessary precondition for their candidature.

Sinn Fein and the IRA developed as 'symbiotic movements' with a considerable overlap of personnel (Horgan and Taylor, 1997a, p. 2).

This allowed the development of the 'armalite and ballot box' strategy, famously if inadvertently articulated by Sinn Fein's Danny Morrison at the 1981 *ard fheis*. Eventually electoralism was to subsume the militarism of the republican movement. Such a development had been predicted by 1970–83 the president of Sinn Fein, Ruairi O'Bradaigh, after the party's 1986 *ard fheis* decision to end abstention from *Dail Eireann*. O'Bradaigh immediately formed Republican Sinn Fein, a group that adhered to the historical principles outlined in 1918–19 and reiterated in 1970. He argued that the departure from the fundamental principle of refusing to recognize 'partition parliaments' was an attempt to ride two horses of constitutional and revolutionary politics, the ultimate destination of which was Stormont. Later, in 1998, O' Bradaigh would claim vindication of his predictions. Yet for most within the republican movement the failure to recognize the 26-county southern state amounted to outdated dogma, at variance from the thinking of the vast majority of Irish people. Recognition of the southern state was accompanied by pledges from the republican leadership that the war would continue, an assertion that was designed to reassure internal doubters but nullified any prospect of immediate electoral progress in the Irish Republic, where Sinn Fein captured only 2 per cent of the vote.

By 1988 there were clearer indications that the Provisional IRA was seeking a way out of the conflict. A series of meetings between the SDLP and Sinn Fein leaderships ended in disagreement, primarily over whether the British government could be regarded as a neutral actor. However the argument by the SDLP leader, John Hume, that the IRA's campaign was detrimental to Irish unity and to Sinn Fein's electoral fortunes was to impact on republicans. Unknown to participants, the Hume–Adams dialogue built on private initiatives by Gerry Adams as president of Sinn Fein. By the mid 1980s Adams was in contact, via an intermediary (Father Alec Reid, a Belfast priest), with the British and Irish governments in an attempt to construct a formula for Irish self-determination, which would not necessarily mean rapid British withdrawal from Northern Ireland (Moloney, 2002). The eventually agreed formula, as outlined in the 1993 Downing Street Declaration by the British and Irish governments, fell short of true self-determination, but nonetheless yielded an IRA ceasefire.

The IRA campaign, when measured in terms of financial and human cost, gathered strength in the run-up to the 1994 ceasefire. The organization wished to demonstrate that it had not been defeated. Furthermore IRA 'spectaculars' might strengthen Sinn Fein's hand in any eventual negotiations. In 1991 the IRA came close to destroying the British cabinet in a mortar attack on Downing Street. Huge bomb explosions at the Baltic Exchange and the NatWest Tower in the financial centre of London caused hundreds of millions of pounds of damage. When the IRA temporarily called off its ceasefire in 1996 due to the exclusion of Sinn Fein from talks, the detonation of huge IRA bombs at Canary Wharf in London and in Manchester emphasized the continuing potency of the organization. Such actions later led the chair of Sinn Fein, Mitchel McLaughlin (2000), to claim that the IRA had 'stopped when it had never been stronger'. Nonetheless the bombings in the 1990s, and certainly those in 1996–97, were not efforts to force British withdrawal but were mainly concerned with securing a place for Sinn Fein in political negotiations and an eventual settlement, even though an agreement would fall short of republican objectives. In Northern Ireland, IRA violence ensured that the nationalist community paid a high price in terms of the response by loyalists. Actions such as the bombing of a fish shop on the loyalist Shankill in October 1993, killing nine plus the bomber, in a failed attempt to kill loyalist paramilitary leaders, were followed by indiscriminate loyalist retaliatory violence against Catholics.

The failure of political initiatives prior to the 1990s

Several broad theses have been advanced on British policy in Northern Ireland. The first is the existence of a discernible strategy of 'long withdrawal' from the province (Fisk, 1975; Kennedy-Pipe, 1997). The second is that Britain has no particular strategy other than to minimize its involvement and the cost to itself (Bew *et al.* 1996; Dixon, 2001). As such the 'policy' of the British government merely amounts to lowest common denominator politics, in which peace and political processes are conducted by harnessing willing participants if they can deliver relative stability. The third thesis is that a new Northern Irish politics has been created through a painfully slow policy learning process for political actors, including the British government (O'Leary, 1997). This culminated in a political settlement based on the consociational principle of power sharing with minority veto rights, linked to broader political arrangements involving the totality of relationships between Northern Ireland and the Irish Republic, and the United Kingdom and the Irish Republic.

The lack of ambition in British policy from August 1969 to March 1972 can be attributed to structural factors. Devolution for Northern Ireland meant that interference by Westminster, although possible, was more likely to be waived in favour of a hands-off approach. It was difficult to raise Northern Ireland issues at Westminster, to the chagrin of a small number of Labour MPs but the indifference of almost all others. The recall of parliament to discuss the introduction of internment in 1971 was only the tenth such reconvention since the Second World War. Internment was favoured by the unionist government, tentatively backed by the British government and opposed by the British Army. Supporters who cited its success in the 1956–62 IRA campaign ignored several new factors. First, the IRA now possessed a strong northern urban base. Second, there was no prospect of a reciprocal arrangement with the Irish government, whose distaste for the unionist government was reflected in bellicose statements, if little else, other than isolated support for the provisionals, by sections of Fianna Fail. Third, army intelligence was inadequate as most Provisional IRA recruits were young and had no previous record of paramilitary or political activity. Fourth, as Kennedy-Pipe (1997, p. 58) notes, internment was a surrogate political strategy that assumed the removal of 'troublemakers' would solve a political problem. Finally, loyalist violence was now endemic, but internment would concentrate on the nationalist population and was thus seen as a highly partisan measure.

After Bloody Sunday it was apparent that the unionist government was doomed, so the introduction of direct rule from Westminster within two months came as little surprise. The imposition of direct rule allowed greater clarity in security policy and offered scope for political dialogue. Although the British government's insistence that it would 'not talk to terrorists' became a mantra, indirect dialogue was commonplace. During the 1970s, dialogue was even public. The leader of the Labour opposition, Harold Wilson, held talks with the leadership of the Provisional IRA in 1971, and in July 1972 the home secretary, William Whitelaw, met a Provisional IRA delegation. By recognizing the Provisional IRA the British government gave credence to the republicans' claim to be an army fighting a legitimate war, with the support of a sizeable section of the population. Given the republican absolutism that prevailed at the time it was difficult to see what such talks could achieve. The British government, lacking clear political goals other than defence of the union, hoped to bring about a Provisional IRA ceasefire, an unrealistic aspiration given the lack of political gains it could offer the republican movement. Republicans believed that they could force British withdrawal and would settle for nothing less than notification of intent to withdraw.

Unsurprisingly the 1972 talks quickly collapsed, to be followed by increased violence. Republicans attempted to make Northern Ireland ungovernable through widespread attacks. 'Bloody Friday', a concerted bombing campaign in Belfast, followed the collapse of the Whitelaw talks. The British government asserted its authority by eliminating 'no go' areas through Operation Motorman, a move that made it more difficult for the IRA to operate. Twenty-five years later, greater sophistry on both sides, allied to political realism, offered a more fruitful agenda.

In 1973 the British government issued a white paper on the likely shape of a future settlement in Ireland (HM Government, 1973). Although the problem continued to be described as intractable for many years, the basis of an agreement was clear from that point onwards. A settlement would contain a Northern Ireland elected assembly, an Irish dimension and an Anglo-Irish intergovernmental arrangement. Outlining a possible solution was, of course, far easier than drawing republicans and loyalists into its framework. The essential difference between the Sunningdale Agreement of 1973 and the Good Friday Agreement of 1998 was that the former was based on the exclusion of paramilitary groups and their political representatives; the latter was based on their inclusion. The change was produced partly through policy learning by the British government, but was mainly facilitated by moderation of the republican agenda. In constitutional terms the agreements were broadly similar and the comment by Seamus Mallon that the Good Friday Agreement amounted to 'Sunningdale for slow learners' was apposite (Tonge, 2000). For a consociational settlement to work, however, there had to be some degree of loyalty to the state, or at least a willingness to abandon attempts at its overthrow. For republicans, this abandonment did not arrive until the 1990s.

The Sunningdale Agreement did not fail merely because of the marginalization of paramilitary groups; it also lacked majority support among the unionist community, as evidenced by the February 1974 British general election results, in which 11 of the 12 elected unionist MPs were opposed to the agreement. The Northern Ireland

Assembly elections in 1973 yielded 26 unionist opponents of power sharing with an Irish dimension, compared with 24 in favour. For unionist opponents the agreement contained an inherent contradiction, rectified 25 years later in the Good Friday version. The recognition by the Irish government that there could be no change in the status of the northern province unless a majority in Northern Ireland consented was undermined by its continuing constitutional claim to Northern Ireland, with the pursuit of 'national territory', later being declared a constitutional imperative of Irish governments by the courts.

What were the principles upon which the Sunningdale Agreement was based? Like the Good Friday Agreement, it was a three-stranded deal, comprising 'north–north' (Executive and Assembly), north–south (cross-border) and east–west (London–Dublin) arrangements. The agreement was based on the consociational idea of enforced power sharing via a grand coalition, as represented in the 1973–74 model by an executive comprising Faulkner (pro-agreement) unionists, the Alliance Party and the SDLP. The agreement also contained minority veto rights, but lacked specific measures for 'community autonomy', another feature of 'classic consociationalism' (Lijphart, 1977). The major difficulty confronting a consociational settlement in Northern Ireland – loyalty to another sovereign country by a sizeable section of the minority population – was addressed by the establishment of the Council of Ireland, with membership of this all-Ireland body being compulsory for members of the Northern Ireland executive. There was much ambiguity over the remit of the all-Ireland body. Famously, it was described by an SDLP member, Hugh Logue, as the 'vehicle by which Unionists would be trundled into a united Ireland' (quoted in Coogan, 1995, p. 177). This assertion, reflective of the thinking of a section of the SDLP leadership, did little to bolster unionist confidence or foster the development of nationalist loyalty to Northern Ireland, which would be essential to the long-term functioning of a consociational settlement.

The similarities between the Sunningdale and Good Friday Agreements, not merely in constitutional architecture but also in terms of the British policy approach, have led to the events in the 1972–74 period being labelled as the first peace process (Dixon, 2001). Yet although a political process was developed, a peace process was nonexistent. While the IRA feared marginalization through the successful implementation of the Sunningdale Agreement and therefore attempted to increase its contact with loyalist paramilitary groups, there was little prospect of the Provisionals abandoning the 'armed struggle' at that stage for a deal that fell so short of their avowed objectives. As such the political process continued, but it was devoid of realism in that it was based on the defeat of terrorists through their exclusion from the political framework. By the 1990s policy makers were prepared to countenance the idea that paramilitaries could be, if not defeated, then relatively comfortably accommodated within a power sharing arrangement, provided they were offered a stake in the system. The Provisionals did attempt a ceasefire in the mid 1970s, but this collapsed amid a growing tide of sectarian killings.

The collapse of the Sunningdale Agreement was followed by security-oriented efforts to defeat the IRA. Ulsterization – the attempted replacement of the British Army by the Royal Ulster Constabulary in parts of Northern Ireland – was perhaps less important than criminalization: the attempt to undermine the IRA's claim to be fighting a political war by treating IRA prisoners as common criminals. The denouement of criminalization was the republican hunger strike to achieve political status for prisoners in 1981, which transformed republicanism into a two-pronged movement of military action and electoral politics. Retrospectively, criminalization might be said to have been successful, in that it squeezed the IRA and set republicans on a political path that eventually led to abandonment of the military campaign. Nonetheless the late 1970s and early 1980s appeared to be a barren time for Northern Ireland politics. Local politicians were rendered impotent during a succession of security initiatives, which were followed by a modest Anglo-Irish intergovernmental cooperation in 1980 and a failed attempt to bring devolution back to Northern Ireland in 1982–86.

The attempt by James Prior, the reluctant secretary of state for Northern Ireland, to revive devolution in 1982 was doomed from the outset as even the SDLP was unwilling to participate in a reconstituted Northern Ireland Assembly. The SDLP derided the scheme as unworkable due to its lack of an all-Ireland dimension. In taking such a 'green' line the SDLP was conscious of the looming electoral rivalry with Sinn Fein. In the 1983 British general election, Sinn Fein won 100 000 votes and secured the election of Gerry Adams as MP for West Belfast.

The 1985 Anglo-Irish Agreement marked the climax of a period of intergovernmentalism that had begun in 1980, wobbled two years later and was revived under pressure from nationalists in 1984. With no prospect of local agreement, political initiatives had to be pursued via

Anglo-Irish governmental dialogue. Since 1972 the British government had conceded that it would be desirable for Northern Ireland policy to be approved by the Dublin government (HM Government, 1972), hence it was merely an incremental step for that government to be given consultative rights on northern policy. In this respect the Anglo-Irish Agreement amounted to policy continuity.

Constitutional nationalists had to be seen to be making gains if the electoral advance of Sinn Fein was to be checked. This produced a dawning community of interest between the two governments, given that Sinn Fein appeared to pose a radical threat to the security of the British and Irish states (Fraser, 2000). Partly at the behest of the SDLP, constitutional nationalists had met in 1983–84 to produce the New Ireland Forum Report. The report's conclusions were in many ways a restatement of traditional nationalist views. Certainly its recommendation for Irish unity, federalism or joint sovereignty had not the remotest hope of being adopted by the British government. The articulation of a fairly basic form of nationalism nonetheless pre-empted any possibility of the British government requesting the abandonment of the Irish Republic's 1937 constitutional claim, which might otherwise have been demanded by the moderate Fine Gael government led by Garret Fitzgerald. The Conservative government, hit hard by the IRA bombing at the Conservative Party Conference in Brighton in 1984, recognized that doing nothing was perhaps no longer an option. The Anglo-Irish Agreement placed the problem of Northern Ireland in a permanently binational context. Whilst it was true that 'almost everyone was surprised that Thatcher was prepared to sign such a document', the consultative rights awarded to the Irish government were arguably less than those which were to have been awarded to the Council of Ireland eleven years earlier (McKittrick and McVea, 2001: 163).

The Anglo-Irish Agreement also produced the last gasp of civil war politics in the Irish Republic. Although republicans partly blamed the Fine Gael government for the temporary breakdown of the peace process in 1996–97, there was little difference in substance between the two main Irish parties in respect of Northern Ireland. This perhaps makes all the more surprising the finding that members of Fine Gael still rated Northern Ireland as the issue over which their party differed most from Fianna Fail (Gallagher and Marsh, 2002, p. 182). In 1985, however, Charles Haughey, as leader of Fianna Fail, opposed the Anglo-Irish Agreement. Haughey argued that Article 1, which indicated that there would be no change in the status of Northern Ireland without the consent of a majority of its citizens, was a unionist veto that 'copper fastened partition'. Indeed the agreement received only a modest majority of 88 votes to 75 in *Dail Eireann*. Haughey's opposition amounted to the final rhetorical flourish of the 'republican party' and Fianna Fail did little to oppose the agreement. Indeed by the time a formal review of the agreement was undertaken in 1989, Fianna Fail's dissent had been put aside. Given that even elements within Sinn Fein privately accepted that the agreement, although partitionist and counterinsurgent, did offer concessions and constituted a shift in British policy, it was difficult for Fianna Fail to oppose the deal. More important to Fianna Fail than the private agonies of Sinn Fein, however, was the fact that the agreement appeared to be popular with the electorate in the Irish Republic. A deal that aroused such vociferous unionist protest was seen as beneficial for nationalists.

Although the Anglo-Irish Agreement offered no obvious threat to Northern Ireland's place in the United Kingdom it prompted a hostile unionist response. Unionists believed that the agreement amounted to a 'slippery slope' to Irish unity, even though the consultative rights afforded to the Irish government, while comprehensive, were far short of the executive powers that might have indicated a shift to joint authority. The agreement was characterized by the extensiveness of the consultative rights rather than their intensity, and there would be no role for the Irish government in the actual governance of Northern Ireland. In effect it would serve as a consultative body on many aspects of how Northern Ireland ought to be governed. The agreement did serve to emphasize the conditionality of Northern Ireland's place in the United Kingdom, and that there would be no unionist veto over internal political developments in Northern Ireland. The agreement also highlighted that there would never be a return to the British government's 1969 position that the affairs of Northern Ireland were a purely internal concern. For the integrationist leader of the Ulster Unionist Party, James Molyneaux, an international agreement on the future of a supposedly integral part of the United Kingdom was anathema and he argued that unionists were 'going to be delivered, bound and trussed like a turkey ready for the oven, from one nation to another nation' (quoted in Arthur and Jeffery, 1996, p. 18). In an attempt to embarrass the Dublin government, the unionist McGimpsey brothers urged the Irish courts to rule the Anglo-Irish Agreement illegal as it breached the constitutional claim to Northern Ireland lodged by the Irish Republic under Articles 2 and 3. The verdict of the courts was that British rule in Northern Ireland was a *de facto* reality, but that the pursuit of Irish unity via Articles 2 and 3 of the Irish constitution was still a requirement of Irish governments.

The agreement hinted at a reconstituted northern state, in which the Irish Republic might act as a guarantor of the rights and interests of the northern nationalist minority. Furthermore it represented the death of the integrationist aspirations held by sections of the UUP leadership as the Conservative government formally abandoned any hope of persuading nationalists to adopt a British identity. Although the Anglo-Irish Agreement, unlike its 1998 Good Friday successor, did not dwell on identity politics, its implication was clear: competing nationalisms within Northern Ireland could only be managed through that form of politics, managed at this stage by the two governments.

Despite a variety of obstructions by unionists, the agreement's permanent secretariat at Maryfield continued to undertake its business. The bulk of unionist opposition was based on the withdrawal from state institutions. Loyalist paramilitary groups were also revived by opposition to the agreement. The UDA, in particular, increased its actions, often in the form of killings conducted under its UFF cover. The UDA offered some serious political thought beyond the Anglo-Irish Agreement impasse, however, through the document *Common Sense*, issued by the New Ulster Political Research Group in 1987 (NUPRG, 1987). The document advocated proportionality in government and substantial protection for the nationalist minority. Meanwhile other loyalists, including mainly law-abiding rural evangelicals, flirted with extraconstitutional activities. Ian Paisley briefly offered support and leadership for Ulster Resistance, a movement that pledged to stay within the law but would operate as a 'third force' if there was any attempt to coerce loyalists to accept a united Ireland. For this section of loyalists, the duty to obey the state was important, provided that the state maintained its obligations to the citizenry. According to loyalists, the state had abandoned this covenant by enforcing the Anglo-Irish Agreement (Bruce, 1994).

The unionist siege mentality was exacerbated by the tentative steps taken towards pan-nationalism in 1988 under the Hume–Adams initiative. Loyalist paramilitaries responded by increasing the targeting of republicans and threatening action against members of the 'pan-nationalist front'. Whilst enticing republicans to come in from the political wilderness, the secretary of state, Peter Brooke, did little to reassure unionists when he asserted in 1989 that Britain had 'no selfish strategic or economic interest' in Northern Ireland. Brooke's words were hardly encouraging to unionists, and his declaration that the role of the British government was to encourage 'free democratic choice' merely highlighted the continuing centrality of the 'consent principle' in respect of the future constitutional status of Northern Ireland (Mallie and McKittrick, 1996, p. 107). Unionist recognition of the futility of continuing to oppose to the Anglo-Irish Agreement arrived early, via the *An End to Drift* document of 1987, but there were few political developments, other than a 1989 review of the agreement, until the bilateral Brooke talks with political parties in 1991. These talks collapsed before proceeding to the 'strand two' discussions on the future role of the Irish government (Arthur, 1992). Although they did not progress far, the Brooke talks heralded a three-stranded approach in subsequent discussions, based on the future of, respectively, Northern Ireland, Northern Ireland–Irish Republic and British–Irish relations.

Brooke's successor, Patrick Mayhew, revived the bilateral talks soon after his appointment in April 1992 (indeed the discussions are often referred to as the Brooke–Mayhew talks). Mayhew's attempt to make political progress also ended in failure as the talks were abandoned in November. The main difficulty had been the reluctance of the Irish government to commit itself to a referendum on the scrapping of Articles 2 and 3 of its constitution. Without a guarantee of this, unionists were not prepared to enter into any negotiations on cross-border arrangements. Mayhew attempted to reassure the unionists by insisting that he would not contemplate 'any change to the status of Northern Ireland that does not represent the self-determination of the people living in Northern Ireland' (quoted in Elliott and Flackes, 1999, p. 349). The parameters of a prospective settlement were now apparent: consent within Northern Ireland for constitutional change, abandonment of the Irish Republic's constitutional claim to Northern Ireland, a power-sharing arrangement in the north, economic cross-border institutions and a continuing British–Irish intergovernmental arrangement. However the balance of these factors was far from clear. It was not yet obvious that republicans would accept an arrangement that fell too far short of joint authority, let alone relinquish their traditional demand for an independent, united Ireland. Brooke and Mayhew's private communications with the IRA had yet to be made public, but such contacts indicated that an end to the war was sought and that republicans *might* compromise their long-held ambitions.

By December 1993 the British and Irish governments were in a position to outline the broad set of principles upon which a settlement would be based. The Downing Street Declaration, couched in the green language of Irish self-determination but coated in the unionist demand for consent, was sufficiently appealing to paramilitary groups to mark the beginning of the end of the Troubles.

Between 1969 and 1998 the conflict was seen as one of low intensity, but if it were applied proportionately to the entire population of the United Kingdom it would have produced 111 000 deaths (Hayes and McAllister, 2000). While the Troubles were not borne of an enduring vision of an independent and united Irish Republic, the allegiance of the Provisional IRA leadership to this vision provided a framework within which nationalist discontent with the northern state could be harnessed. Such discontent was sparked mainly by the majoritarian and sectarian nature of the unionist administration in Northern Ireland, in which a recognizable system of government and opposition failed to emerge. Nationalist abstention and the nature of the southern state did not help north–south or intercommunal relations, but the key point was that any rotation of power was unthinkable.

Discrimination against nationalists was largely the product of fear of a republican resurgence and partly due to the distaste for Catholics held by a sizeable proportion of the ruling Unionist Party, in which membership of the Orange Order was of considerable importance. This political and religious hostility inhibited some in unionist politics from supporting a modest reform programme in the 1960s, as demanded by the civil rights movement. The failure to accommodate protest ensured its rapid translation into armed insurrection. Although the outline of an accommodation with the nationalist community had emerged by 1973, British insistence on the defeat of terrorism and the republican assertion of fundamentalist ideals combined to prevent a settlement until 1998. The 1970s and 1980s constituted a period of ideological politics, in which republicanism offered a holistic vision of an independent Ireland, pitted against unionist integrationist or majority rule ideals. The 1990s witnessed the development of identity politics, under which competing national identities and aspirations came to be respected by both sides. This new emphasis on identity politics created space for the application of consociational principles in the 1998 Good Friday Agreement. Power could be shared and community identity recognized through new institutions.

2

The Solution? The Logic of the Good Friday Agreement

A possible framework for agreement in Northern Ireland had been apparent for most of the three decades of conflict, based on consociational ideas of power sharing between the rival ethnic blocs, mutual vetoes, parity and community autonomy. The difficulty lay in brokering a viable deal and the antecedents were not encouraging. In 1974 a power-sharing executive comprising unionists and nationalists had lasted a mere five months, and the British and Irish governments preferred an intergovernmental deal to risky local consociationalism in the 1985 Anglo-Irish Agreement. Nonetheless, as Article 4 of that agreement made clear, intergovernmentalism was a holding operation pending devolved power sharing on the basis of 'widespread acceptance'. As such, a further attempt to broker a consociational deal was inevitable. The improved political climate after the paramilitary cease-fires of 1994 allowed the revival of efforts in this direction. By 1998 it seemed that there might be 'widespread acceptance' of the principle of power sharing, but it was far from clear that the modalities of power sharing would command such a consensus. A sizeable number of unionists would accept power sharing with nationalists, but not with Sinn Fein, even though that party was representing an ever-larger proportion of the nationalist electorate.

The 1998 Good Friday Agreement (GFA) marked the climax of a protracted political process. Compromise was reached after months of formal multiparty bargaining, following a slow dilution of the republican agenda over several years. By coming to this agreement, the British and Irish governments, together with all the main parties except the DUP, which had remained aloof from the negotiations, confounded those cynics who had believed that such a deal could never be attained. Although sceptics wondered whether the GFA would follow the route of the Sunningdale Agreement, the changed political climate and the fact that the deal was subtler than its predecessor gave the GFA a better chance of managing Northern Ireland's political divisions. The deal was more inclusive as it embraced the main paramilitary groups, it enjoyed popular backing from the electorate and it was endorsed by three of the four main political parties. It appeared possible that the time was finally ripe for consociationalism, but the deal would test unionists' commitment to power sharing and republicans' depth of conversion to exclusively constitutional modes of operation.

Sunningdale revisited or policy learning? Shaping the Good Friday Agreement

The claim that the GFA amounted to a 'Sunningdale for slow learners' was understandable, given the similarity of the agreements' constitutional architecture (Seamus Mallon, quoted in *The Sunday Times*, 2 April 1997). The slow learners – most unionists and all republicans – had rejected a less elaborate deal 25 years earlier. For republicans, Sunningdale had amounted to British colonialism, abetted by a compliant nationalist party, the SDLP, and a supine Irish government. Although the IRA's campaign had peaked in 1972, the movement had still been conducting a vast range of military operations at the time the Sunningdale Agreement was brokered and it had no intention of making political compromises. Article 5 of the agreement had made clear that there could be no change in the status of Northern Ireland without the consent of the majority of its citizens. Tacit republican acceptance of the consent principle was still two decades away. During the 1970s and 1980s, the belief that the northern state was illegitimate and unreformable had been fundamental to republican thinking.

The Sunningdale Agreement had offered a cross-community governing executive, combining moderate elements from the Faulkner Unionist Party with Alliance and SDLP representatives. The executive had presided over an elected assembly, which had been linked to the Council of Ireland. For a majority of unionists, however, Sunningdale had represented a substantial step towards joint British–Irish authority over Northern Ireland and the creation of structures of Irish unity (Gillespie, 1998). Unionists had been perturbed even by the internal component of the deal, with many viewing power sharing as essentially undemocratic. Having enjoyed unbridled power from 1921 to 1972, many unionists had been reluctant to cede authority to any of the new bodies of governance or influence. There had been lack of clarity over the remit of the Council of Ireland, which had contained representatives from the Northern Ireland Assembly and *Dail Eireann*. Sunningdale had been an ambitious project undertaken in unfavourable political circumstances. Given the lack of political support, in effect it had been stillborn.

When developing the GFA the British and Irish governments attempted to avoid the mistakes of the Sunningdale deal. There was greater clarity over the Irish dimension and, even more importantly, the earlier attempts to marginalize paramilitary groups were recognized as having been futile. In the 1998 version of power sharing, Sinn Fein and the small loyalist parties, the Progressive Unionist Party (PUP) and the now defunct Ulster Democratic Party (UDP), were included in the bargaining process, ensuring that a historic compromise would have the blessing of the main paramilitary organizations. Naturally these parties stressed their formal organizational separation from the paramilitary groups with which they were associated. Furthermore the IRA explicitly stated that, contrary to Sinn Fein, it was not a signatory to the 1996 Mitchell Principles of non-violence to which all groups were supposed to adhere. Nonetheless both governments recognized the ability of republican and loyalist political organizations to 'deliver' on behalf of paramilitary groups. Significantly, much of the subsequent destabilization of the GFA was due to its lack of clarity on the decommissioning of paramilitary weapons.

An institutional framework for the inclusion of paramilitary groups was provided through the derided Northern Ireland Forum, established in 1996. The idea of Forum elections was tentatively recommended by Senator George Mitchell in an attempt to circumvent the problem of paramilitary groups' failure to decommission their weapons. The Forum election was seen by republicans as a tactic to delay Sinn Fein's entry to multiparty talks and was perceived by many as a contributory factor in the temporary fracture of the IRA's ceasefire in 1996. Nonetheless the Forum set the electoral bar low, using a 'top-up' system to give the top ten parties in the poll access to Forum talks. This enabled loyalist parties to enter the prenegotiation process alongside Sinn Fein, even though the PUP and UDP won only 3.5 per cent and 2.2 per cent of the vote respectively (Elliott, 1997).

Following the election of the Labour government in May 1997 the prenegotiation process was turned into multiparty negotiations, proceeding on the basis of sufficiency of consensus. The 1998 elections to the 108-member Northern Ireland Assembly were fought under a more conventional system of proportional representation, based on six seats per Westminster constituency boundary and without top-up representation for the ten best-supported parties. The fall in electoral support for the UDP to a mere 1.1 per cent resulted in its exclusion even from the overgenerously populated Assembly. The absence of representation for the UDP had negative consequences for the conduct of politics in small sections of the working-class loyalist community, but loyalist paramilitaries, pre-feud, were still represented by the PUP, its 2.6 per cent vote share having secured two Assembly seats (Elliott, 1999).

The inclusion of representatives of paramilitary groups in the bargaining process ensured that the Good Friday Agreement was a much more detailed and comprehensive document than the Sunningdale Agreement. By offering prisoner releases – the non-negotiable demand made by paramilitary groups – the GFA addressed the players in the conflict. Sunningdale had studiously ignored combatants, thus eliminating the prospect of a deal that would stick. Furthermore the GFA had a wider agenda, designed primarily to eliminate lingering aspects of second-class citizenship for nationalists. The agreement established new commissions on human rights, equality and policing. Yet the policy learning by the British government had arrived late (O'Leary, 1997). Earlier in the 1990s the Brooke–Mayhew talks, mainly bilateral discussions between the parties and the successive secretaries of state (Peter Brooke and Patrick Mayhew), had pointlessly revived the idea of a settlement that would exclude Sinn Fein. Crucially, this had been decisively rejected by the leader of the SDLP, irrespective of the short-term benefit that might accrue to his party from the marginalization of its nationalist rival. As the leader of the Alliance Party of Northern Ireland (APNI), David Ford, commented, 'it is a legitimate basis of argument that Hume personally ensured that we didn't reach another 1974-style deal' (quoted in Leonard, 1999, p. 43).

A combination of changes in republicanism, greater inclusivity, political balance and war-weariness gave the GFA greater popularity than the Sunningdale Agreement, as indicated by the result of referendums, north and south, in May 1998 (Table 2.1). The referendum in Northern Ireland was simply on acceptance of the agreement, whilst electors in the Irish Republic voted on whether to accept the changes to Articles 2 and 3 of the constitution, thereby downgrading the territorial claim to Northern Ireland to one of mere aspiration.

Table 2.1 *The Good Friday Agreement referendums, 1998*

	Yes	Percent	No	Percent	Turnout (%)
Northern Ireland (to support/reject the GFA)	676 966	71.1	274 879	28.9	81.1
Republic of Ireland (to amend Articles 2 and 3)	1 442 583	94.4	85 748	5.6	56.3

The substantial majority of votes in favour of the agreement did not mask the division within the unionist population. Only 57 per cent of Protestants voted yes, compared with an overwhelming 99 per cent of Catholics (Hayes and McAllister, 2001). The holding of referendums allowed the British and Irish governments and the SDLP to claim that Irish self-determination had been achieved. For the first time since partition, all the people of Ireland were given the opportunity to determine the constitutional future of the island. However in the Republic only half of the electorate availed themselves of the opportunity to amend Articles 2 and 3. There were also 17 064 spoiled votes, 'indicating some republican dissatisfaction with the Agreement's explicit recognition of the constitutional position of Northern Ireland' (ibid., p. 79). In Northern Ireland the high turnout of 81 per cent was less significant than the breakdown of bloc voting.

Whilst the agreement might still have survived if it had been favoured by only a minority of Protestants, this would have yielded an anti-agreement majority of unionist Legislative Assembly members in the June 1998 Assembly elections. The subsequent disappearance of the pro-agreement unionist majority in the Assembly and the unionist electorate by 2001 indicated the importance of parallel bloc support.

Consociational themes

There is some truth in Hazelton's (2001) claim that whilst there were elements of Lijphart's (1977) consociationalism in the GFA, they were the product of political bargaining under pressure, not the consensual acceptance of a particular theoretical approach. However the consociational framework within which the parties bargained was a construct of a process of policy learning over the previous 24 years. Consociational principles underpinned both the GFA and the Sunningdale Agreement, although the details of their implementation differed. At the heart of the GFA was a belief that, through recognition of the equal validity of two competing ethnic groups and their respective aspirations, both could be reconciled to peaceful power sharing in Northern Ireland, the constitutional status of which would continue to be determined by the will of its people.

The agreement was based on group rights and communal recognition, although it has been argued in a wider context that the establishment of equal citizenship through group rights is also a means of guaranteeing individual rights (Kymlicka, 1989). Individuals could participate in the ratification of the agreement, but what mattered was the aggregate 'score' of their bloc. The construction of the agreement was largely devoid of genuine citizen involvement, as distinct from support, in that it was produced by negotiations between government and party elites. None of the parties balloted its members on the agreement, although 94.6 per cent of Sinn Fein's *cumann* (branch) delegates endorsed it (by 331 votes to 19) at the party's 1998 *ard fheis* (annual conference).

The GFA attempted to harness cultural and political pluralism within an institutional framework. It aimed to manage, even nurture, difference in the hope that the Northern Ireland polity would be recognized as one in which the rights and aspirations of a national minority could be comfortably accommodated. As such the GFA was a binational and bicultural agreement, in which Britishness and Irishness were equally legitimate political identities and cultures. To accommodate potentially contesting identities the symbols of the (British) state were to be made neutral, whilst in civil society expressions of a particular cultural identity would be fostered. The agreement aimed to divert political identity into the cultural sphere, although given the link between political and cultural identity this aim would have limited value.

The obvious question was whether the Northern Ireland polity was ripe for the application of consociational principles. Consociationalism had offered a model for the bridging of societal divisions in other European countries, notably Belgium, the Netherlands, Austria and

Switzerland, although globally there have been few successful cases (Horowitz, 2001). Clearly, society in Northern Ireland was fractured between Irish nationalists and British unionists. Consociationalism appeared to be a viable model of conflict management as it did not deny identity or aspiration and thus provided all sides with a stake. There was also a dearth of suitable alternatives. The immediate integration of Northern Ireland into a united, independent Ireland was likely to provoke civil war, given the willingness of loyalist paramilitaries to use violence to defend their Britishness. Unionist majoritarianism in Northern Ireland had failed to stabilize the state between 1921 and 1972 and there was scant prospect of securing peace through its return. Although the form of unionist rule that could have been introduced would have been less discriminatory that its pre-1972 predecessor, it would nonetheless have left a substantial minority without a proper stake in political institutions. Moreover direct British rule since 1972, although useful in eliminating much of the discrimination against the minority community, had failed to produce long-term political progress.

Consociationalism might be seen as a least bad option. The features of grand coalition, minority (and mutual) veto and segmental autonomy could be seen as positive developments, designed to foster societal reconciliation within a secure state, free from political violence. The selling of the GFA to the various constituencies took a different form: as a transition to Irish unity by Sinn Fein, which exaggerated the all-Ireland aspects; as the embodiment of an agreed Ireland by the SDLP; as a possible, if not ideal, route to creating a sense of Northern Irishness by the centrist Alliance Party; and as the best way to secure the union by the pro-agreement section of the UUP and the PUP. Against these forces the DUP and UKUP took a line that was not dissimilar from that of pro-agreement Sinn Fein: that the deal meant the end of the union was nigh. Republican dissidents meanwhile poured scorn on the idea that the agreement paved the way to Irish unity, arguing that as a stepping stone to that end the GFA was about as useful as the 1921 Anglo-Irish Treaty, which had consolidated the partition of Ireland.

The immediate pre-agreement conditions for consociation met some of Lijphart's preferences, but not all. Lijphart (1977) preferred a multi-cleavage society, fearing that in dual cleavage societies such as Northern Ireland, competitive, zero-sum-game politics might remain. Elite accommodation was only partial as the political leadership of the DUP, which represented a substantial section of unionist opinion, had declined to take part in the negotiations. Furthermore consociation-alism would require a degree of loyalty to the state. Critics of the deal argued that this was absent among republicans and that internal loyalty was diminished by the cross-border element of the agreement. Such caveats, however, overlooked the abandonment of the Irish government's territorial claim to Northern Ireland and the willingness of Sinn Fein to accept the Northern Ireland state as a *de facto* reality, as evidenced by its participation at Stormont. Although denounced by republican ultras as 'Crown ministers', Sinn Fein's presence in the Northern Ireland executive, after the agreement's institutions were established, was indicative of its willingness to suspend its wider polit-ical goals in favour of making the governance of Northern Ireland a viable proposition. Indeed it was unclear, post-GFA, what constituted the party's strategy for dismantling Northern Ireland and creating a united Ireland, other than wishful thinking. One sympathetic com-mentator, Tom McGurk, predicting that the 2001 census would put the proportion of Catholics at 45–6 per cent, claimed that the 'Adams/ McGuinness project has the unstoppable smack of both historical and demographic forces about it' (*Sunday Business Post*, 27 October 2002). This would destabilize the GFA and render it no more than a staging post to Irish unity.

Historical determinism would not yield a united Ireland however, and the touching faith in a 'demographic timebomb' awaiting union-ists was shattered by the 2001 census, which showed a modest rise in the Catholic population to 41 per cent, a sizeable minority of whom did not want a united Ireland. What mattered to the British and Irish governments, in terms of the success of the GFA, was that the Provisional IRA would cease to pose a destabilizing threat to the state and Sinn Fein would be prepared to work in its institutions. Hence the 'cutting edge' of the IRA, which was capable of preventing North-ern Ireland from being anything other than a failed entity, had to be neutered. In this respect, as the British diplomat Sir David Goodall commented, 'actually, it's all working out almost exactly to plan (quoted by A. McIntyre in *The Blanket*, 6 September 2002, 'Controlling the Streets', *Saoirse*, October 2002, p. 2). Destabilization of the GFA arose from the inability or unwillingness of some unionists to compre-hend the extent of change. The problems with the GFA, although a nuisance to the British government, were of less concern than ending IRA violence. Power sharing had always been a desired, but non-essential, aim of British strategy in Northern Ireland (Bew *et al.*, 1996).

Critics of segmental consociational arrangements have been accused of 'utopianism, myopia and tacit partisanship' (O'Leary, 1999, p. 258). Indeed it has not been proven that consociationalism increases sectarianism or the pursuit of vigorous ethnic bloc politics. Sectarian politics have existed under devolved, single-party government, direct rule and consociational governance in Northern Ireland. The fuelling of unionist or nationalist bloc agendas and the conduct of zero-sum-game politics cannot be directly attributed to a post-GFA dispensation, even though its contents, in the short term, legitimized a unionist–nationalist dichotomy. The pursuit of robust ethnic politics can occur independently from the implementation of consociational political arrangements.

With sufficient commitment by the respective parties to the new political institutions and, more broadly, Northern Ireland, the prospect of a consociational agreement appeared much brighter by the late 1990s than during the 1970s. The 1995 framework document suggested the format upon which elite accommodation could be based. The 1998 deal modified these proposals, mainly to the advantage of unionists in terms of the all-Ireland 'add-ons' to the deal. The application of consociational principles to the governance of Northern Ireland is shown in Table 2.2.

The idea of grand coalition, evident in the Sunningdale Agreement, was extended to allow the inclusion of a (vastly changed) Sinn Fein, although the power-sharing executive was, at best, a loose coalition. The executive was arguably oversized, a common characteristic in

Table 2.2 *The application of consociational principles in the Good Friday Agreement*

Principle	Application
Grand coalition	Cross-community power-sharing executive, headed by first/deputy first minister duopoly
Proportionality in government	Use of the D'Hondt system for executive formation and proportional representation in elections
Minority veto rights	Parallel consent/weighted majority voting within the Assembly
Segmental autonomy	Limited. Respect for the rights of both communities and language provision, but little else

consociational democracies, although the executive was palpably less inflated than the Assembly. Between 1999 and 2002 the Assembly contained eleven different parties, including seven unionist groupings. Again, the presence of a large number of parties is common in European consociational systems, with the exception of Austria (Pennings, 1999). At the head of the executive lay the 'quasi-presidential dual premiership' of the first minister and deputy first minister (O'Leary, 2001).

The idea of a grand governing coalition was more apparent in the GFA than in the Framework Document, the pre-GFA outline of a settlement having been floated tentatively by the Conservative government in 1995. The Framework Document proposed that a three-member elected panel, drawn from the UUP, DUP and SDLP as the best-supported parties at the time, would adjudicate on controversial issues. The UUP argued that the presence of the panel and the requirement for unanimity among its members would render the Northern Ireland Assembly 'paralysed and ineffective' (UUP, 1995).

Selling elite accommodation within political parties

The obvious test was whether the GFA, as an accommodation among political elites, would find favour among the highly politicized and polarized electorate. An apolitical electorate would be one to which consociational ideas need not be applied. Northern Ireland's citizens were more politically engaged than those elsewhere in the United Kingdom, as measured by electoral turnout, engagement in community activity and willingness to engage in political violence. The size of the rejectionist group within the unionist community posed problems for the consolidation of accommodation. Among subelite members of political parties in Northern Ireland there was substantial support for the GFA. The 94.6 per cent of Sinn Fein delegates who actually voted in favour of the agreement at their party gathering were joined in their support of the deal, according to survey evidence, by 98.6 per cent of SDLP members, 94.7 per cent of Alliance Party members and 70.4 per cent of UUP members (Tonge and Evans, 2002).

Historical evidence showed that the support of party members would be vital to the functioning of a devolved government in Northern Ireland. The ill-fated Sunningdale experiment had collapsed not merely because of a loyalist strike but also due to the lack of support by a majority of UUP members, which had fatally damaged the position of the party leader, Brian Faulkner (Gillespie, 1998). Similarly, if the GFA and devolved government were to be sustained, and if the deal's brokers were to retain their credibility, majority support among pro-agreement party members was required. Within the UUP, such support was tested on numerous occasions. Although the votes consistently resulted in victories for pro-GFA supporters, the narrowness of the margins and the frequency of such votes did little to instil confidence in the ability of the party leader to deliver on the deal.

The success of the GFA depended on rival interpretations of the deal being sold to unionist and nationalist parties and electorates, each of which held different political ambitions. The agreement aimed to manage differences in both national identity and constitutional preference. In these areas there was little common ground among 'moderate' pro-GFA party memberships. Eighty per cent of SDLP members had adopted an exclusively Irish identity; 90 per cent of UUP members had adopted a similar exclusive stance in terms of their Britishness. In the centre, the Alliance Party persistently promoted the concept of 'Northern Irishness', but this was a minority aspiration even among party members. Catholics in the Alliance Party leaned towards an Irish identity; Protestants towards a British identity. Unsurprisingly the overwhelming majority of UUP members advocated that Northern Ireland should remain in the United Kingdom, a position supported by only 8 per cent of SDLP members.

The argument by pro-GFA unionists that Northern Ireland's place in the United Kingdom was confirmed by the agreement was accepted by a majority of party members, who did not see the agreement as a move towards Irish unity. Nonetheless the margin was uncomfortably narrow (Table 2.3).

A substantial minority of unionists feared that constitutional aspects of the GFA would create embryonic structures of Irish unity. On this point there was agreement from nationalists: a majority of SDLP members concurred that a united Ireland had come closer as a consequence of the agreement. Added to a similar argument by the Sinn Fein leadership, this nationalist interpretation exacerbated unionism's internal problems. The argument by the UUP leader that the agreement would shore up the union was greeted with scepticism by some in the party leadership as well as ordinary members. The difficulty of selling this argument lay in the intended creation of cross-border bodies, which was supported by the SDLP and Alliance memberships

Table 2.3   *Perceived implications of the Good Friday Agreement among party members in terms of it being a step towards a united Ireland (per cent)*

	Strongly agree	Agree	Neither agree nor disagree	Disagree	Strongly disagree
UUP	27.1	18.2	6.9	30.2	29.4
SDLP	14.2	55.1	21.6	7.0	0.6
APNI	0.3	16.3	32.6	43.1	7.8

(Table 2.4) but seen as an undesirable concession by many in the UUP, a majority of whom favoured power sharing without cross-border bodies.

Most of the UUP leaders argued that unionists need not fear the expansion of all-Ireland structures, given that they would have control over such a development. Despite this the constitutional provisions of strand one of the agreement failed to reassure a large proportion of the party members who in turn were unable or unwilling to convince their electorate. This enabled the DUP to make sizeable electoral gains and it replaced the UUP as the leading unionist party in the 2003 Assembly contest. The problems arising from the agreement often appeared to be less to do with its constitutional direction than other measures which formed part of a process of conflict management. For many UUP members there was no conflict, only terrorism. As such the package of conflict resolution items, which were designed mainly to satisfy nationalists, were based on a false premise. Within the UUP, policing reforms and the early release of paramilitary prisoners were seen as politically and morally wrong, particularly given the reluctance of the IRA to decommission its weapons. According to the author's

Table 2.4   *Attitudes towards the idea that the best solution for Northern Ireland would be power sharing with cross-border bodies (per cent)**

	Strongly agree	Agree	Neither agree nor disagree	Disagree	Strongly disagree
SDLP	35.9	43.0	9.4	3.1	2.3
UUP	11.8	32.2	3.5	28.7	23.9
APNI	39.6	48.9	7.6	3.5	0.0

* No figures are available for Sinn Fein.

survey, fewer than one in ten UUP members would support Sinn Fein's indefinite participation in the Assembly if the IRA failed to lay down all its arms.

Among unionists there was considerable hostility to the early release of paramilitary prisoners. Seventy per cent of UUP members opposed the releases, with only 18 per cent in favour. A slight majority (51 per cent) of Alliance Party members also opposed the deal on prisoners, but 59 per cent of SDLP members supported their early release, with only 18 per cent opposed. If party members had been consulted systematically it is probable that the GFA would never have been brokered, given the contentiousness of this aspect of the package. Accommodation between party elites, protected from their members, was therefore necessary to create a deal. However the lack of support for parts of the GFA among UUP members rendered it vulnerable to challenge from the DUP, whose opposition to its 'unpalatable' aspects was shared by many members of the party's main political rival.

Consociational weaknesses: intrabloc division

Power sharing arrangements carried the advantage of mutual veto, thus preventing dominance by the political representatives of either community. However the arrangements were based on the assumption of solidarity within each political bloc, a characteristic that was missing among unionists. The mutual reliance on which the power-sharing structures were built was evident in the posts of first minister and deputy first minister, neither of the holders of which could survive without the other. The assumption was that each incumbent had to be acceptable to the other community. What had not been anticipated was the unacceptability of proposed representatives of one's own community, an oversight that became apparent with the DUP's refusal to support the UUP's nominee for the post of first minister in 2001. In 1999 Seamus Mallon, the SDLP deputy first minister, resigned, a move that was later declared null and void on the dubious grounds that the Assembly was not fully functioning.

In February 2000 the first minister, David Trimble, used the threat of resignation to force the secretary of state, Peter Mandelson, to suspend devolution. The Assembly and executive were restored in May that year, after an IRA commitment to decommission some of its weapons. However little further progress was made on the issue so

Trimble quit as first minister in 2001. Despite the commencement of decommissioning by the Provisional IRA in October 2001, the confidence of unionist Assembly members (MLAs) in the GFA had diminished and Trimble lacked the necessary unionist majority to secure reinstatement. His position was rescued only by the redesignation of three Alliance MLAs and one Women's Coalition (NIWC) MLA as 'unionist' in November 2001. However the reprieve was only temporary and the Assembly was dissolved in October 2002.

The GFA created an executive in which all the main parties – Sinn Fein, the SDLP, the UUP and the DUP – were supposed to share power. Their choice of departments was based on the D'Hondt mechanism, a formula that rested on the number of seats gained in the Assembly election in June 1998. What emerged was a disparate body rather than a coherent, coalitional executive, indicating the limits of consociation when four ethnically based parties, two from each side, attempt to manage inter- and intraethnic divisions. The factionalism of the governing executive gave lie to the basic consociational assumption that there was a desire among political elites to share power. Although desirous of devolution and claiming only a wish to renegotiate the agreement, the DUP's executive ministers repeatedly objected to the presence of Sinn Fein 'colleagues' in government prior to the disbandment of the IRA. The involuntary nature of the coalition not only made devolution in Northern Ireland a fundamentally different entity from that in Scotland and Wales; it also rendered the executive vulnerable to grandstanding by executive members at the expense of collective action.

The terms of the GFA made it difficult to remove an incompetent minister. A party could supply a replacement minister in the (unlikely) event that its minister was ousted by the Assembly. Elite accommodation within the governing executive and Assembly was also devoid of the recognized system of opposition that existed in standard democracies. Opposition was not present in the bloc system, nor in the Assembly structures. Strong criticism of a Sinn Fein minister, for example by a committee member drawn from the same party, was unlikely. Minority veto rights within the new political framework were based on parallel consent or weighted majority voting. These were, respectively, the requirement that a majority of the MLAs present supported a measure, including a majority of the unionist and nationalist who were present and voting, or that a measure was backed by 60 per cent of the members present and voting, including at least

40 per cent of each of the unionist and nationalist members. Cross-community support was compulsory for votes on the election of the chair of the Assembly, the first minister and the deputy first minister, plus standing orders and budget allocations. On other matters the requirement for cross-community support could be initiated by a petition of concern from 30 of the 108 MLAs. The insistence on measured cross-community support meant that the GFA constituted a rigid form of consociationalism, but it is difficult to think of an alternative. Unqualified proportionality would have been unacceptable to nationalists, being tantamount to a revised form of unionist majoritarianism.

The least clearly defined consociational aspect of the GFA was segmental autonomy, which was minimal for both the unionist and the nationalist bloc. The nationalist community in Northern Ireland was subject to the same legislation emanating from Stormont as its unionist counterpart. The minimalist model of segmental autonomy protected minority political and cultural rights, but a more accurate term for describing community rights under the GFA would be segmental protection. The proposal in the Patten Report in respect of local policing boards would have enhanced local control, but this suggestion was diluted. Segmental autonomy might have been appropriate in Northern Ireland if the territory inhabited by nationalist and unionist communities had been more segregated. Territorial north–south division is apparent in a number of societies where consociational rules apply. For example, Belgium is broadly divided between the northern, Dutch-speaking Flemish community and the southern, French-speaking Walloons. There is segregation in Northern Ireland in terms of the urban delineation of territory and the 'greening' of the three westernmost counties. However the unionist–nationalist territorial divide is far from neat and Belfast is a patchwork quilt of unionist, nationalist and mixed areas. As a result the form of segmental autonomy permitted under the GFA is more akin to the corporate federalism identified by Lijphart (1977), in which 'each individual should be able to declare to which nationality he or she wished to belong ... these nationalities should then become autonomous non-territorial cultural communities' (Harris, 2002, p. 31).

In October 2002 the institutions established under the GFA were suspended for a fourth, indefinite, period. It was evident that the GFA was enduring a crisis of confidence among the unionist population, with the erosion of confidence becoming even more evident when the DUP became the largest unionist party in the 2003 Assembly election.

Although the IRA had begun to decommission its weapons, a series of allegations that it was continuing its activities undermined unionist confidence. Allegations of gun-running from Florida, the arrest in Columbia of three republicans who were linked to FARC guerrillas, a break-in at Castlereagh police headquarters and a police raid on Sinn Fein's office at Stormont, together with claims of an IRA spying operation on political rivals and the security forces, contributed to a sharp reduction in unionist support for the agreement, which fell from 57 per cent in the GFA referendum to 33 per cent in autumn 2002 (BBC Northern Ireland Hearts and Minds Poll, 17 October 2002). Meanwhile loyalist violence increased sharply between 1998 and 2001. Only 38 per cent of the members of the Ulster Unionist Council, the ruling body of the ostensibly pro-GFA UUP, stated they would have voted yes if a second referendum on the agreement had been held in 2001 (Tonge and Evans, 2001c).

Two broader factors need to be considered in respect of the GFA. The first is a cost–benefit analysis of applying consociational principles to a polity that lacked a tradition of parity between two competing communities. Any process of equalization could have been seen as disadvantageous to the formerly dominant community and benefi-cial to the minority community, which had started from a lower political or economic base. As such the costs to the formerly dominant community could have been seen as too great a burden to bear, given that the overall prize – relative peace and security – was demanded as a right.

The second factor was the ability of parties to shape political preferences among voters. By presenting itself as the embodiment of a new, peaceful republicanism, involving fundamental policy changes, Sinn Fein managed to gain the support of a community that might otherwise have been hostile to governmental control from Stormont. Had Sinn Fein opposed the deal the level of support for the GFA by the republican community would have been substantially less and might have been strangled at birth. Instead the nationalist community, weary of an unwinnable war, desirous of peace and willing to accept that a united Ireland was merely a distant possibility, overwhelmingly backed the agreement. The British and Irish governments were assisted by the fact that two strong and popular leaders, John Hume and Gerry Adams, worked in common cause on the nationalist side. The most popular demagogue on the unionist side, Ian Paisley, worked in the opposite direction, damaging an agreement that the DUP saw as morally and politically flawed. Support for the GFA by Sinn Fein heightened unionists' suspicions and reinforced the sceptical DUP view that the agreement amounted to a series of concessions to republicans. The GFA was an incomplete accommodation, given that a section of the political elite, the DUP, opposed the deal whilst the unionist elite broker, the UUP, was vulnerable to erosions of support for the Agreement among its members and supporters. The UUP's response was to support the GFA while simultaneously criticizing aspects of it, particularly changes to policing and the release of prisoners. Electorate preference-shaping was thus hindered by ambiguity, reservation and intra-unionist bloc rivalry.

Self-determination, codetermination, or neither?

Although the language of Irish self-determination preceded the GFA, the 1993 Downing Street Declaration offered a particular interpretation of what this constituted. Endorsement of the agreement was achieved through codetermination, in which the citizens of Northern Ireland and the Irish Republic voted in separate referendums. The form of self-determination permitted to the northern nationalist community did not extend to secession from Northern Ireland and unity with the remainder of the island, as this (leaving aside the obvious practical barriers) was contingent on the approval of the majority of citizens in Northern Ireland. No alternatives to the deal were placed before the electorates of Northern Ireland and the Irish Republic, and whichever way the referendum had gone in the Irish Republic it would not have made any difference to Northern Ireland's constitutional status as part of the United Kingdom. Hence the 1998 referendum was not an exercise in Irish self-determination, but rather a limited device for partial codetermination. The continuing territorial and political integrity of Northern Ireland was justified on the basis of group differentiation; specifically, that its dismantling would impinge upon the right of the unionist majority community to self-determination.

A key issue for British and Irish policy makers was the extent to which the 'Irish dimension' would form part of the GFA. This needed to reflect the identity of northern nationalists and acknowledge, via institutional means, the desire of the majority of the people of the island for Irish unity. Successive Irish governments, beginning with Garret FitzGerald's Fine Gael administration in the 1980s, had supported Irish unity, 'not as the fulfilment of irredentist claims, but as reconciliation within a pluralist context' (Cox, 1985, p. 40). This approach led to the rewording of Articles 2 and 3 of the constitution, which no longer defined the national territory as the 'whole island of Ireland' (Article 2), and deletion of the reference to the reintegration of the national territory as 'pending' (Article 3). The new articles accepted the principle of consent in Northern Ireland as a prerequisite for a united Ireland. The revised Article 3 declared that it was:

> the firm will of the Irish nation, in harmony and friendship, to unite all the people who share the territory of the island of Ireland, in all the diversity of their identities and traditions, recognising that a united Ireland shall be brought about by peaceful means with the consent of a majority of the people democratically expressed, in both jurisdictions in the island.

For diehard republicans the Irish government's willingness to forgo the South's constitutional claim to the north in favour of limited influence amounted to a denial of the national will. The slight binationalism of the agreement and the (even slighter) enhanced conditionality of Northern Ireland's place in the United Kingdom were unacceptable trade-offs for the abandonment of 'national sovereignty'. Support for a united Ireland in the Irish Republic varied considerably according to whether the proposition was put as a long-term aspiration or a short-term workable reality. During the IRA's armed campaign, over 80 per cent of the population aspired to unity (Hayes and McAllister, 1996). One poll in 1999 found that 96 per cent of those with a view on the matter supported the eventual establishment of a united Ireland (*Irish Independent*, 21 December 1999; Coakley, 2001). However the same poll found that only 10 per cent would be prepared to pay higher taxes to facilitate unity.

Opposition to British withdrawal from Northern Ireland grew during the 1970s and 1980s because some in the Irish Republic were fearful of inheriting almost a million 'dissident' unionists. While British withdrawal remained the most favoured option, in contrast to the position in the 1970s and 1980s it was no longer a majority aspiration. As Coakley (2001) notes, the passing of the prepartition generation had led to a greater association of the Republic with just 26 counties, rather than an all-encompassing 32-county nation. Successive Irish governments paid lip service to the notion of Irish unity, but had little

Table 2.5   *Constitutional preferences in Northern Ireland (per cent)*

	Protestant	Catholic	Total
Remain part of the UK	79	15	50
United Ireland	5	59	28
Independent Northern Ireland	5	6	6
Other	2	3	2
Don't know	10	17	14

Source: Adapted from Northern Ireland Life and Times Survey, 2001.

desire to inherit the dissident unionists. A united Ireland remained the most popular choice among Catholics in Northern Ireland, but support was far from overwhelming. Protestants were much more united in their constitutional preference (Table 2.5).

According to combined survey evidence from Hayes and McAllister (1996) and the Northern Ireland Life and Times Survey (2001), 2.5 million people on the island (400 000 in the north and 2.1 million in the south) would like to see a united Ireland, against 1.1 million who do not (roughly 600 000 in the north and 500 000 in the south). The strength of the pro-union aspiration is likely to vary considerably, but the willingness of half the electorate in the Irish Republic and the overwhelming majority of nationalists in Northern Ireland to support an essentially partitionist agreement (or at least in the short or medium term) indicates the lack of a strong desire for Irish unity. This is due to a variety of reasons: the legacy of Britain's colonial claim to territory, the threat of loyalist violence, a genuine willingness to recognize the unionist claim to self-determination and a lack of desire to coerce the pro-Britain population into a united Ireland.

Nonetheless, given the aggregate preference for Irish unity (as acknowledged in the GFA), the claim that a single-option referendum that excluded this option from the ballot paper, whatever the pragmatic grounds for its exclusion, constituted a true exercise in Irish self-determination is dubious. Assuming, not unreasonably, that the electoral process is designed to facilitate the unfettered will of the people, a UK election in which the Labour Party appeared as the only choice on the ballot paper could hardly be called a democratic contest. None of this is to dismiss the symbolic importance of both parts of the island voting on essentially the same topic for the first time since 1918, when of course the result of a genuine exercise in Irish self-determination was ignored. Rather it is merely to puncture the grandiose claims made about the 1998 referendums, which in fact were limited exercises in codetermination in that no alternative choices were put to the people, for pragmatic reasons and perhaps for fear of producing the 'wrong' result.

Binationalism, confederalism and the Irish political process

Given that the GFA was declared by successive British secretaries of state to be 'the only show in town' (an interesting take on self-determination), the question begged was the extent to which acknowledgement of the aspiration for Irish unity would be reflected in the creation of binational structures to link the two parts of the island. The agreement amounted to 'consociationalism plus', in that internal power-sharing arrangements in Northern Ireland were linked to wider associations involving Britain and Ireland. The Northern Ireland Assembly, North–South Ministerial Council, intergovernmental conference and British–Irish Council were established as interlinked institutions. The agreement created a 'consociational federacy' as the British and Irish governments transferred power to a devolved, power-sharing institution, with a remit across different countries and with linkages to other cross-national institutions (O'Leary, 2001, p. 460). The removal of the Republic of Ireland's constitutional claim to Northern Ireland facilitated a more fruitful environment for the conclusion of the strand 1 and 2 talks. The contrast with the Sunningdale Agreement could hardly have been starker. After the conclusion of that agreement, the Irish attorney general had insisted that 'any person living in this island and knowing our history could not possibly construe the Sunningdale declaration as meaning that we did not lay claim over the six counties' (*Irish Times*, 22 April 1974; O'Leary and McGarry, 1993).

There followed growing convergence in preferred policy towards Northern Ireland, between the post-nationalist discourse offered by John Hume as leader of the SDLP and the neo-, or civic, nationalist approach of the Irish government. Hume's argument was that the disagreement between unionists and nationalists over the modalities of the means of national self-determination could be resolved by separate referendums in the north and south, a view accepted by the Irish and

British governments. The intergovernmentalism imposed via the 1985 Anglo-Irish Agreement angered unionists, whilst eventually helping to convince sufficient militant nationalists that goals could be advanced within a framework devoid of violence. The say afforded to the Irish government in the affairs of Northern Ireland was used constructively, being aimed at convincing republicans that politics offered a superior route to Irish unity than did violence.

The cross-border dimension of the GFA created six new all-island implementation bodies, overseen by the North–South Ministerial Council (NSMC). The institutional model of all-island cooperation was 'top down'. There was little support from unionists for such a development and this was not a civic society model of cooperation. For the British government, limited joint authority did not amount to joint sovereignty as the two governments were exercising sovereignty in their own states to create new political institutions. The NSMC was made accountable to the respective legislatures in Northern Ireland and the Irish Republic, and the UUP was successful in ensuring that the NSMC did not have executive power, which instead was dispersed to individual bodies (Hennessey, 2000). In addition to the implementation bodies, six areas were identified for cross-border cooperation, but with policy implementation remaining separate, according to jurisdiction. The Irish dimension was minimal, being confined to largely insignificant policy areas, EU programmes aside, and ringfenced by the requirement for Assembly approval for expansion. As the chair of Sinn Fein, Mitchel McLaughlin, conceded, the 'Assembly does have a controlling input in terms of both the establishment of the bodies and their functions' (quoted in ibid., p. 171). Concerned with selling the deal to its own constituency, Sinn Fein negotiated much harder on issues such as prisoner releases and equality than on the all-island agenda, which ought to have been the party's domain.

The British–Irish Council has been likened to the Nordic Union in that it acts as a facilitator for interparliamentary contact, policy discussions and the development of common frameworks for dealing with problems (Walker, 2001). The Ulster Unionist Party favoured the British–Irish Council as a means of securing Northern Ireland's place within a restructured United Kingdom. By linking the Assembly in Northern Ireland to other devolved institutions in the UK, the new legislature might be less isolated. The GFA also made clear that the intergovernmental machinery of the Anglo-Irish Agreement would be subsumed (but not abandoned) under the revised administrative arrangements. British–Irish summitry was retained, but broadened to involve the heads of the devolved administration in Northern Ireland.

The British and Irish governments moved towards a position of neutrality on the future of Northern Ireland, as asymmetry replaced irredentism. There remained differences between them, given that the revised Article 2 of the Irish constitution stated that citizens in the north had the right to belong to an Irish nation, whilst Article 3 indicated the preferred outcome of Irish unity. However Article 2 made no territorial claim and Article 3 was explicit in its assertion of the need for northern consent for a united Ireland. Poor relations between the British and Irish governments on the question of Northern Ireland between 1969 and 1972 healed with remarkable rapidity as both moved against the IRA. Suspicion of the Irish government came almost exclusively from the unionist parties. According to a UUC membership survey conducted by the author in 2001, only 3 per cent of the Ulster Unionist Council believed that the Dublin government could be trusted on constitutional issues (Tonge and Evans, 2002). The influence of the Republic on the affairs of Northern Ireland has been derided as an exercise of power without responsibility (Aughey, 1989).

The Sunningdale Agreement and the Anglo-Irish Agreement offered new institutional contexts for Anglo-Irish relations, with little pain for the Irish government. Abandonment of the constitutional claim to Northern Ireland was more difficult, given its symbolic importance, but it was clearly a non-negotiable item if cross-border executive authority was to be conceded by unionists. The *taoiseach* could also present the Good Friday Agreement as a possible route to Irish unity. A more realistic appraisal of the Irish government's perception of the GFA was offered by one of its advisers, Fergus Finlay, who insisted that 'this was never about unity' but instead concerned 'stability and peace' (Finlay, 1998, pp. 182–3). Given that an agreement without republicans was 'not worth a penny candle', the main ambition of the Irish government was to bring Sinn Fein and the IRA onboard by promoting the Hume–Adams conclusions as much as possible with the British government. The difficulty for the Irish government was to articulate the merits of a document that association with was described as the kiss of death by John Major's Conservative government. Some input from loyalist paramilitary groups was also offered to the Irish government, with a Protestant clergyman, Roy Magee, acting as intermediary (Mallie and McKittrick, 1996). The language of pronouncements on Northern Ireland, stressing the need for self-determination but exercised on a north and south basis, reflected a compromise between the forces of Irish nationalism and robust British assertions of the consent principle. Even a very senior party official in Sinn Fein conceded privately that he 'never believed that the Good Friday Agreement would bring about unity in twenty to thirty years' time' (private discussion, December 2000).

Non-constitutional agendas

The main thrust of the GFA was reconstituting Northern Ireland, rather than moving towards binational authority or joint sovereignty (despite genuflections in those directions). Reconstitution involved a new form of governance and the 'quangofication' of Northern Ireland, via the establishment of various commissions. The most striking conflict resolution measure was the release of all paramilitary prisoners associated with groups that had declared ceasefire by 2000. Other measures were more permanent attempts to end inequality and perceived injustice. Their net effect was to falsify the common currency among republicans that Northern Ireland could not be reformed as a political entity. Post-GFA, few could argue that Catholics were the subjects of serious and systematic disadvantage. Indeed the inequalities in Northern Ireland appeared to owe more to social position than to religious denomination. It was social and economic inequality that had fuelled nationalist protest at the start of the Troubles and many nationalists could be assuaged by the promise of equality within the existing territorial boundaries. For true republicans, however, it was denial of the political right to national sovereignty that needed to be addressed. Thus Bernadette Sands-McKevitt – sister of Bobby Sands, the republican hunger striker who died in 1981 – insisted that he 'did not die for nationalists to be equal British citizens within the Northern Ireland state' (*Irish Times*, 8 January 1998; Hennessey, 2000, p. 112).

A Human Rights Commission (NIHRC) and an Equality Commission have been established under the GFA. The Human Rights Acts of 1998 and 2000 enshrined the European Convention of Human Rights in the law. The HIHRC is headed by a full-time commissioner, assisted by nine part-time commissioners. Its task is to ensure that laws comply with human rights, and therefore it scrutinized Assembly legislation until the collapse of the Assembly in 2002. It is entitled to bring proceedings when it suspects contraventions of human rights (Harvey,

2001). Individuals are entitled to take cases of alleged breaches of human rights to the NIHRC, which is also charged with promoting awareness of such rights. A key role of the Equality Commission is to monitor Section 75 of the 1998 Northern Ireland Act, which places a statutory responsibility on public authorities to offer equal opportunities to all. The Equality Commission, which is headed by a chief commissioner and deputy commissioners and supported by 18 part-time commissioners, is a consolidation of the pre-GFA 'fairness' commissions, covering fair employment, equal opportunity, racial equality and disability.

A review of the criminal justice system was set up under the GFA. Its purpose was to monitor the workforce to ensure religious balance in the system, monitor judicial independence, assist victims of injustice and explore north–south cooperation (Bryan, 2001). The Criminal Justice Review Group (2000) recommended the introduction of a Law Commission to review legal processes, plus the establishment of a Judicial Appointments Commission. An Independent Commission on Policing was also established under the GFA, with the Patten Commission's recommendations soon becoming a source of considerable consternation to unionists. Meanwhile the Independent International Commission on Decommissioning, itself reformist in the sense of diminishing paramilitary culture, presided over a slow process of weapons decommissioning, the Provisional IRA having completed three acts of decommissioning by the end of 2003.

Rectifying the democratic deficit

The Good Friday Agreement was sold by New Labour not merely as a means of consolidating peace, but also as a remedy for the long-standing democratic deficit in the governance of Northern Ireland. Devolution was offered as part of a wider process of democratization. The parties in Northern Ireland were at least able to agree that there was a democratic deficit. For diehard republicans the continuing presence of the British government was the reason for, not the solution to, that problem, whilst some unionists believed that total administrative integration offered the ideal remedy for the problem. Electoral integrationists argued that redress through devolution was only a partial solution, and that to ensure true democracy the citizens of Northern Ireland ought to be able to join and vote for the three main parties at

Westminster. In 2003 a Labour Party supporter in Northern Ireland took court action to win the right to join the party. It appears that Labour conceded the right of Northern Ireland citizens to join the party, but there was no indication that the party wished to contest elections in the province. Electoral integrationists in the Labour Party were heavily criticized by Irish nationalist sympathizers in the same organization, including Kevin McNamara, who (correctly) perceived a unionist agenda in the pro-integration organization, Democracy Now, which had been launched in 1992 (McNamara, 1992). There was little evidence of widespread sympathy for the integrationist cause within the party as only 12 per cent of Labour MPs supported the idea (Elliott and Flackes, 1999, p. 224).

The main problem with direct rule in the post-1972 period was the lack of scrutiny of policy. Ministerial orders could not be amended by the Council for Northern Ireland, only approved or disapproved (Hazleton, 1994). Few Westminster MPs displayed an interest in or knowledge of Northern Ireland. Scrutiny improved slightly with the establishment of the Northern Ireland Select Committee in 1994, but its birth was seemingly a case of a beleaguered Conservative government under John Major offering succour to the unionists, whose parliamentary votes it needed. Nonetheless the idea had been mooted for some time. If the establishment of the committee was a sop to unionists, they were not hugely rewarded as only five (one of whom was the first chair) of the 13 committee members were from Northern Ireland, a ratio that remained unchanged when a non-Northern Ireland MP (Peter Brooke) became chair immediately after the election of the Labour government in 1997. More cohesive than effective, the committee achieved little in its first term, one member even describing as 'a joke' the idea that it had increased the accountability of direct rule (Wilford and Elliott, 1999).

Consociationalism and conflict resolution

The ultimate success of the consociational solution offered by the GFA depended on whether it could offer an appropriate means of conflict management, through its interrelated institutions, mutual community vetoes and equality agenda, all of which are discussed in detail elsewhere in this book. Under the GFA power was diffused, although much remained at Westminster. Of the devolved responsibilities, most lay with the 'grand coalition' executive, but were also delegated to the wider Assembly, the intergovernmental conference and the NSMC. Diffusion of power was accompanied by interdependence. The failure of one arena of power had a negative impact on another, given that the executive and the North–South Council were interdependent. That risked a domino effect, in which the collapse of one institution would lead to the destruction of much of the entire edifice, as occurred in 2002.

A second means of reducing conflict – the elimination of inequalities between rival groups – was a clear feature of the GFA, although inequality within each bloc was also of great importance. The equality agenda carried risk, as the formerly dominant community, itself far from homogeneous, feared there would be overcompensation. There was also a possibility of intra-ethnic conflict, as the unionist and nationalist parties promoted party interests above the collective good laid down in the agreement. As Horowitz (1985, pp. 597–99) argues, intra-ethnic conflict can be functional if it moves a problem away from traditional interethnic conflict. However in Northern Ireland, pro- versus anti-GFA political and electoral rivalries within the unionist bloc destabilized the agreement and overshadowed the diminution of interethnic conflict.

Long-term conflict reduction can depend on the parties in new political institutions being capable of developing agendas to encourage the development of non-ethnic alignments and interethnic bloc cooperation. There need to be incentives for moderation in bloc parties. Clearly these existed for Sinn Fein, which was anxious to remain in the executive. The alleged continuation of paramilitary activity by the IRA led to the recurrent suspension of the Assembly and executive in 2000–2, even though Sinn Fein had distanced itself from armed struggle. The incentive for moderation rested on the assumption that all parties wished to remain in the political institutions and risked being expelled by the electorate if they failed to adhere to the rules of the game. Under this model Sinn Fein acted as a centripetal force, attempting to move all parties towards the political centre, rather than as a centrifugal party, permanently promoting vigorous ethnic bloc politics.

For the DUP, which opposed the GFA, there were fewer incentives for moderation, given the increased electoral mileage in rejecting the terms of the deal. Having acquired the coveted status of leading unionist party through such opposition, there was now the incentive that moderation could lead to the party acquiring key posts, including that of first minister, in a revived executive. With less significant portfolios, the DUP had remained within the Assembly and executive between 1999 and 2002, despite its criticism of aspects of the GFA.

The longer-term hope is that non-ethnic alignments can be forged, given that many of the issues determined by the Assembly are not ones in which a particular 'ethnic view' is held. Therefore party competition, or intraparty rivalries, based on factors such as class, gender or age, may pertain, rather than interethnic hostility.

The GFA did not offer a model for assimilation of the ethnic identities of the two communities in Northern Ireland. Rather it presented an elite accommodation, based on the classic consociational features of grand coalition, mutual veto, proportionality and, to a much lesser extent, community autonomy. It recognized two ethno-nationalisms and offered institutional facilitation of cooperation. At the societal level, it cherished and celebrated diversity, with the emphasis on mutual tolerance. The alternative, single-community approach favoured by the political centre was seen as too ambitious. Tolerance and acceptance, before integration, underpinned the thinking behind the GFA. Co-identity, rather than shared identity, was a recurring theme. The GFA assumed that there would be sufficient all-party loyalty to the institutions it created to develop consensus politics. As such politics took root, segmentation would no longer be seen as threatening or harmful.

From the outset the functioning of the institutions suffered from the lack of a system of government and opposition, the latter being based on hostility to aspects of the GFA by members of the government. For the consociational settlement to become fully embedded, acceptance of cross-segmental responsibilities by all parties was necessary, as was the need for the institutions of the state to command authority and respect. The attempted institutional reconstruction of Northern Ireland was not matched by developments in civil society, where only a slow thaw occurred, or greater segregation developed in some localities. This led to the GFA being criticized as a consociational, elite accommodation that froze ethnic divisions and denied a common humanity. Social transformationists argued for a bottom-up approach, in which reconciliation through cross-community initiatives would unpick the sectarian log jam that consociational deals supposedly enshrined (Taylor, 2001). The consociational school perhaps offered a more realistic appraisal of the fracture in Northern Ireland and its management, but as later chapters will discuss, both schools, whilst readily agreeing to a binational approach to conflict resolution, under-stated the impact of partition on the perpetuation of sectarian division. The primary focus of the GFA was on internally reconstituting the northern state, rather than, as might have been preferable given the long-term aspirations of the majority of the island's citizens, attempting to turn the province into a more explicitly binational entity.

3

Unionism New and Old

The Good Friday Agreement heightened the unionist rivalries that had existed since the rise of Paisleyism in the late 1960s. Although unionists had enjoyed near unanimity in respect of constitutional preferences, they had often been divided on the most appropriate means of maintaining the constitutional *status quo*, itself a defensive position. The brief period of unionist unity following the 1985 Anglo-Irish Agreement had long dissipated as work on the GFA began in the 1990s. Intra-unionist rivalry destabilized the GFA, and Paisley's DUP prospered in opposing the deal. The divisions within unionism were partly tactical and strategic in terms of how best to counter the perceived growth of pan-nationalism, seemingly led by Sinn Fein. More fundamentally, intra-unionist contests raised questions about the essence of unionism.

Unionism and the GFA: from modest support to opposition

The Good Friday Agreement exacerbated long-standing divisions within unionism. There was 57 per cent support among Protestants for the GFA in the May 1998 referendum on the deal (Hayes and McAllister, 2001), and one month later this narrow margin was translated into a precariously narrow majority of pro-GFA unionists in the Northern Ireland Assembly. The discomfiture of pro-GFA unionists was exacerbated by ebbing support among Protestants, with only one in three backing the agreement by 2001 (Northern Ireland Life and Times Survey, 2001). In 2002 the UUP withdrew its ministers from the North–South Ministerial Council (NSMC), which had been boycotted from the outset by the DUP. Unionist disenchantment climaxed amid allegations of an IRA spy ring at Stormont in October 2002, with a police raid on Sinn Fein's Assembly office being followed by the arrest elsewhere of republicans suspected of targeting the army, the police, opposition parties and even civil servants. As unionists would not continue to work alongside Sinn Fein until the Provisional IRA disbanded, the Assembly and executive were suspended for an indefinite period. The Joint Implementation Plan issued by the British and Irish governments in 2003, designed to revive the GFA, was rejected by several prominent figures in the UUP. When the latter was defeated in the 2003 assembly election, outpolled by the DUP, it was apparent that a realignment of unionism had occurred.

Many in the ostensibly pro-GFA UUP shared the hostility of the unionist electorate to the agreement, whilst unionism's other major electoral force, the Democratic Unionist Party (DUP), had voiced clearly its distaste of the deal from the outset. Unionist disunity was scarcely novel: after the demise of Unionist Party hegemony at the beginning of the 1970s, unionist unity had been rare, and had occurred mainly in the immediate aftermath of the 1985 Anglo-Irish Agreement. The common unionist distaste for the unsold 1995 Joint Framework Document was replaced by deep differences over the GFA. These divisions were played out in unionism's largest party through a succession of special votes by the ruling body of the UUP, the Ulster Unionist Council (UUC), on whether to remain in Northern Ireland's new political institutions alongside Sinn Fein. As in the wider unionist community, confidence in the GFA ebbed among the UUC membership. Almost 70 per cent of its members claimed to have voted in support of the agreement in the 1998 referendum, but by 2001 only 38 per cent said they would vote again the same way.

This chapter explores the basis of the fragmentation of unionism by examining economic, social, religious and political variables. It suggests that transition from an ethnic and cultural form of unionism to a civic and pluralist form is possible, but may require changed leadership and a clearer commitment to power sharing with republicans from the DUP, whilst within the UUP the need for structural change is evident.

Who were the players?

It was once remarked by Brendan Behan that the first item on the IRA's agenda was the split, yet a similar jibe could be made of unionism in recent decades. Whilst the notion of unionist hegemony from 1921 to 1969 has perhaps been overplayed, the Unionist Party was unquestionably dominant, assisted by the abolition of proportional representation in the 1920s, a move that inhibited the growth of rival unionist parties. After the onset of the Troubles in 1969, unionist parties proliferated. Later, 35 per cent of the population declared that they regard themselves as unionist, although half of the electorate identified themselves as Protestant (Northern Ireland Life and Times Survey, 2001). The 1998 Assembly election yielded a plethora of anti-GFA parties. The cast of characters included the Northern Ireland Unionist Party (NIUP), whose three MLAs were elected as United Kingdom Unionist Party (UKUP) candidates but split from the party in January 1999, leaving a solitary UKUP MLA, Robert McCartney, who was also staunchly anti-GFA. A total of four UKUP MLAs left to form the NIUP, but one, Roger Hutchinson, was expelled from the new party in December 1999 and sat as an independent unionist. Members of the United Unionist Assembly Party (UUAP) stood as independents but formed an Assembly alliance in September 1998. In the 2003 Assembly election the DUP hoovered up these disparate anti-GFA groups, only the UKUP surviving with a solitary seat. The DUP's dominance of anti-GFA unionism was complete, its 30 Assembly seats being boosted to 33 by the defection from the UUP of the anti-GFA MLAs Jeffrey Donaldson, Arlene Foster and Norah Beare. After the defections, the UUP was reduced to 24 seats, with only a solitary Progressive Unionist Party (PUP) member adding to the pro-GFA unionist representation in the Assembly. The PUP accepted unionism as a form of political pluralism and forged a 'new loyalism' that interpreted the constitutional aspects of the GFA in a similar way to the pro-GFA wing of the UUP. Hitherto the dominant unionist party, other than in European elections, the UUP, with 22.7 per cent of the vote, found itself outpolled by the DUP's 25.7 per cent.

The struggle between the UUP and DUP for unionist votes was vigorous from the time the latter was formed in 1971 from the Protestant Unionist Party. Post-GFA the rivalry reached new levels, as pragmatic versus fundamentalist and civic versus ethnic faultlines within unionism became starker. Despite its opposition to the deal, the DUP participated in all the institutions created by the agreement, except the NSMC. Attracting a combination of urban loyalists and rural evangelicals, the DUP had a hardline constitutional approach, but attempted to marry this to a progressive social agenda. A signifi-cant number of activists were drawn from the Free Presbyterian Church, itself a tiny organization (Bruce, 1986). The DUP's critique of the GFA was based on political and moral factors. The party out-lined its 'seven principles' in respect of any replacement for the GFA. These included insistence that there would be 'no negotiating with the representatives of terrorism' and that 'terrorist structures and weaponry must be removed before the bar to the Stormont execu-tive can be opened' (Democratic Unionist Party, 2003, p. 2). These demands were not greatly different from the UUP's insistence that the Assembly should be restored 'only when republicans have dealt conclusively with the issues of decommissioning, continued paramili-tary activity and the effective winding-up of their paramilitary activity' (Ulster Unionist Party, 2003). With an increasing number of unionists disillusioned with the GFA and the UUP leadership admitting to feeling 'short-changed' by an IRA act of decommissioning in October 2003, the DUP was entrusted to pursue what was demanded by Protestants from any deal. The DUP critique was not confined to the GFA's ambiguity on the requirements placed on paramilitary groups. Whilst the UUP welcomed ring-fenced cross-border cooperation, the DUP argued that executive cross-border bodies were insulated from control. Thus the DUP asserted that 'any relationship with the Republic of Ireland should be fully accountable to the Assembly', rather than the NSMC (Democratic Unionist Party, 2003, p. 2).

Working-class loyalists split over the GFA. At one stage the two loyalist parties, the PUP and UDP, which were linked to the para-military UVF and UDA respectively, supported the agreement and campaigned for a yes vote in the 1998 referendum. Assisted by its presence in the Assembly, the PUP remained on-side in that respect, although in 2002 the UVF admitted breaching its ceasefire during sectarian riots in Belfast. Without a foothold in the Assembly the UDP collapsed, the UDA and UFF withdrew their support for the GFA and their ceasefire was ruled invalid by the secretary of state, John Reid, in 2001. The UDA ceasefire was revived in 2003 after the expul-sion of the imprisoned leader of 'C Company', Johnny Adair, and the enforced exile of his allies after an internal feud. Meanwhile main-stream unionists maintained their divisions over whether the GFA was the most appropriate means of securing the union and bickered over the painful side effects of its various measures.

A crisis of identity, tactics or ideology? Approaches to the study of unionism

There are three broad approaches to the study of divisions within unionism. The most common is to concentrate on a supposed crisis of unionist identity, distinguishing between Ulster loyalists and Ulster British (Nelson, 1984; Todd, 1987). Whilst not disputing the existence of such distinctions *per se*, assertions of a crisis of identity become less convincing when subjected to empirical testing (Aughey, 1989, 1997; Tonge and Evans, 2001c). Seventy per cent of Protestants describe themselves as British, 17 per cent use the label Northern Irish, 9 per cent prefer an Ulster identity and only 2 per cent view themselves as Irish (Northern Ireland Life and Times Survey, 2001). These variations are less than those found among Catholics, yet there has been scant talk of a crisis of nationalist identity.

The internal divisions plaguing unionist parties do not stem from an identity crisis. The DUP's Britishness is starkly expressed in cultural and ethnic forms, while the UUP's 2003 manifesto ('Simply British') makes clear the party's national identity. Indeed surveys suggest that the degree of clarity about national identity within the UUP surpasses that found among nationalist and centrist party members (Evans *et al.*, 2000; Tonge and Evans, 2001a, b, c; Evans and Tonge, 2003). The large (858-member) ruling body of the UUP, the Ulster Unionist Council (UUC), appears to be more in harmony in respect of national identity than even the wider Protestant population, a considerable achievement given the solidity of Protestant national identity. National identity and political strategy clearly require separation. Table 3.1 shows the overwhelming sense of British identity within the UUC, transcending internal party divisions.

Unionists' sense of Britishness, which became more acute after the loss of the Ulster identity particularly associated with the pre-1972 devolved parliament, has remained strong. There is also greater cohesion among Protestants over constitutional questions than there is among Catholics. Seventy-nine per cent of Protestants believe that the long-term policy for Northern Ireland should be for it to remain part of the United Kingdom; no other option merits support of greater than 5 per cent. Only 59 per cent of Catholics support a united Ireland (Northern Ireland Life and Times Survey, 2001). Unionists do not appear to be confused about their identity or their political aspirations.

Table 3.1   *The self-ascribed national identity of UUC members**

National identity	Per cent
British	94.3
Northern Irish	3.7
Irish	0.7
Other	1.3

* N = 299.

In short, they know who they are and where they want to be. What concerns unionists is where they are being taken, however groundless the concern.

Among a section of working-class loyalists, tapped by the PUP, there is greater acknowledgement of an Irish dimension to identity than hitherto. This is due to their newly found confidence, only partly eroded since the GFA, about Northern Ireland's constitutional future, which was also a crucial factor in bringing about the loyalist ceasefires. Growing disaffection among loyalists about perceived concessions to loyalists prompted the secretary of state, in a speech at the Institute of Irish Studies at Liverpool University in 2001, to caution against Northern Ireland becoming a 'cold house for Protestants' in the way it once had been for Catholics.

The second broad approach to the problems within unionism, similar to the line taken by the leader of the UUP, David Trimble, sees division as tactical rather than strategic or ideological. Thus the fault lines within unionism are the product of short-term issues such as the debate on whether to share power with Sinn Fein prior to the disbandment of the Provisional IRA. Clearly some post-GFA debates within the UUP have been tactical, including how best to enforce a 'no guns, no government' stance.

However to view the divisions within unionism as reducible merely to the activities or existence of the Provisional IRA is to risk ignoring wider contesting forces. The third approach looks at fundamental ideological divisions within unionism that may have particular social and political bases, such as concern about the appropriate response to the novel challenges of a vibrant pan-nationalism and the attempted implementation of a form of consociational democracy, nodding towards a binational approach to solving Northern Ireland's political difficulties. The basic choice for unionists lies between a 'no' unionism that is heavily reliant on cultural expressions of a distinctive Protestant Britishness, and a pragmatic 'yes' unionism that is prepared to over-look the imperfections of an emotionally difficult political deal with historical enemies in favour of what Porter describes as civic unionism, designed to preserve the union (Porter, 1996). The contest appears to be between two broad categories of unionist: rational civics who are willing to concede the validity of nationalism and are supportive of an Irish dimension to Northern Ireland's political arrangements, and Orange sceptics who are fearful of any dilution of the Britishness of the state and distrustful of the changed strategies of Irish republicans.

The impact of structure

The divisions within the UUP have been exacerbated by its structural problems. In contrast the DUP has had the advantage of a semi-autocratic leadership, a loyal membership and an absence of overly democratic structures. Indeed the DUP was once described as 'Paisley's fan club' (Bruce, 1986, p. 107).

Despite the existence of the UUC and an executive committee to endorse and confirm policy, the UUP is one of the most decentralized political parties in the United Kingdom, often resembling a movement rather than a formal organization (Hume, 1996). The party comprises 18 virtually autonomous constituency associations, over which the leadership exerts little authority. Its members have derided the party's 'quaint 100 year old system' of decision making and the UUP has begun a process of reform (Michael McGimpsey, quoted in the *Belfast Telegraph*, 27 March 2000). The UUC comprises 680 delegates from constituency associations, plus representatives of the Orange Order and a small number of delegates of other affiliated bodies. Its diverse make-up reflects its historical status as the ruling body for all unionist thought, prior to the party schisms that have afflicted unionism since the late 1960s. It remains, however, a diverse, coalitional body of interests whose remit is to secure the political interests of the Ulster British people.

The decentralized structure and diverse make-up of the UUC mattered relatively little during the decades of unionist hegemony. Indeed participation during part of that period by bodies such as the Ulster Unionist Labour Association emphasized the cross-class alliances within unionism. Since then, however, challenges have come from a variety of forces: the strident loyalism of the DUP, the overarching nature of the Anglo-Irish intergovernmental axis, and the vibrancy of pan-nationalism since the 1990s.

The UUP's status as a coalitional movement means that internal dissent is possible. Its Westminster MPs were almost evenly divided over whether to back the GFA. Its Assembly MLAs were mainly pro-GFA from 1998 to 2002, but two refused to support the re-election of David Trimble as first minister in November 2001. Constituency autonomy allowed the selection of a number of anti-GFA candidates in the run-up to the Assembly 2003 elections. Finally, the Union First 'ginger' group offered persistent criticism of aspects of the agreement.

Measuring UUP division

Although the phrase 'crisis in unionism' has often been uttered there is little data on the basis of division. How do we measure and analyse the divisions within unionism? In part, this can be undertaken by examining the relative strengths of the UUP and DUP (Table 3.2).

Whilst Paisley's popularity as the DUP's representative in the 'beauty contests' of single constituency European elections was evident between

Table 3.2   *UUP–DUP electoral rivalry, 1997–2004*

Election	Share of vote (%)	
	UUP	*DUP*
Pre-GFA:		
1997 Westminster	32.7	13.6
1997 Local	27.9	15.6
Post-GFA:		
1998 Assembly	21.3	18.1
1999 European	17.6	28.4
2001 Westminster	26.8	22.5
2001 Local	22.9	21.4
2003 Assembly	22.7	25.7
2004 European	16.5	31.9

1979 and 1999, his party was an oppositional force until it became the leading unionist party in 2003. The DUP gained three Westminster seats in the 2001 general election and 40 council seats in the local elections held on the same day. In 2003 the DUP gained nine Assembly seats, subsequently increased to 12 by UUP defections, and the party accounted for 56 per cent of the unionist bloc in the Assembly.

Within the UUP, the first Assembly term saw a consistently narrower majority in favour of the party's continued involvement in government alongside Sinn Fein. In November 1999 the UUC members voted by 480 to 329 (59.3 per cent to 40.7 per cent) to allow the UUP to join an all-inclusive executive. This pro-GFA majority narrowed slightly in subsequent UUC ballots, but the pragmatic, rational civic wing still held sway. When entering government with Sinn Fein the UUC built in its own default mechanism, indicating that it would withdraw by February 2000 if progress on decommissioning failed to materialize. As that date arrived without the requisite progress, it was clear to the secretary of state for Northern Ireland, Peter Mandelson, the UUP would not remain in government. In a pre-emptive move on 11 February he suspended the executive, the first of a series of collapses.

In addition to regular UUC votes on whether to govern with Sinn Fein, the contest between rational civics and Orange sceptics was played out in 2000 in a UUP leadership contest between the incumbent, David Trimble, and the challenger, the Reverend Martin Smyth. This amounted to a contest between the pro-GFA rational civic wing of unionism and its anti-GFA Orange sceptics. This section analyses data from the first academic survey of the voters in that contest – the members of the Ulster Unionist Council – to examine the social and attitudinal differences between the two types of unionist outlined above (299 replies to a detailed postal questionnaire were received from 858 UUC members). All UUC members are required to be UUP constituency members and the vast bulk (four fifths) of delegates are representatives of their constituency parties. It is of course possible that the membership of the UUC is unrepresentative, in sociodemographic and attitudinal terms, of the wider party, but this is unlikely, given the non-hierarchical nature of the party and the presence of so many constituency delegates in the ranks of the UUC.

As challenger, Smyth insisted he had 'no real desire to be leader of the party' (*The Times*, 24 March 2000). He also took a 'tactical division' line, arguing that his decision to stand was due to widespread disillusionment over the failure to achieve IRA decommissioning.

Specifically, he rejected Trimble's assertion in Washington during the previous week's St Patrick's Day events that it might be possible for the UUP to re-enter government with Sinn Fein 'without [IRA] guns upfront' (*Belfast Telegraph*, 24 March 2000). Smyth was certainly not the only prominent Orange critic of Trimble; another, Jeffrey Donaldson, removed himself from the GFA negotiations on the day of signing, due to ambiguities about decommissioning, and eventually headed for the DUP.

The margin of Trimble's victory over Smyth was much narrower than predicted. The incumbent party leader defeated his challenger by 457 votes (56.8 per cent) to 348 (43.2 per cent). Five years earlier Smyth had been the first to be eliminated in the UUP leadership contest won by Trimble, having polled only 60 votes. Although the 2000 leadership contest showed that the pro-Trimble, pro-GFA section of the UUC was still larger than the anti-Trimble wing, the assertion by the Trimble supporter Michael McGimpsey that the triumph was based on a 'rock solid majority' convinced few (*Guardian*, 27 March 2000). At the same meeting as the Trimble–Smyth contest, the UUC passed a motion prohibiting UUP participation in the Northern Ireland Executive unless the name and symbols of the Royal Ulster Constabulary were preserved. Clearly there was considerable division within the UUC over the desirability of continuing the pragmatic form of unionism exercised by Trimble. The leadership contest was indicative of the divisive nature of the debate on the ideology and politics of unionism. Trimble survived a further leadership challenge in 2004.

The pro- and anti-GFA wings of unionism each sought the decommissioning of IRA weapons, so Trimble was able to argue that divisions within the UUP were tactical rather than strategic. Trimble supporters believed that the Provisional IRA had concluded its paramilitary campaign, and that the GFA offered a framework for the development of a new politics in Northern Ireland and heralded a necessary change in unionism. The pro-GFA wing of the party wished to develop a civic form of unionism, accepting the diversity of traditions in Northern Ireland and emphasizing the principle of consent. It argued that the consent principle enshrined in the GFA ensured that the pursuit of nationalist goals would not threaten unionists. The nationalist political tradition could be safely accommodated in Trimble's new version of Stormont, which was outlined in his opening address to the Assembly as a 'pluralist parliament for a pluralist people'. In developing this civic unionism the UUP could be the primary shaper of unionist destiny, unlike the pre-GFA situation, in which an intergovernmental axis had dominated from the time of the 1985 Anglo-Irish Agreement.

For opponents of the GFA the deal constituted a baseline for republican advances, which would transfer Northern Ireland into a binational state and ultimately a united Ireland. Meanwhile a residual subculture of paramilitarism would flourish. Whilst anti-GFA unionists were not a cohesive body, most of them saw republicanism as a form of cultural and political expansionism that could best be countered by resolute displays of cultural and political unionism, emphasizing faith and crown, alongside a tough position on the constitution. Smyth's prominent role in the Orange Order, of which he had been grand master for 25 years, linked unionist resolution to Protestantism and Orangeism, allied to determined expressions of Ulster Britishness. According to the *Belfast Telegraph* (27 March 2000) Smyth had 'first been an Orangeman, then a politician'. Thus the debates on decommissioning were indeed tactical, but they masked more fundamental questions about the future of unionism.

Figure 3.1 *Voting by age in the Ulster Unionist Party leadership contest, 2000 (per cent)*

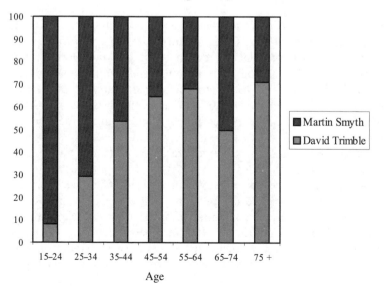

A sociodemographic breakdown of the voting in the Trimble–Smyth leadership contest facilitates assessment of whether factors such as occupation, age and region are significant indicators of support of or hostility to Trimble's leadership, and by extension the Good Friday Agreement. The pro- versus anti-GFA debate within unionism was sometimes portrayed as a battle between progressives and dinosaurs. True or otherwise, the composition of the respective 'camps' was not as might be expected. Most notably, the forces of modernization were predominantly older members of the UUC. Perhaps the most striking aspect of the Trimble–Smyth leadership contest was that the veteran, non-progressive challenger enjoyed majority support among those aged 34 or under. In contrast the strongest support for Trimble was among the 55–64 and 75 plus age groups (Figure 3.1). Trimble, as a modernizer, was forced to query whether the Young Unionists should be permitted to hold seats on the Ulster Unionist Council. In 2004 the Young Unionists dissolved, amid a general crisis of discontent within and defection from the UUP following its relegation to second place by the DUP in the previous year's Assembly elections.

The influence of the Orange Order

Smyth's prominent showing indicated a further fault line within unionism, based on the Orange Order. An organization with formal voting rights (one sixth of UUC votes) in the UUP, the Orange Order opposed the GFA as politically unsound and morally unacceptable, most obviously because of its provision for the early release of paramilitary prisoners. This opposition was of importance in a highly religious, overwhelmingly Protestant party and Orange Order membership was an important variable in the vote on the GFA, although in the post-GFA honeymoon period even a majority of Orange Order members voted for the deal (Table 3.3).

Most UUP members belong to the Presbyterian Church (52 per cent) or the Church of Ireland (36 per cent); just 0.6 per cent are Roman Catholic. Protestant denomination is insignificant as an attitudinal variable. The vast majority of UUP members describe themselves as 'practising' in respect of their faith – A survey of Young Unionist Council delegates in the 1990s found that only 7.5 per cent did not go to church at all (Hume, 1996).

Table 3.3 *Support for the Good Friday Agreement by Orange Order Members of the Ulster Unionist Council (per cent)*

	For	Against	Total*
Orange Order members	56.6	43.4	100.0
			(weighted n = 152)
Non-Orange Order members	72.1	27.9	100.0
			(weighted n = 136)

* Weighted N = 294 ($\chi^2 = 7.46$, 1df, $p < 0.01$).

The UUC is divided over whether the Orange Order should have a continued role in the UUP, with 49 per cent opposing the maintenance of the Order's rights and 42 per cent supporting their continuation. Although his re-election had been supported by a substantial section of the Orange Order following his insistence on the Order's right to parade in the nationalist area of the Garvaghy Road in Drumcree in 1995, relations between Trimble and the Order soon deteriorated. In the 2000 leadership contest Trimble's vote was evenly split between Orange Order members and non-members, while only one third of Smyth's vote came from non-members (Tonge, 2002, p. 57).

With slightly more than 50 per cent of UUC members belonging to the Orange Order, removal of the Order's UUC voting rights is a vexed question for the party leader. There is a significant association between Orange Order membership and support for the retention of the voting rights of the Order, controlling for the Smyth–Trimble vote ($r = 0.24$, $p < 0.01$, one-tail significance). An OLS regression (Table 3.4) demonstrates the strength of each variable. Whilst the effects of both are significant, the predicted values show that Smyth supporters were more supportive of voting rights than were Trimble voters, irrespective of Orange Order membership. Effectively, membership provided an intensity effect, where the leadership vote indicated direction. Trimble supporters were much less vehement in their opposition to the removal of the Order's voting rights, whereas among Smyth supporters, non-members of the Order were much less vehement in their support for the retention of voting rights.

The fault line within the UUP is also apparent when occupation is considered, but party division is not reducible merely to social class. Support for Trimble and the GFA was strongest among senior managers, farmers, teachers and the retired; junior and middle managers,

Table 3.4   *OLS regression of the ballot on Orange Order voting rights, by Orange Order membership and leadership contest vote, 2000**

	B (SE)	P	Member of Orange Order?	
			Yes	No
Member of the Orange Order	0.57 (0.13)	0.000		
Voted for Smyth	1.97 (0.13)	0.000		
Constant	−3.57 (0.26)	0.000		
Adjusted $R^2 = 0.481$				
Weighted N = 292				
Predicted values of the vote in the leadership contest				
Trimble			−0.47	−1.03
Smyth			1.50	0.93

* Dependent variable: 'Orange Order should retain voting rights on the UUC' (-2 = strongly disagree; $+2$ = strongly agree).

civil servants and other professionals were far less favourably disposed. With the exception of professionals, who tended to be young, in general support for Smyth was greater among the lower social classes and non-senior management. This may have been the section of the unionist community whose confidence had been reduced to the greatest degree, a situation exacerbated by the increased status of the nationalist community. In the eyes of this group the GFA was based on two falsehoods: that republicanism could safely be harnessed within the political institutions of Northern Ireland, and that these institutions should implement a nationalist equality agenda. Fewer than 2 per cent of UUC members saw nationalists as 'second-class' citizens of Northern Ireland.

A multivariate analysis (Table 3.5) shows the salience of demographic variables as independent predictors of the leadership vote. Occupation, income and age were selected as core variables along which a unionist fault line might run. These variables were used to test the hypothesis that there existed a social class dimension and age factor in support for or hostility to Trimble's attempt to forge a new, civic unionism. The possibility of an east (urban) versus west (rural) division was explored via county of residence. Finally, gender was introduced as a control.

Table 3.5 *Logistic regression of Trimble–Smyth voting in the Ulster Unionist Party leadership election, 2000.*

	B	SE	Wald	p
Gender	0.15	0.23	0.46	0.50
Age			21.72	0.00
15–24	2.59	1.07	5.84	0.02
25–34	0.76	0.51	2.21	0.14
35–44	−0.22	0.42	0.26	0.61
45–54	−0.69	0.38	3.28	0.07
55–64	−0.97	0.33	8.66	0.00
65 and over	−1.45	0.46	10.03	0.00
Orange Order	0.46	0.17	7.76	0.01
Income			6.91	0.03
£40 000 and above	−0.65	0.26	6.34	0.01
£19 999 and below	0.49	0.23	4.76	0.03
Occupation			17.35	0.01
Secretary/clerical/trade	0.82	0.42	3.73	0.05
Junior/middle management,				
civil servant	0.56	0.27	4.20	0.04
Farmer	−0.26	0.35	0.56	0.45
Professional	0.88	0.42	4.32	0.04
Teacher/academic	−1.24	0.51	6.00	0.01
Senior management	−0.43	0.50	0.76	0.38
County of residence	−0.18	0.18	1.00	0.32
Constant	−0.38	0.29	1.68	0.20

Model: $\chi^2 = 75.69$, 17*df*, $p < 0.001$
Nagelkerke pseudo $R^2 = 0.33$

Note: Reference categories (deviation coding): gender, female; age, 65–74; income, £20 000–39 999; Orange Order, not a member; occupation, other (manual worker, student, housewife); county, counties Down, Antrim, Armagh.

It can be seen that Orange Order membership had a significant independent effect on the vote, although other variables were also important, including age (the young are more anti-Trimble), income (high earners were more pro-Trimble) and occupation (teachers and academics were pro-Trimble, but other professionals were not). Membership of the Orange Order provides an important indicator of attitudes within the UUC to Trimble's revisionist unionism and could prompt the leader to revisit his idea of assessing the value of the formal historical link between the party and the cultural–religious organization. However individual membership and its influence on attitudes would not be affected.

Income also had a clear independent effect, with the affluent supporting the relative security of peaceful change and non-violence offered by the Trimble vision. Controlling for county of residence, no significant regional effect is discernible. The 'intellectual' wing of the party appeared to support Trimble's position on the GFA, but clearly the biggest problem for the pro-GFA wing of the party will be its advancing years. In terms of the GFA, youth means negativity.

Two unionisms? Rational civic and Orange sceptic

All sections of unionism are united on some questions. Unionists are sceptical about the intentions of the British (and Irish) governments. Scepticism about the value of the GFA has increased within the Ulster Unionist Council, as illustrated by the assertion of 62 per cent of members in 2001 that they would vote no in a new referendum, a figure that was in line with the wider Protestant population. Nonetheless two fairly distinct types of unionist are apparent: the 'rational civics', who see the GFA as a means to secure the unionism, albeit through considerable internal change in Northern Ireland; and the 'Orange sceptics', who believe that the GFA will fail to secure the union and will accommodate a republican micro-agenda. The latter category includes a number of professionals in the UUP, for whom Orangeism may be less important. Orange unionists and a professional class are combined in opposition to the Trimble leadership and the GFA, although the evidence suggests that the Orange wing is the more important.

Rational civics believe that unionism, through the application of the consent principle, has gained a reasonable deal from the GFA. The UUP's position on this 1995 Joint Framework Document was that its cross-border element document was so substantial as to render the consent principle 'meaningless ... through a process of harmonisation' (UUP, 1995, p. 2). The onus was on supporters of the GFA in the UUP to explain why the Framework Document was unacceptable, whereas the negotiated details of the GFA were satisfactory. Rational civics support the pluralist dimensions of the GFA and accept the legitimacy of constitutional nationalism. They are tolerant of power sharing with cross-border bodies. A breakdown of UUC votes according to whether they supported the GFA in the 1998 referendum indicates that rational civics accept the need for mechanisms to enforce power sharing in the Northern Ireland Assembly, including weighted

Table 3.6 *UUC members' views on dual majority voting and power sharing with cross-border bodies**

Mean scalar position (s.d.)	Voted yes to GFA	Voted no to GFA	
Assembly decisions should have a majority on both sides	0.27 (1.31)	−1.36 (0.92)	N = 284
The best solution is power sharing with cross-border bodies	0.30 (1.16)	−0.57 (1.14)	N = 278 (*p* < 0.001)

* Five-point scale (−2 = strongly disagree; +2 = strongly agree).

majority (or parallel consent) voting rules, whilst the anti-GFA section of the party is strongly hostile to it (Table 3.6). Rational civics also accept the need for an Irish dimension to any solution. Overall, only 44 per cent of UUC members (almost exclusively pro-GFA Trimble supporters) believe that 'the best solution for Northern Ireland is power sharing with cross border bodies, with 53 per cent disagreeing' (Tonge and Evans, 2002).

The issue of IRA decommissioning, rather than theoretical or long-term misgivings, troubles the rational civics, given its propensity to destabilize political arrangements. Fewer than one in ten UUC members believe that Sinn Fein should be allowed to participate in the Northern Ireland Assembly, irrespective of whether or not IRA decommissioning takes place; but for rational civics the evident progress on decommissioning means that there are no particular barriers to devolved power sharing. This group acknowledges that there can be no return to the straightforward majoritarianism of 'Old Stormont'. Since 1974 Orange sceptics have also moved away from objecting to enforced power sharing *per se*; their concern now is with the 'consociationalism-plus', all-Ireland dimension attached to power sharing. The sceptic wing of unionism is still struggling to come to terms with the new relationship that has developed between Northern Ireland and the Irish Republic since the 1985 Anglo-Irish Agreement.

Among rational civics and Orange sceptics there is also disagreement over the overall policy direction represented by the GFA. For Orange sceptics the GFA constitutes a transition towards a united Ireland and they have little faith in the ability of the British government to maintain the consent principle. According to them, the basis of the agreement is binationalism, not consent. The asymmetry in the relationships between the British government and Ulster unionists, and the Irish government and northern nationalists, has become more marked during the peace process (Cochrane, 1994, 1995; Dixon, 1995). Rational civics, in contrast, contend that the consent principle in the agreement will secure the union. They point to the following: the insistence of successive secretaries of state for Northern Ireland that the consent principle is paramount, Tony Blair's assertion that he 'values the union', and the relegation of the Irish government's constitutional claim to Northern Ireland to mere aspiration (Tonge, 2002).

The general acceptability of the political framework does not mean that pro-GFA unionists accept all aspects of the micro-agenda of the deal. Opposition to the implementation of recommendations in the Patten Report on policing in Northern Ireland is strong in both wings of unionism. Only 18 per cent of the UUC members view the recommended changes to policing as necessary, the same percentage as those who believe that the early release of paramilitary prisoners was justifiable. These members not only view the GFA as a good guarantor of the union, but are also prepared to accept substantial non-constitutional changes as part of the process of conflict resolution. Other rational civics share the sceptics' dislike of the conflict resolution aspects of the deal, but feel that these are outweighed by the protection the GFA affords to the union. Ranged against these forces are the Orange sceptics, who see little value in any aspects of the GFA, with changes to policing being an example of the dilution of Britishness. This group is also strident about contentious issues that are not addressed by the GFA, notably Orange Order marching rights. Whilst a small majority of UUC members (51.5 per cent) support the right of the Orange Order to march through nationalist areas, this majority contains far fewer pro-GFA supporters than opponents of the GFA, who are strongly in favour of the right to march. Unsurprisingly, Orange Order membership is a key variable.

A realignment of unionism?

As Arthur Aughey (1997, p. 31) points out, 'there is no clear answer anyone can give' to the question of where unionism is going. The question can however, be made somewhat simpler through disaggregation, permitting analysis of the likely party, political and electoral future of unionism. The DUP has emerged as the main representative of the unionist bloc, supported by a majority of unionists on the basis that it can act as a stouter defender of their interests than can the UUP.

Structural changes within the UUP are likely to embrace a new centralism that is akin to the leadership-oriented axis of the DUP. The UUP compares the relationship between the party and the Orange Order to that of the British Labour Party and the trade unions, missing the obvious point that there has been a dramatic change in that particular relationship. The UUP has not undergone serious reorganization since its foundation in 1905, a weakness that has been exposed by the public playing out of divisions over the GFA. These divisions beg the question of how such diversity can be accommodated within a single organization. Those members who are hostile to the GFA and would have preferred devolved power sharing without cross-border bodies share a similar political position to the DUP. For such members, pan-unionism offers the best means of resisting the supposed pan-nationalist agenda of Sinn Fein, the SDLP and the Irish government. Over half (54 per cent) of UUC members believe that the party should form an electoral pact, with a majority (53 per cent) declaring that this alliance should be with the DUP and a further 25 per cent naming all unionist parties as viable partners.

The overwhelming preference is for vote transfers to remain within the unionist family. There are significant differences in outlook towards other unionist parties between those who supported the GFA in the 1998 referendum and those who voted no, as Table 3.7 demonstrates.

As expected, those in the UUP who are hostile to the GFA are much more likely to transfer votes to the DUP. Both groups are hostile to the pro-GFA PUP, which was born of the paramilitary UVF and is thus seen as beyond the pale even by some moderate unionists. Pro-GFA unionists appear to be largely uninterested, albeit less so than anti-GFA unionists, in making common cause with the pro-GFA SDLP across the communal divide. Unsurprisingly there is no willingness to transfer votes to Sinn Fein. Among GFA supporters and opponents alike there is considerable hostility to transfers even to the SDLP, although the level of hostility, again as might be expected, is greater among anti-GFA unionists (3.51 to 2.9).

Table 3.7   *Potential UUC vote transfers to other unionist parties, according to yes or no votes for the 1998 Good Friday Agreement**

Scalar mean (s.d.)	Voted yes to GFA	Voted no to GFA	
DUP	2.65 (1.14)	1.52 (0.95)	N = 264
UKUP	2.72 (1.09)	1.46 (0.82)	N = 251
PUP	2.85 (1.03)	3.37 (0.86)	N = 226

* Four-point scale (1 = very likely; 4 = no possibility); $p < 0.05$.

Ulster unionists are divided over whether to embrace a rational civic or traditional cultural form, although the consent principle may have ensured unionism's future in the short to medium term. In viewing the GFA as a constitutionally satisfactory deal, rational civics overcame the 'paranoia which infests the political imagination of contemporary Unionism' (Coulter, 1997, p. 138). Emotionally, however, it was a difficult bargain to accept, given the early release of prisoners, changes to policing and acceptance of Sinn Fein in government. Amid allegations of continued IRA activity, Sinn Fein's presence in the executive became too much to bear. The difficulty for unionism lies in articulating a coherent vision for the future, given the fear – not confined to anti-GFA unionists – that the GFA constitutes the baseline for irredentist nationalism.

Unionists offer a diverse, sometimes conflicting range of strategies for maintaining the union. The consequence of this is that, even beyond a devolved power-sharing agreement, long-standing tensions between the integrationist and devolutionist wings of the party are being maintained. Despite the granting of devolution for Scotland, Wales and Northern Ireland, 53.8 per cent of UUC members believe that the best solution for their province is full integration into the United Kingdom. This percentage masks significant differences between the pro- and anti-GFA wings. Part of the anti-GFA section of the UUP has yet to abandon hope of the full integration of Northern Ireland into the United Kingdom, despite the restructuring

Table 3.8 *UUC members' attitudes towards Northern Ireland's political integration into the United Kingdom, by GFA vote in the 1998 referendum**

	Voted yes for GFA	*Voted no for GFA*	
Best solution – full integration into the UK	−0.05 (1.37)	1.14 (1.03)	N = 282
Best solution – direct British rule	−0.98 (0.88)	−0.10 (1.26)	N = 279
British parties should contest elections in Northern Ireland	0.00 (1.27)	−0.30 (1.25)	N = 285

* Five-point scale (−2 = strongly disagree; +2 = strongly agree).

of the United Kingdom by means of devolution (Table 3.8). These integrationist sympathies mark Orange sceptics as potentially different from the anti-GFA unionists in the DUP, a strongly prodevolution party that is adamantly opposed to the terms of the GFA.

Integrationists in the UUC tend to shy away from the political implications of this unlikely move. As might be expected, backers of the GFA are more opposed to direct rule, but there is also hostility to this idea in the rational civic and Orange sceptic camps. The idea of electoral integration divides the UUC. On the qustion of whether the Labour, Liberal Democrat and Conservative Parties should be granted the right to contest elections in Northern Ireland, 39 per cent favour the idea and 34 per cent are opposed. There are slight but significant differences between the pro- and anti-GFA forces. A possible challenge to a confessional, ethnically based party system – electoral integration (an unlikely prospect) – has less support amongst opponents of the GFA, despite their overall support for integration. A summary of rival policy positions within unionism is provided in Table 3.9.

Many in the anti-GFA wing of the UUP have little in common with the members of the DUP, but their differences could be overlooked, particularly among former UUP voters defecting to the DUP, amid overriding hostility to the terms of the GFA. For unionist voters, the main political problem has been the provision in the agreement that permits Sinn Fein to share power with unionists whilst the Provisional IRA remains intact, rather than divisions over the longer-term strategic vision of unionism between the anti-GFA forces of rival parties.

Table 3.9   *Summary of policy positions in the UUC and DUP*

	UUC, pro-GFA	UUC, anti-GFA	DUP
Good Friday Agreement	Pro	Anti	Anti
Devolution	Pro	Anti	Pro
Direct rule	Anti	Neutral	Anti
Integration	Anti	Pro	Anti
Electoral integration	Neutral	Neutral	Anti
Pan-unionism	Anti	Pro	Anti

Conclusion

Unionism's divisions owe far less to a supposed crisis of identity than to fundamental differences over the implications of the GFA. As Loughlin (1995) states, the lack of constitutional alternatives and reliance on the British state mean that, in terms of identity, unionists are more British than ever before. Identity politics may be important, but the divisions among unionists deepened with different understandings of how the GFA might challenge Northern Ireland's long-term future in the United Kingdom and threaten the existing securities that unionists associate with aspects of their polity. Division over the province's political future should not be conflated with an identity crisis.

The divisions within unionism are between those who take a rational view of the centrality of the consent principle in the GFA and ultra sceptics who perceive that binationalism, rather than local political pluralism, forms the foundation of the agreement. Dissent at this supposedly binational approach is exacerbated by an alleged micro-agenda to undermine the symbols of Britishness. Rational civics believe that the GFA offers a reasonable bet on securing the union and neutering its opponents, notably Sinn Fein. While the agreement contains unpleasant short-term provisions, notably on policing and prisoners, for rational civics the agreement's nod to binationalism is an inevitable outworking of the 'necessary nonsense' agreed by a former UUP leader, Brian Faulkner, decades earlier.

Disquiet over aspects of the GFA, created partly by ambiguity over decommissioning and fuelled by the electoral threat by the DUP, has increasingly discomfited pro-GFA unionists. Fewer than one in ten UUC members support Sinn Fein's participation in the Assembly before the IRA decommissions all its weapons. In short,

IRA surrender outside the terms of the agreement is required. Acquiescence to this demand is not impossible, given that the IRA has minimal utility to a (provisional) republican movement that is now dominated by electoralism. The pro-GFA wing of the UUP claimed its approach had been vindicated, in that the IRA had, for the first time in its history, decommissioned some weapons. A voluntary process of decommissioning envisaged by Sinn Fein and the IRA became an imperative, clothed by Sinn Fein as a move to 'save the peace process', but indicative of Sinn Fein's concern to maintain its electoral momentum and keep its ministerial offices intact.

The anti-GFA wing of the UUP comprises mainly, but not exclusively, the working class and the petty bourgeoisie, plus a number of young professionals. Orange Order membership is a major attitudinal variable. Structural reform of the UUC, involving removal of the Orange Order's voting rights, could result in a shift towards modern civic unionism by the main unionist party. The 'natural party of unionism' has now been overtaken by the DUP. DUP voters are more disciplined, more prepared to support their party's candidates at the expense of others, particularly pro-GFA unionists. The UUP has relied on other factors to inhibit its members from defecting to the DUP: UUP rebels cannot expect the freedom to dissent from party policy in the DUP; the DUP is palpably leadership-driven; the opportunities for advancement in the DUP could be restricted; and there remains unease about the informal links between the Free Presbyterian Church and the DUP. However this combination of deterrents has been less potent since the DUP became the dominant electoral force in unionism. As unionist electors realigned, it became evident that the DUP would be the party responsible for any reformulation of a power sharing deal that would be more acceptable to unionists.

To quote the British prime minister, it may be almost impossible to 'see Northern Ireland as anything but part of the United Kingdom' (Hennessey, 2000, p. 104). The paradox is that, while the union now appears to have been made safe, those unionists who brokered the deal that ensured this have been made vulnerable. The defence of the post-GFA unionist position has not been entrusted by the electorate to a party that is divided over the contents of the agreement and uncertain about its preferred direction for unionism.

4

The Diminishing Centre Ground: Whither the Third Tradition?

Given that the centre ground in Northern Ireland has been described as 'mythical', the dedication of an entire chapter to an apparently non-existent entity may appear strange (Arthur and Jeffrey, 1996, p. 51). Yet Northern Ireland is a polity in which 35 per cent of the population claim to be neither unionist nor nationalist, compared with 35 per cent who identify themselves as unionist and 27 per cent as nationalist (Northern Ireland Life and Times Survey, 2001). Despite this, the 1998 Good Friday Agreement has provided a new political dispensation based on management of the competing aims of unionism and nationalism, rather than the eradication of contestatory ideologies. This approach is understandable, as the large segment of the population that claims to be neither unionist nor nationalist either vanishes or changes its mind at elections. The non-unionist, non-nationalist Alliance Party of Northern Ireland (APNI) has never managed to win more than 14 per cent of the vote, and it obtains far fewer votes nowadays. The only other significant centre party in recent times, the Northern Ireland Women's Coalition (NIWC), lost its representation in the Assembly after the 2003 election, having achieved negligible support. Sections of the pro-GFA wing of the UUP and a sizeable portion of the entirely pro-GFA SDLP hoped that the GFA would promote cross-community consensus, allowing the forging of a new, moderate centre. However the segmental autonomy that is evident under the consociationalism of the agreement poses questions about the existing political centre in Northern Ireland.

Traditionally the centre, as represented by the Alliance Party, has rejected unionism and nationalism, believing them to be ideologies to be overcome, rather than accommodated. Under the post-GFA political arrangements, the Alliance Party was sometimes obliged to bolster pro-agreement unionism. Using the first ever membership survey of the main centre party in Northern Ireland, this chapter examines whether its vision of a radical third tradition is sustainable in a polity in which unionist and nationalist politics are legitimized. The data is drawn from a party membership survey carried out by the author in 2001. Questionnaires were posted to each of the 1025 party members. Seven hundred and two replies were received, a response rate of 68 per cent.

The Alliance Party and the Good Friday Agreement: critical support and a compromise on principles?

As a long-standing advocate of devolved power sharing, the Alliance Party endorsed the GFA. Yet the agreement posed theoretical and practical problems for Northern Ireland's main biconfessional centre party. The consociational underpinnings of the GFA appeared to institutionalize a unionist–nationalist dichotomy in Northern Ireland politics, at odds with the Alliance view that the construction of 'one community' was required (Alliance Party of Northern Ireland, 2000). Since the party's establishment in 1970 it had clung to the belief that a third tradition – post-nationalist or non-unionist – could be established. In practical terms the GFA threatened to reduce further the narrow centre ground occupied by the Alliance. By obliging Northern Ireland Assembly members to designate themselves as 'unionist', 'nationalist' or 'other', allied to weighted majority provisions with no role for the 'other' bloc, the GFA arguably further entrenched ethnic bloc politics. Support for the Alliance Party dropped to a very low 3.7 per cent in the 2003 Assembly elections. Nonetheless the party survived as the recipient of lower preference vote transfers from both sides of the community divide, and the party retained its six Assembly seats in the 2003 contest. Low support for the party had also prevailed during the time of Northern Ireland's earlier experiment in consociationalism, the Sunningdale power-sharing executive of 1974, although during that period the party had played an important part in the executive.

The lack of a pro-GFA unionist majority caused the Alliance Party to compromise its stated principle of being neither nationalist nor unionist. In November 2001 three Alliance Members of the Legislative Assembly (MLAs) redesignated themselves as unionist to ensure the re-election of the Ulster Unionist Party leader, David Trimble, as first minister, and thus to shore up the GFA. Candidates for the posts of first minister and deputy first minister required parallel majorities – that is, each had to enjoy majority support among unionist MLAs and nationalist MLAs. In the first contest in November 2001, Trimble failed to obtain majority unionist support and his subsequent re-election was thus dependent on redesignation by sufficient Alliance MLAs. Although only temporary, the redesignation of three MLAs occurred against the wishes of the majority (60 per cent) of Alliance Party members. Indeed two other Alliance MLAs declined to be re-designated (the sixth Alliance MLA served as speaker). Furthermore, redesignation compromised long-held Alliance principles. The NIWC also went through ideological contortions as part of the 'Save Trimble/ Save the GFA' process in 1999–2002, with one member being re-designated as unionist and another, to avoid allegations of bias, being redesignated as nationalist. Given that the NIWC had a less explicitly one-community approach (it accepted unionism and nationalism as ideologies), the redesignation of its MLAs was of less significance in ideological terms than that of the Alliance MLAs.

The basis of Alliance policy was rejection of the 'two communities' approach to politics in the GFA as this 'undermines the legitimate expression of political identity by many people; it denies the individual choice over identity' (Alliance Party of Northern Ireland, 2000, p. 7). The party did not dwell on why the two communities had emerged. It offered a vision of societal integration but did not explain the origins of the fracture. Instead it tended to regard the pursuit of ambitions – unionist or nationalist – as innately sectarian and thus pernicious. Whatever the limits of unionist or nationalist analyses, immersed in blame location, they at least offered a 'how we got here' component, with historical referents. For the Alliance Party, however, there was the difficulty of explaining why the differences between the competing populations on the island were sufficient to justify partition and separate states, but so minimal as to be compressed into a one-community approach in Northern Ireland.

A common criticism by nationalists was that the Alliance was a unionist and British party. The party's statement at formation – that it supported Northern Ireland's position in the United Kingdom as this offered the best guarantee of social and economic rights – carried an implicit condemnation of the Irish Republic. The party insisted that its politics did not amount to a mix of unionism and nationalism, or a historical compromise between the two traditions. Instead it favoured a radical third way: devolved government with power sharing. Yet acceptance of enforced power sharing, with its attendant weighted majority voting rules and acknowledgement of the two traditions, belied the party's belief in one-community politics. In defence of its support for such arrangements, the party offered a vision of what might be termed consensual consociationalism. In its model of ethnic conflict reduction, incentives for moderation would accompany power-sharing institutional arrangements.

The party opposed the rigid segmental designations of the Northern Ireland Assembly created through the GFA, which contravened the party's one-community approach and arguably breached its liberal principles. Non-key decisions in the Assembly, including the pro-gramme for government, could be taken on the basis of a simple majority. Key decisions, however, required cross-community sup-port. Under the GFA, cross-community support for a measure could be required when a petition of concern from 30 of the 108 Assembly MLAs was lodged. The insistence that MLAs be designated as 'unionist', 'nationalist' or 'other' could *breach* consociational ideas. Consociational institutions should fully accommodate parties without bloc identities. Elections and institutional representation should be based on the self-determination of the universal populace, rather than be rigidly based on representation via predetermined ethnic blocs (Lijphart, 1977; Horowitz, 1985). However this desire was perhaps contradicted by the requirement that segmental autonomy be facili-tated by consociational structures. Whilst supportive of the GFA, some Alliance members urged the executive, elected through proportion-ality, to stand 'aloof' from a legislature in which MLAs would not be required to designate themselves as unionist, nationalist or other (Leonard, 1999). The Alliance Party has recently declared itself to be opposed to the legitimation of 'mutually exclusive identities' that have allowed the 'conflict to rumble on' (Alliance Party, 2004, p. 1). Hence it proposes not only a reconstituted Assembly free of bloc designa-tions, but also, for example, opposes Protestant and Catholic quotas for police recruitment.

Intra-ethnic rivalries, with defence of the bloc being the priority of parties of similar size within the unionist and nationalist communities, have impeded cross-community cooperation. This has led to the association of the GFA with the strengthening of the centrifugal forces of Sinn Fein and the DUP, a situation that had been feared by the Alliance Party. However the two parties have moderated their agendas. Having spent many years attempting to destroy the state, Sinn Fein turned its hand to managing its education and health services. Whilst it has changed far less, the DUP claims to accept the principle of devolved power sharing in Northern Ireland. In 2000–2 all parties cooperated to some extent in the Assembly. Admittedly the new moderation of the 'extremists' was evident prior to the GFA, but criticism of the agreement as an institutional entrenchment of sectarianism in Northern Ireland is naïve and exaggerated. Sectarianism has been a feature of Northern Ireland since its foundation on a religious–political headcount. The country is a sectarian entity in terms of the rationale for its existence, a contrived unionist majority dwelling within an artificial territorial enclave on the island of Ireland. Elite accommodation does not guarantee the withering of sectarianism, but consociational arrangements may lead to its mitigation and ultimate redress, although, as argued elsewhere in this book, far more explicit recognition of the case for a binational state may be required.

The Alliance Party offers a vision of integrative power sharing in Northern Ireland, attached to north–south structures. The party lays great stress on the democratic accountability of such structures, arguably reflecting its unionist-leaning opposition to any all-Ireland dimension to Northern Ireland's political arrangements. The party's support for the GFA is based on the premise that consociational democracy is merely a transitional stage towards more integrative forms of association. Senior party figures have expressed pessimism about the ability of consociational settlements to work in societies with clear ethnic or ethnonational divisions, describing the GFA as a mere 'band-aid' agreement that cannot itself resolve the conflict (Farry and Neeson, 1999). The party favours what it sees as a milder form of consociationalism, based on structures that emphasize inter-communal reconciliation and cooperation. Frustrated at the absence of measures to improve community relations, the party opposed the second programme for government produced by the Northern Ireland executive.

The party has always been anxious to avoid definition as unionist or nationalist. Rather it sees itself as a Northern Irish party that is promoting the replacement of the unionist–nationalist dichotomy with a liberal, pluralist, non-ethnic form of politics. However there are indications that this position is idealized at best, and does not conform to the membership's views of the party, let alone those of outsiders. For instance the party leadership has asserted that 'only Alliance supporters more strongly associate with a concept of Northern Irishness ahead of Britishness or Irishness' (ibid., p. 1224). This is untrue, however, of the party members, for whom the largest single category of identification is British (Table 4.1). Moreover there are clear differences in national identity according to religious affiliation. Whilst the party may reject the sectarian basis of politics, the differing national affiliations suggest that the religious divide may still form the basis of divergent and thus potentially divisive perceptions of identity.

The party membership overwhelmingly supported the GFA in the May 1998 referendum, with 95 per cent voting in favour and only 1 per cent opposing. However there is disagreement within the party over the party's vision of what to do about unionism and nationalism, and whether the GFA will exacerbate the ethnic bloc politics that the party disdains (Table 4.2).

For a party that is trying to promote a coherent vision of Northern Ireland's future, the level of support for the idea of separate unionist and nationalist blocs is perhaps surprising. The party's ideal is consensual power sharing amongst the various communities, making such blocs redundant. The view of some party members that Assembly votes should be taken on the basis of a simple majority, rather than weighted majority voting, favours the unionist bloc. The nationalist

Table 4.1 *Alliance members' national identity by religious affiliation (per cent)*

National identification	All	Protestant	Catholic	None
Irish	16.2	11.0	32.8	17.3
British	29.1	34.4	10.4	30.6
British-Irish	27.2	30.8	20.9	19.4
Northern Irish	22.9	21.8	30.6	17.3
European	2.7	1.3	3.7	7.1
Other	1.9	0.7	1.5	8.2
N	677	417	134	98

Source: Evans and Tonge (2003). Reproduced by permission of the Political Studies Association/Blackwell Publishing.

Table 4.2   *Alliance visions and the Good Friday Agreement (per cent)*

	Strongly agree	Agree	Neither agree nor disagree	Disagree	Strongly disagree
'The Alliance vision is of unionists and nationalists separate but equal' (N = 689)	11.5	28.7	13.2	33.8	12.8
'The GFA increases sectarianism by dividing parties into blocs' (N = 680)	8.8	20.9	20.4	42.2	7.6
'Decisions in the Assembly should require a simple majority only' (N = 674)	11.0	37.8	12.3	32.0	6.8

Source: Evans and Tonge (2003). Reproduced by permission of the Political Studies Association/Blackwell Publishing.

jibe that Alliance members are 'unionists without the sashes' appears to find some foundation in this view, although the party sees itself as a a pro-consent rather than a pro-unionist party. Of course, the party's ideal is a Northern Ireland community – devoid of sectarian divides – that can vote on issues without the need for weighted or dual majorities. Despite the party's sensitivity to the charge that it is the party of 'soft' unionism, 28 per cent of its members believe this to be true, with fewer than half (49 per cent) disagreeing. The party sees itself as a radical centrist organization, although only about one third of members agree that the party is radical. The reluctance of the party to be considered as unionist, even with a small 'u', is understandable: application of a unionist label would destroy its *raison d'être* as a party promoting the eradication of unionist and nationalist communal politics. Yet the self-perception of even the party's core supporters brings into question its vision of a radical third tradition. Is the party's clinging to its 'other' status a construct borne of the circumstances of the GFA, which could be set aside in favour of tactical redesignation to the unionist bloc to boost the pro-GFA element there?

Decline of the centre and the implications of bloc designation

From its inception the Alliance Party attempted to operate as a biconfessional party in a confessional party system (McAllister and Wilson, 1978). The party has attracted support from Protestants and Catholics and its members are drawn from both communities, although only 20 per cent are Catholics. Averaging 7.3 per cent support in elections, its electoral tale is one of slow decline, as Table 4.3 shows.

Although the demise of the centre has been associated with the implementation of the GFA, it is apparent that the decline in Alliance support preceded the deal. Northern Ireland's 'third pillar' crumbled during periods of, successively, political stalemate, intergovernmentalism and consociationalism. Even senior party figures do not necessarily attribute the decline of the party to the birth of a consociational political settlement, but instead blame previous failures of leadership (interviews with Tom Ekin, chair of the APNI, 21 August 2001, and Jayne Dunlop, vice chair of the APNI, 22 August 2001). One interpretation of the party's performance might be that it has been remarkably successful in attracting cross-community support. Certainly it does not mirror the religious exclusivism associated with other parties in Northern Ireland, in terms of both support and membership

Table 4.3   *Alliance Party electoral support, 1973–2003 (per cent)*

Election	Support	Election	Support
1973 Council	13.7	1989 Council	6.9
1973 Assembly	9.2	1989 European	5.2
1974 Westminster	3.2	1992 Westminster	8.7
1974 Westminster (Oct.)	6.3	1993 Council	7.6
1975 Convention	9.8	1994 European	4.1
1977 Council	14.4	1996 Forum	6.5
1979 Westminster	11.9	1997 Westminster	4.7
1979 European	6.8	1997 Council	4.7
1981 Council	8.9	1998 Assembly	6.5
1982 Assembly	9.3	1999 European	2.1
1983 Westminster	8.0	2001 Westminster	4.8
1984 European	5.0	2001 Council	3.6
1985 Council	7.1	2003 Assembly	3.7
1987 Westminster	10.0		

(Evans *et al.*, 2000; Tonge and Evans, 2001c). This positive reading of the party's performance suggests that the party has offered a persistent challenge to the communalism of Northern Ireland politics.

An alternative interpretation is that the Alliance Party has failed to develop centrist, non-sectarian politics among the electorate. Whilst the electorate or particular types of political system are often held as culprits, the relative success of the Northern Ireland Labour Party (NILP), which polled only 8000 fewer votes than the unionist parties in Belfast during the 1960s, offers some historical evidence that a political centre might have been cultivated (Elliott and Flackes, 1999). The NILP, like the Alliance Party, found little nationalist support due to its support for the constitutional *status quo*. The unrepresentative class base of the Alliance Party prevented the furtherance of any labourist tradition in the centre. The party was not in a position to promote cross-community politics from below.

Should the Alliance Party quit the centre ground and bolster moderate unionism?

There are various future possibilities for the political centre in Northern Ireland. One is the collapse of the traditional centre amid the new moderation of most republican and some unionist politics. Given the Alliance Party's avowed hostility to unionism and national-ism, compromises between ethnic blocs would not amount, in the party's view, to genuine centre politics. The second, remote, possibility is of a revival of the party's fortunes, with its radical, post-nationalist, post-unionist concept of one-community Northern Irishness being endorsed by the electorate in post-conflict Northern Ireland. The third scenario is a shift by the party towards the pro-GFA unionists to bolster these beleaguered supporters of the agreement, a deal that would require the consent of representatives of both communities. When moderate unionism was pressurized by the centrifugal force of the anti-agreement DUP, three Alliance MLAs temporarily redesig-nated themselves as unionist in 2001 to bolster overall unionist support for the unstable GFA. However this move was anathema to many in the party: the party organizer, Stephen Farry, argued that 'hell would freeze over' before the party's MLAs engaged in the 'false solution' of redesignation (interview by the author, 21 August 2001). The balance of unionist forces after the 2003 elections and defections to the DUP (34 anti-GFA ranged against 25 pro-GFA) meant that even maximum Alliance redesignations would not produce a unionist majority in favour of the GFA within the Assembly.

Yet Farry, in common with several of the party's other prospective parliamentary candidates, effectively redesignated Alliance supporters as pro-GFA moderate unionists during the 2001 Westminster election campaign. He withdrew as the party's candidate for North Down to encourage Alliance voters (7500 in the 1997 general election) to vote for the pro-GFA UUP candidate Sylvia Hermon. Although this tactic was successful, facilitating the defeat of Robert McCartney, the anti-GFA, United Kingdom Unionist Party incumbent, it was not easy to reconcile the Alliance's electoral strategy with its 'plague on both houses' attitude towards unionism and nationalism. The party's idea of a radical centre politics appeared to be compromised. The party prides itself on being untainted by association with unionism or nationalism. Indeed it is critical of the Northern Ireland Women's Coalition (NIWC), the alternative centre party, arguing that it offers mere difference-splitting between unionism and nationalism (Leonard, 1999). In the contest to re-elect Trimble, as noted earlier in this chapter, two NIWC MLAs redesignated themselves: one as unionist, the other as nationalist.

Positioned as it is in the 'other' bloc, the Alliance Party may be experiencing electoral decline, but it has at least retained its status as the main non-sectarian party. Relocating itself in the unionist bloc would remove its *raison d'être* – if one is voting moderate or 'soft' unionist, why not vote UUP (or at least for its moderates) rather than for the emasculated Alliance Party? In this regard there is a clear risk of the party falling prey to the negative logic that affects many small partners in coalitions, whether explicit or *de facto*: the larger partner may capture the support of its smaller partner. For some in the party, whatever their religious or ideological position, redesignation could herald doom.

The 'acid test' of the party's adherence to its radical vision lies in its attitude towards redesignation. For those who believe that the Alliance is in reality a unionist party, redesignation might be acceptable under certain circumstances. For those for whom the radical vision of a third tradition is paramount, redesignation would be unacceptable under any circumstances. Two bases of opposition can be hypothesized: social and ideological. The principal social group against redesignation would be Catholic. Whilst the party has always attracted a Catholic minority who are happy to reject the nationalist bloc in favour of the third pillar, it is likely that a move into the unionist bloc would be rejected by this section of the membership. Rejection of bloc affiliation by the party members from higher socioeconomic strata could also be expected. Due mainly to residential location, the middle class has been less affected by the Northern Ireland conflict than the working class. Over-represented in the Alliance Party, this affluent group has disdained the 'political tribalism' of unionist and nationalist politics. Hence members in this stratum would be more likely to reject redesignation under the sectarian banner than those upon whom the conflict has had a more direct impact.

In ideological terms, one can expect greater rejection of redesignation by those who are more distant from unionist ideals than by those who are closer to unionism as regards constitutional settlements and power sharing with the nationalist bloc. Alliance, however, argues that the unionist–nationalist divide is largely irrelevant to its members, given its espousal of the third tradition. The party remains keen to move the political agenda to non-constitutional issues. Indeed this is also an important part of its redesignation argument. If it were to redesignate, then ideological factors beyond constitutional settlement and power-sharing questions would become important – 'normal' politics within the unionist bloc would become an issue for cohesion between the Alliance and the other unionist parties.

Two questions are begged. First, would the Alliance membership support further redesignation? Second, if redesignation did occur, to what extent would there be the convergence between the Alliance Party and the UUP not just on constitutional or power-sharing issues, but also on normal political matters? Alternatively, are Alliance members actually closer in their views to the nationalist SDLP? These hypotheses were tested using a pooled data set, constructed from the Alliance survey and a similar survey of Ulster Unionist Council members. As with the Alliance survey, the UUC survey was carried by means of a postal questionnaire (see Chapter 3). In the final section of the analysis, the findings of a survey of the SDLP membership in 2000 are used (see Chapter 5).

possibility of tactical redesignation of the Alliance Party is ted by examining the likely compatibility of the party and the ey were united in a single bloc. The relative positions of oderate parties – the UUP, Alliance and SDLP – are in ideological terms to assess their compatibility. The

Alliance membership, as the dependent variable, is subgrouped into pro- and anti-redesignation groups. The original variable included four categories of attitudes towards redesignation: (1) yes, (2) yes, for tactical advantage, (3) yes, but only to save the GFA and (4) no under any circumstances. All positive responses have been placed in one category, the negative ones in the other. The multinomial logistic regression model contrasts anti-redesignation Alliance members and UUC members with the pro-redesignation Alliance reference.

Two social explanatory variables were included. Religion (there were only two Catholics in the UUC survey) is trichotomized into Catholic, Protestant and a secular reference. For class the Goldthorpe schema is used, despite the absence of manual workers in the Alliance Party (the retired are classified according to former occupation). An 'unclassified' category is used as the reference, made up of those with no current/ former occupation. Four other social variables are employed in the models as controls. Region is controlled for by employing a variable based on county of residence, with Fermanagh, Derry and Tyrone as 'west counties' and Down, Antrim and Armagh as 'east'. Gender is classified by male, and age is included as a four-category variable, with the 75 years and older category as the reference. Finally, education is classified as a four-category variable.

Four attitudinal scales are included to tap dimensions that are potentially relevant to political cohesion within the Alliance Party, and between parties that might be thrown together in the 'unionist' bloc in the Assembly. The principal dimension is evidently the nationalist–unionist one, which is assessed by means of seven Likert items that ask respondents to (strongly) agree, (strongly) disagree or neither agree nor disagree to the statements listed below:

- A United Ireland is the best solution to the Northern Ireland question.
- Joint British–Irish sovereignty is the best solution to the Northern Ireland question.
- Full implementation of the Patten Commission's recommended changes to the RUC is necessary.
- Republican violence was never justified.
- IRA decommissioning should take place within two years.
- Early republican prisoner releases were justified.
- The Orange Order should have the right to march through nationalist areas.

The two ideological dimensions of 'normal' politics are tapped by means of a single item for each. To tap the economic dimension, respondents are asked about the extent of their agreement with the statement 'Northern Ireland's universities should not charge tuition fees to undergraduate students'. To tap the liberal–conservative dimension, respondents are asked about their support for the legalization of abortion in Northern Ireland. In both cases, negative scores correspond to left/libertarian positions, positive scores to right/authoritarian positions. Finally, two 'strategic' items are included to look at non-ideological bases for opposition to redesignation. The first of these ask respondents whether they think that their party should form electoral pacts. Individuals who are unhappy with the idea of compromising the Alliance's third pillar position by allying with other parties, or are worried about the strategic implications of such a move, are more likely to reject the notion of redesignating as unionist. The level of openness to electoral cooperation with the UUP is coded as a dummy variable, that is, 'yes' to the possibility of pacts. Also included is an item asking respondents about their perceived influence within the party, on the basis that individuals who feel themselves to have influence within the party are more likely to reject redesignation. Testing the position of Alliance members in relation to others allows a more nuanced analysis of the ideological differences between the three moderate parties. Table 4.4 provides basic details of Alliance and UUC members.

Social differences, particular by terms of education and class, and ideological differences in the nationalist–unionist and abortion dimensions suggest incompatibilities between the parties that could limit the cohesion of a post-redesignation bloc.

The Alliance Party is, however, divided on whether to engage in redesignation to support the GFA. The variables have been tested elsewhere, with religious affiliation being the only significant social predictor of pro- or anti-redesignation, when all the other items listed above have been tested (see Evans and Tonge, 2003, p. 39, for the results). Catholics in the Alliance Party are significantly less happy with the idea of redesignating as unionist than are their Protestant or secular counterparts. In response to redesignation, one might expect the Catholic members to leave the party (see Hirschman, 1970, for a general theoretical discussion). Were this indeed the outcome it would clearly undermine the party's key claim to uniqueness, namely its cross-community support and membership. Perceived level of

Table 4.4 *Descriptive statistics (means and percentages) for the explanatory variables in the Alliance and UUC comparison*

	All	Alliance	UUC
Gender			
Male	62.0	54.2	80.6
Age			
15–34	7.5	6.3	10.5
35–54	22.0	20.5	25.3
55–74	50.5	50.2	51.0
75 plus	20.1	23.0	13.2
Education			
No qualifications/O-level	23.3	14.8	43.2
A-level/ILC	12.6	12.7	12.8
University degree	49.3	58.0	30.4
Other	14.1	14.5	13.5
Class			
Professional/managerial	55.3	59.7	44.9
Routine non-manual	22.3	24.0	18.4
Self-employed	10.3	3.9	25.5
Unclassified	12.1	12.5	11.2
Region			
West	17.1	13.5	25.4
Party should engage in electoral pacts	49.6	49.2	50.4
Influence within party	−0.46	−0.63	−0.05
University tuition fees should be abolished	−0.72	−0.80	−0.53
Abortion should be legalized in Northern Ireland	−0.21	−0.40	−0.23
Nationalist–unionist dimension	0.59	0.31	1.24

Notes: University and abortion scores are calculated according to a five-point Likert scale: $-2 =$ strongly agree (left/libertarian); $+2 =$ strongly disagree (right/authoritarian). The seven-item nationalist–unionist dimension is also calculated according to a five-point scale: $-2 =$ nationalist; $+2 =$ unionist. Influence within the party is calculated according to a three-point scale: $-1 =$ little or no influence; $+1 =$ considerable influence.
Source: Evans and Tonge (2003). Reproduced by permission of the Political Studies Association/Blackwell Publishing.

influence is also important, with those who feel themselves to be influential being more likely to be against redesignation. Unsurprisingly the result for the nationalist–unionist dimension suggests that the more towards the unionist end of the dimension an Alliance member is placed, the less likely it is that the member would oppose redesignation. This indicates that the party, despite claiming a third tradition, can be placed on the nationalist–unionist continuum.

The party enjoys a certain brand loyalty that could be threatened if tactical shifts towards the unionist bloc became regular. The party leadership might be able to justify the movement of the party's elected representatives into the unionist camp as a necessary 'one-off', but if this were accompanied by electoral withdrawal in favour of unionist candidates and the possibility of future redesignation, the party could lose its *raison d'être*. Redesignation (in 2001) was taken without reference to the party membership, which was thus denied a voice. Furthermore many members joined the party to escape the unionist–nationalist game. The insulation of political elites from members could of course be useful more generally for the construction and maintenance of a consociational settlement. The non-insulation of the UUP leadership, which was subject to frequent recall by the large Ulster Unionist Council, helped to destabilize the GFA.

Table 4.5 shows that anti-redesignation Alliance members tend to be younger than pro-redesignation members, older members having joined when the party was often seen as innately unionist. The higher age profile of the pro-unionist members is closer to that of the Ulster Unionist Council (for the full attitudinal model see Evans and Tonge, 2003).

Table 4.5　*Significance of age in respect of Alliance Party's possible redesignation as unionist**

	Alliance Party anti-redesignation			UUC		
	Coeff.	*S.e.*	*Sig.*	*Coeff.*	*S.e.*	*Sig.*
Age						
15–34	0.78	0.46	0.09	1.30	0.57	0.02
35–54	0.05	0.27	0.79	1.08	0.38	0.01
55–74	0.06	0.22	0.79	0.51	0.33	0.12

* N = 864.
Source: Adapted from Evans and Tonge (2003).

The difference between the UUC and pro-redesignation Alliance membership is that the UUC membership is significantly more weighted towards males, the less well educated, younger people and the self-employed. The Alliance Party would risk alienating its younger members, who are less receptive to unionist politics, if it tried to prop up the UUP through some kind of realignment with moderate unionists. On important issues in Northern Ireland politics the disparity between 'closet unionist', pro-redesignation Alliance members and the UUC is large, and the possibility of close cooperation is obstructed at a number of levels: in the willingness to redesignate in the first place, in broad differences over key constitutional and power sharing issues, and in the day-to-day policies to be legislated by a revived Northern Ireland Assembly. The electoral pact item demonstrates that the UUC is not as open to electoral cooperation as those Alliance members who would be willing to join the unionist bloc. Within the UUC there is an almost equal split between those who favour and those who are against electoral pacts. For many in the UUC, mainly those who oppose the GFA, their ideal partner in an electoral pact would be the DUP, rather than the Alliance Party.

Finally, the relative party positions along a nationalist–unionist dimension are depicted in Figure 4.1, which includes an error bar showing the mean position and its 95 per cent confidence interval. This examines the distance between the three 'moderate' parties, including the SDLP. Clearly there is no possibility of relocating the Alliance Party in the nationalist bloc, given that it is the pro-GFA unionist forces that have needed bolstering. However the distance between all three moderate forces is important from the interbloc consensual perspective.

The distance between the Alliance and SDLP memberships is significantly less than that between the memberships of the Alliance Party and the UUC. However, despite this the Alliance membership is situated just within the unionist bloc. The centrist position on the dimension suggests that there may well be divergence amongst the constituent items – the centre may be a hybrid rather than a discrete position. This is confirmed by the individual item positions (see Evans and Tonge, 2003). Broadly, the Alliance Party tends to be closer to the UUP on constitutional questions, but closer to the SDLP on other issues, including the decommissioning of paramilitary weapons, changes to policing, early prisoner releases and Orange Order parades.

Figure 4.1   *Relative positions of party memberships along
the nationalist–unionist dimension*

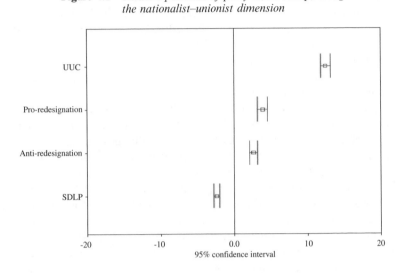

95% confidence interval

Alternative centre ground: the Northern Ireland Women's Coalition

Since its foundation in 1996 the NIWC has offered a different centrist
position from that of the Alliance Party, one that would not inhibit
temporary tactical redesignation when this was necessary to support the GFA. Instead of adopting a one-community approach, the
NIWC sees itself as a cross-community party, comprising nationalists,
unionists and others. The party seeks to reconcile differences between
nationalists and unionists, supporting the concept of a 'more shared
but pluralist society', based on human rights, inclusion and equality
(Northern Ireland Women's Coalition, 2003). The NIWC claims that
it wishes to build a country where diversity is celebrated, but also calls
for the moderation of extremes of difference (NIWC, 2003). What
constitutes these 'extremes' is not stated, although one assumes this is
a tacit criticism of deeply held republican, loyalist or possibly Orange
identities. The celebration of diversity does not extend to Catholic
schools as the party argues that education should take place in integrated or non-denominational schools, although it would not abolish
denominational schools.

Whilst supporting the GFA as a realistic consociational approach to
the management of Northern Ireland's differences, the NIWC argues

for 'strong reconciliation' via institution building and societal transformation (Porter, 2003). At the institutional level, the party envisages a greater role for the Civic Forum, including a closer relationship with the Community Relations Council. It also wishes to develop a greater role for local councils in the promotion of better community relations. The NIWC has also tentatively supported the establishment of an independent monitoring body to assess sectarianism. At the local level, the party argues that *ad hoc* interface initiatives, whilst useful, need to be replaced by more sustained measures to develop the 'minimal peace' in post-GFA Northern Ireland. Unlike the Alliance Party, the NIWC supports the rectification of religious (and gender) imbalances via a rigid quota system, as exemplified by its support for 50–50 Protestant–Catholic police recruitment. The party's commitment to inclusion means that it has opposed attempts to remove Sinn Fein from the political institutions, arguing that decommissioning must be voluntary to avoid the appearance of surrender.

Notwithstanding its title, the NIWC has male members. Its supporters tend to be drawn from middle-class areas. In 1998 the party contested eight seats in the Assembly elections and won two. In the 2003 elections it contested six seats but won only 2 per cent of first preference votes and lost representation in the Assembly. In South Belfast the party leader, Professor Monica McWilliams, polled highest for the NIWC (4.2 per cent) and outpolled the Alliance Party, but fell from third to eighth place, with a 2.8 per cent fall in vote share. The party's other representative, Jane Morrice, lost her seat in North Down. Fifty-eight per cent of Morrice's terminal vote transfers went to the Alliance Party, with the nearest party to this, the UUP, trailing far behind at 21 per cent. In South Belfast, Alliance terminal transfers to the NIWC amounted to 41 per cent, but the UUP also picked up 33 per cent. Hence there appears to be a lack of centrist solidarity in respect of the NIWC and the Alliance Party, with supporters of the latter offering lower preference transfer votes to moderate parties in the blocs they oppose.

As the GFA declined in popularity, the NIWC's role in negotiations came to be seen as less laudable and the party had difficulty defining a post-GFA agenda. Overall the NIWC has attracted only low levels of support, despite its distinctiveness as a centrist party that is attempting to accommodate, rather than necessarily overcome, nationalism and unionism. The party may continue to play a role in agenda setting, but institutional representation appears to have been less important since the collapse of the Stormont Assembly in 2002.

Conclusion: blocked out? The future of the traditional centre

The Good Friday Agreement further marginalized the already diminishing political centre ground in two ways. First, although it floated the idea of a larger moderate centre it eschewed the one-community approach to politics offered by Northern Ireland's existing centre parties. The two-communities approach undermined the value of Alliance representation in the Northern Ireland Assembly. Second, the instability of the agreement and diminished enthusiasm among unionists obliged the Alliance Party to compromise its rejection of the unionist–nationalist model of politics by sometimes aligning itself with the unionist bloc in order to rescue the agreement. The reward for this political altruism was scant, as the political institutions eventually collapsed and the centre continued to be squeezed.

The redesignation of Alliance MLAs as unionist in 2001 was unpopular with the party members. Their loyalty, derived from the monopoly position of the party as an advocate of a particular type of politics, was sorely tested and a membership haemorrhage remains possible, although, unlike supporters of the nationalist and unionist parties, Alliance members have no natural 'second home' and their instincts match the words of the party leader, David Ford: 'if the GFA is so flawed it requires me to tell lies, it is an agreement not worth saving' (interview by the author, 27 August 2001). On constitutional questions the Alliance Party has always been pro-consent and thus pro-union. Yet it does not see itself as a unionist party, and on several important political issues its members have views that are nearer those of the nationalist SDLP. Given the party's persistent rejection of unionism and nationalism as political ideals, it is unsurprising that a majority of its members oppose redesignation. Movement by the party's MLAs into a unionist bloc, even for the purely tactical reason of shoring up the GFA, would alienate many in the party and risk the loss of its Catholic members. Instead the party argues that the institutional arrangements of the GFA need to be reconfigured, with less emphasis on rigid ethnic bloc politics, ideological designation and parallel consent.

The political centre in Northern Ireland has a distinctive radical tradition and the Alliance Party cannot be comfortably accommodated in either of the ethnic blocs. Yet if power sharing ever becomes fully embedded the party might find its centre ground being occupied by others as greater cross-community cooperation emerges.

As constitutional questions diminish in importance, liberal, pluralist unionists might combine with moderate nationalists and gradually lay claim to the Alliance's centre ground. Alternatively bloc polarization might further marginalize the centre, as rival electorates eschew compromise and defend their bloc by aligning with centrifugal forces. The centre party has already compromised its ideological purity by supporting an agreement that it believes legitimizes or even deepens sectarian politics. Alliance MLAs could again engage in tactical redesignation as unionist, but this seems unlikely, given the limited utility of such a tactic since the growth of anti-GFA unionism and the insistence of the party's leadership that it will not happen. Alignment with the unionist bloc would not merely be at odds with long-held principles, but it would also conflict with the party's position on a range of issues and be contrary to the expressed wishes of the remaining party stalwarts in Northern Ireland's vanishing centre ground.

5

New 'Green' Politics: Growing Electoral Dominance by Sinn Fein

The most important factor in the progress of the Irish peace process was the change in republican politics. The provisional republican movement, which had been committed to the overthrow of British colonial rule, ended its armed campaign upon entry to Stormont and the management of Northern Ireland under British rule. The Good Friday Agreement offered an all-island dimension (a similar offering had been denounced as neocolonial tokenism by republicans during the 1970s). At the end of the twentieth century the determined but ultimately futile attempt to unite Ireland by force was replaced by 'republican' politics, which rested mainly on the long-term hope that changing demographics might one day prove useful. Sinn Fein urged the Irish government to be more proactive on the issue and to make plans for structures of unity – not quite the 'repelling the colonial invader' stance that had dominated traditional politics. Republicanism has entered a new phase, in which, as has been the case at earlier junctures, politics and compromise have displaced theology and militarism (Laffan, 1999; Feeney 2002).

This chapter explores why republicans abandoned absolutism in favour of pragmatism, and assesses the political and electoral consequences for Sinn Fein and its nationalist rival, the Social Democratic and Labour Party (SDLP). It suggests that there is broad nationalist convergence, enhanced by solid support for the GFA. As Sinn Fein has occupied the SDLP's political territory, the long-term future of the latter is increasingly being called into question. The SDLP acted as the architect of the three tiers of the political arrangements for the GFA. In enticing Sinn Fein into the new political dispensation, however, the party may have done itself a disservice. Sinn Fein's new constitution-alism, which was allied to successful promotion of nationalist bloc politics, was appealing to the nationalist electorate, many of whom had previously been disdainful of the republican movement's association with violence.

To assess the direction of constitutional nationalism, this chapter draws on data from a postal questionnaire survey of over 500 SDLP members, completed in 2000.

Nationalist convergence stage one: the greening of the SDLP

Convergence of the nationalists during the peace process had a long gestation. Although its beginnings are often attributed to the Hume–Adams dialogue of 1988, it is evident that Gerry Adams, as president of Sinn Fein from 1983 onwards, had already formulated a strategy to forge a pan-nationalist alliance. Adams developed a concept of Irish self-determination that might not necessarily result in physical British withdrawal from Northern Ireland (Moloney, 2002). Furthermore a 'greening' of the SDLP was evident after the collapse of the Sunning-dale power-sharing agreement in 1974 (Evans *et al.*, 2000). In 1970 the party's socialist origins had formed the basis for replacing the Northern Ireland Labour Party, but from 1975 onwards a new type of SDLP emerged, one that was less concerned with 'red' politics and instead favoured a greener, more nationalist outlook. The SDLP was always more nationalist than the NILP: the latter had a partitionist approach, whereas the SDLP made clear that Irish unity, or an 'agreed Ireland', was its preferred solution. According to the first leader of the SDLP, Gerry Fitt, the party's aim was to be a 'social democratic and labour party that would engage the sympathies across the sectarian divide in Northern Ireland' (*Irish News*, 17 August 1995). It failed in this aim as its electoral supporters were overwhelmingly Catholic and its membership was 95 per cent Catholic.

The post-1975 greening of the SDLP involved approaching to the Dublin government for a binational approach to Northern Ireland. This followed the unwillingness of unionists in the 1970s to share power if a cross-border dimension existed. The New Ireland Forum of 1983–84 brought together constitutional nationalist forces on the island of Ireland, to argue, in order of preference, the cases for Irish unity, a federal or confederal Ireland or joint British–Irish sovereignty.

Unsurprisingly the British response was to concede only an 'Irish dimension' to political arrangements for Northern Ireland, with the Republic afforded consultative rights via the 1985 Anglo-Irish Agreement. Although a modest arrangement, the Anglo-Irish Agreement included a bilateral dimension to any solution for Northern Ireland. The new role for the Irish Republic and the willingness of the British government to ignore unionist opposition caused interest among a Sinn Fein leadership that was already looking for a possible route away from republican violence. As early as 1984, Gerry Adams made private approaches to the British government via an intermediary, the west Belfast priest Father Alec Reid. Adams indicated that a formula for Irish self-determination could replace the absolutist 'Brits out' demand by republicans (Moloney, 2002). Secret dialogue with the Irish government also took place in the mid 1980s. By the 1990s a heavily watered down version of Irish self-determination formed the basis of the peace process and eventually the 1998 Good Friday Agreement.

The move away from violence involved the development of pan-nationalist dialogue between the SDLP and Sinn Fein in 1988. Labelled the Hume–Adams dialogue, this paved the way for the development of a broad nationalist consensus. Hume, who assumed leadership of his party in 1979, offered a political, electoral and moral case to the president of Sinn Fein for the end of republican violence. Hume's analysis, shared by a growing number of republicans, was that the IRA was fighting an unwinnable war, as neither violence nor the post-1981 'ballot box and armalite' strategy could force British withdrawal from Northern Ireland. The problem was not the British government's presence in Northern Ireland, but the British people's presence, that is,

Table 5.1 *SDLP members' perceptions of the party 2000 (per cent)**

	Strongly agree	Agree	Neither agree nor disagree	Disagree	Strongly disagree	Missing/ other
The SDLP is:						
Nationalist	32	56	7	2	2	1
European	39	49	8	2	0	2
Social democratic	32	56	10	1	0	1
Socialist	10	41	25	17	3	5
Catholic	7	31	24	30	7	1

* N = 528.

Table 5.2 *Party label correlations among
SDLP members*

	Nationalist	Socialist
Socialist	0.15	–
Catholic	0.17	−0.02

Source: Data from Evans *et al.* (2000, p. 120).

the unionists. Self-determination for all Irish people was a legitimate demand, but this, under the Hume formulation (and the private Adams initiative), would not automatically lead to a united Ireland. There were contradictions in the SDLP approach, notably in respect of whether unionists were a separate people or merely a different tradition, but this did not alter the substance of Hume's approach. The electoral case advanced by Hume was altruistic and ultimately damaging to the SDLP. If the IRA ended its violence, Sinn Fein's vote in Northern Ireland would surely rise. In this respect Hume went beyond narrow sectoral interest. Indeed his leadership of the party was at times incidental to his wider role as statesman (Murray, 1998). The moral case was that the IRA was not fighting a just war; it was not acting against a colonial oppressor, given Hume's argument that the British government was essentially neutral on the future of Northern Ireland. Furthermore the IRA did not enjoy the support of a majority of nationalists.

At the time not everyone in the SDLP felt comfortable about the dialogue with Sinn Fein. Some of this opposition was due to pique at the lack of consultation by Hume, a consistent feature of his tenure as leader (Murray, 1998). More fundamentally, there was a lingering antipathy among those who joined the party in its early days to the increasingly nationalist tone of the party, which partly reflected anxiety about Sinn Fein's electoral threat. The constitution of the SDLP labels the party as socialist and the party remains a member of the Socialist International. The term 'nationalist' does not appear, although the desire to promote the 'cause of Irish unity' is present. However the members of the party clearly do believe they are part of a nationalist organization, as Table 5.1 shows.

The 'socialist' and 'Catholic' labels are the most problematic for party members in that they represent a fault line within the party. As can be seen in Table 5.2, the Catholic and socialist labels correlate positively with the label nationalist. However there is a lack of correlation between the Catholic and socialist labels. This suggests that although different elements in the party are nationalist, they may have differing perceptions of the nationalist agenda.

The lack of association between the socialist and Catholic labels suggests that a common nationalist agenda does not exist and that, crucially, there may well be a wide range of opinions among party members as to the validity of the socialist 'red' agenda and the Catholic 'green' agenda. Furthermore there may exist groups who reject one and accept the other.

In electoral terms, the nationalist identity of the party has delivered most of the Catholic votes. The SDLP filled the vacuum that had been created in nationalist politics by the moribund abstentionism of the old nationalist party and the militarism of republicanism in the 1970s. The red–green divide has always been a sensitive issue for the SDLP, but there is evidence that the red section of the party has been marginalized. Three categories of member can be identified: (1) those who see the party as socialist, not Catholic (the socialist group); (2) those who see the party as Catholic, not socialist (the Catholic group); and (3) those who offer a combination of responses (the mainstream group). The socialist group accounts for 20 per cent of party members, 8 per cent can be placed in the 'green Catholic' section, and the mainstream group accounts for the remaining 72 per cent. This begs the questions of whether there are differences in policy or ideology between the wings, and which group is closer to the mainstream.

A 'red equality' attitudinal scale was constructed on the basis of questions on the equality, job creation and healthcare provisions in the Good Friday Agreement. Another attitudinal scale tested views on desirability of joint British–Irish sovereignty, which is perhaps currently the main nationalist constitutional goal. A separate republican scale asked whether decommissioning should take place, whether the early release of republican prisoners was justified and whether IRA violence was ever justified. The final test was on the views of SDLP members on the desirability of electoral pacts with Sinn Fein. However the utility of formal pacts is now limited, given the propensity of nationalists to transfer votes within the nationalist family and Sinn Fein's diminished interest in pacts, given its electoral ascendancy. As Table 5.3 shows, it is the electoral pact question that differentiates the socialists most from the other two groups, in terms of both direction and effect.

Table 5.3 *Scalar attitudinal indicators among SDLP members*

	Equality	Republican	Joint sovereignty	Electoral pacts
Socialist	0.68	−0.48	−0.20	−0.30
Mainstream	0.55	−0.53	0.00	0.29
Catholic	0.35	−0.26	0.05	0.60

Source: Data from Evans *et al.* (2000, p. 123).

All sections of the SDLP support the equality agenda associated with the GFA, although it is of greatest importance to the socialist wing of the party. The green/Catholic wing is more sympathetic than the remainder of the party to republican positions, there being no significant difference between the red and mainstream groups. On the green/Catholic wing there is even evidence of a lingering sympathy for armed struggle, with one section being much less condemnatory of IRA violence. 'Reds' oppose electoral pacts with Sinn Fein, which are supported by other groups within the party. Reds also oppose joint sovereignty, a matter on which the mainstream and green wings are more ambivalent.

A multivariate model to test the membership profile of these wings has been constructed, the full results of which are reported in Evans *et al.* (2000, p. 125). The Catholic wing of the party is ideologically closer to the mainstream as the SDLP has seemingly moved away from its leftist origins. The key variable in the attitude of party members is year of joining, with those who were members in 1970–74, when it operated as a 'reddish' party, being more likely to belong to the social-ist wing of the party. Age has an independent effect (younger members tend to be greener) but not to the same extent as year of joining. The remaining socialist grouping within the SDLP is most hostile to electoral pacts with Sinn Fein. Although increasingly marginalized, this group remains active within the party. On a self-ascribed scale of 1–4 for degree of activity within the party (1 = highly active; 4 = inactive) the socialist wing scored 2.42, the mainstream 2.66 and the Catholic wing 3.02. The socialist wing also scored highest in terms of (self) perceived influence within the SDLP, whatever the reality.

When the SDLP emerged from the civil rights campaign it disdained previous conservative Catholic politics. After 1975 there was a shift towards a greener approach and the removal from influence of the early, trade-union-based leaders of the party, including Gerry Fitt and

Paddy Devlin. Disillusioned by the collapse of the Sunningdale Agreement the party increasingly looked to the Dublin government to exert influence on British policy towards Northern Ireland. The pursuit of local cross-community politics declined in importance as the SDLP devoted its energy to preventing the greater integration of Northern Ireland into the United Kingdom by boosting Dublin's influence. The climax of this particular phase of politics arrived with the signing of the Anglo-Irish Agreement in 1985. The SDLP emphasized the need for a strong Irish dimension to any settlement. It boycotted the Northern Ireland Assembly from 1982 until its closure in 1986, criticizing the idea of rolling devolution as an unsatisfactory internal solution.

In rejecting a purely internal solution for Northern Ireland whilst insisting on unionist consent for constitutional change, the SDLP offered a GFA type of solution long before its time. Perhaps the main achievement of the party was to persuade the British and Irish governments that a settlement without the SDLP's main political rival was futile. Although both governments were perhaps already aware of this, the British government in particular persisted with futile attempts to broker deals that exclude Sinn Fein, and continued to do so until the Brooke–Mayhew talks of 1992. SDLP leader John Hume's willingness to do business with Sinn Fein offered an antidote to this attempt at the politics of exclusion. Having been scathing of the SDLP's support for an Irish dimension for two decades, Sinn Fein settled for precisely this in 1998. Beyond the constitutional agenda, the two parties shared common approaches. The SDLP members supported much of the micro-agenda of the GFA, which was so important to Sinn Fein. Fifty nine per cent supported the early release of republican prisoners, with 18 per cent dissenting. An overwhelming 94 per cent backed radical reform of the RUC and 79 per cent opposed Orange Order parades through nationalist areas.

Its best days behind: is there a future for the SDLP?

Despite its considerable political achievements in diluting republicanism and producing the GFA, the SDLP has organizational and image problems. The party leader's willingness to take initiatives for peace, it had been argued even by sympathizers, led to neglect of internal party matters (Murray, 1998). With the SDLP far less able to condemn Sinn Fein's association with violence, the party needs to convince the nationalist electorate that it can offer the same benefits from a power-sharing agreement as can be extracted from Sinn Fein's form of politics. The SDLP attempts to portray itself as the party best placed to deal with post-constitutional issues through its longer experience of politics compared with its nationalist rival. Differences with Sinn Fein over Europe and the future role of the nation state are scarcely designed to excite the nationalist electorate.

In immediate post-GFA Northern Ireland the peace process was still considered by the Northern Ireland electorate to be the most important election issue. The NHS and education lay second and third respectively (Northern Ireland 2001 General Election Survey). With Sinn Fein MLAs in charge of these two key ministries, it was evident that the SDLP might struggle to engage the nationalist electorate and maintain its lead over Sinn Fein. Despite the image of a modest campaign, the SDLP canvassed a higher percentage of the electorate in the 2001 election than any other political party in Northern Ireland, but still lost substantial ground (ibid.)

In the 2003 Assembly election the party suffered a severe reverse, losing six seats to Sinn Fein. The party now faces the strategic difficulty of whether its best tactical approach would be to reinforce pan-nationalist commonalities with Sinn Fein, attempt to forge a new centre ground with pro-GFA elements in the UUP, or merely, as it attempted disastrously in 2003, to attack the DUP as 'wreckers' of the agreement. Criticism of the DUP may resonate among nationalist voters, but does not provide a clear reason to vote for the SDLP. However no strategy can be guaranteed to stem the flow of votes to Sinn Fein as the SDLP's problems appear to be terminal. The retirement of John Hume as party leader, replaced by Mark Durkan after the 2001 Westminster elections, removed the SDLP's one highly prominent figure and added to its vulnerability.

The GFA can be viewed as vindication of the SDLP's approach to conflict management. Support for the agreement by Sinn Fein was indicative of a considerable strategic rethink by republicans, prompted by the Hume–Adams dialogue, the first public sign of which was in Sinn Fein's 1992 policy document *Towards a Lasting Peace in Ireland*. While the SDLP's identity and type of membership are not as originally envisaged, changes within Sinn Fein have been much more dramatic. The GFA contained the three types of political institution that were seen by the SDLP as a necessary part of any political accommodation: 'north–north' arrangements, creating devolved, power-sharing government in Northern Ireland; 'north–south' institutions, with cross-border bodies facilitating cooperation between Northern Ireland and the Irish Republic; and continuing 'east–west' intergovernmental relations between London and Dublin. The recycling of old SDLP ideas in the 1974 power-sharing experiment was clearly evident, although the GFA clearly had more end-of-conflict 'additions'. It is little wonder, therefore, that over 80 per cent of SDLP members concluded that the GFA contained most of the party's objectives, although there were additional signs of 'negative unity' in the significant degree of pessimism about the likelihood of its rapid implementation.

Convergence has occurred at the elite, membership and voter levels among Northern Ireland's nationalist rivals. The SDLP rejects the concept of 'pan-nationalism' as a derogatory term used by loyalists (Farren, 1996) and there is not an identikit ideology that transcends homogeneous parties and institutions. Although its members see their party as nationalist, the SDLP regards itself as a post-nationalist party, placing the Northern Ireland problem within wider European and binational contexts. Seamus Mallon, former SDLP deputy leader, admits that nationalism 'will always be a vibrant and legitimate political philosophy on the island of Ireland' (Murray, 1998, p. 221). For the SDLP, achievement of a united Ireland is not a fundamental imperative, as Table 5.4 shows.

The message is clear. More SDLP members are prepared to support the GFA and power sharing than to back the (as yet abstract) concept of a united Ireland. Of course the message from the members is contradictory. Few want Northern Ireland to remain in the United

Table 5.4 *SDLP members' views on the best solution for Northern Ireland's constitutional future*

	Strongly agree	Agree	Neither agree nor disagree	Disagree	Strongly disagree
United Ireland	20.5	29.5	25.8	16.9	2.8
Joint sovereignty	6.8	27.7	21.6	26.9	8.9
GFA/power sharing	41.1	39.4	11.2	4.0	1.3
Remain in the UK	1.5	6.4	18.4	34.8	36.7

Kingdom, yet they back an agreement that will ensure that the province will indeed continue to be part of the United Kingdom for at least several more decades.

The SDLP lacks Sinn Fein's structural and demographic advantages. As an exclusively Northern Ireland party its room for expansion is limited. In the 1990s one possible option was merger with the Irish Labour Party (ILP) to form an all-Ireland organization, a move advocated by the leader of the ILP, Ruairi Quinn, in an address to the SDLP annual conference in 1998. The call fell on stony ground, with only 22 per cent of SDLP members supporting merger. SDLP recruitment has not collapsed: 27 per cent of its members joined between 1996 and 1999. However the average age of party members is 57 and working-class members comprise less than 15 per cent of the party. Sinn Fein has held its working-class base whilst proving its ability to expand into a middle-class nationalist constituency.

Sinn Fein has stolen many of the political clothes of the SDLP. Nonetheless its concept of Irish unity continues to stress territorial factors, despite the party's tacit acceptance of unionists' right to self-determination under the GFA. The party has dropped its opposition to the European Union, preferring a policy of critical engagement. Nonetheless it continues to view the nation state as the most appropriate means of territorial organization. In this respect it continues to offer a form of territorial nationalism that is distinct from that of its northern electoral rival. The party campaigned actively in the Irish Republic for no votes in both referendums on the Nice Treaty. It declined to accept positions on the Policing Board of the Police Service of Northern Ireland (PSNI), arguing that the dilution of the Patten Commission's recommendations for changes to policing prevented the establishment of a sufficiently changed force.

Nationalist electoral rivalries

The SDLP will be confronted by a difficult strategic choice over the next few years. The GFA represented a triumph of SDLP thinking, but the party that offered the greenprint for the agreement cannot reap the electoral rewards. The SDLP began as a party with the intention of capturing both Catholic and Protestant votes. While it failed in this, it did establish itself as the principal representative of nationalist voters in Northern Ireland. Sinn Fein's new constitutionalism has ended

Table 5.5   *Share of nationalist electoral votes,*
1982–2004 (per cent)

Year	Election	SDLP	Sinn Fein
1982	Assembly	18.8	10.1
1983	General	17.9	13.4
1984	European	22.1	13.3
1985	Local	21.1	11.4
1987	General	21.1	11.4
1989	Local	21.0	11.2
1992	General	23.5	10.0
1993	Local	22.0	12.4
1994	European	28.9	9.0
1996	Forum	21.4	15.5
1997	General	24.1	16.1
1997	Local	20.7	16.9
1998	Assembly	22.0	17.6
1999	European	28.2	17.4
2001	General	21.0	21.7
2001	Local	19.4	20.7
2003	Assembly	17.0	23.5
2004	European	15.9	26.3

this supremacy. Support for the SDLP, in raw percentage terms, has remained buoyant, not least due to demographic change (an increase in the number of Catholics), but relative to Sinn Fein the party's position has weakened dramatically in recent years, as Table 5.5 illustrates.

With the GFA having been supported by 97 per cent of nationalists in the 1998 referendum, the electoral rivalry between the two parties now concentrates on which party can best ensure its implementation. In the 2001 contests, Sinn Fein emerged triumphant over the SDLP. Fielding candidates in all 18 constituencies for the first time, it won 51 per cent of the nationalist vote in the British general election, compared with the SDLP's 49 per cent. This confirmed the accelerating growth of support for Sinn Fein since the first Provisional IRA ceasefire in 1994. Overall the nationalist bloc was much more successful than its unionist counterpart in mobilizing voters: the turnout in nationalist constituencies was 10.7 per cent higher (O'Leary and Evans, 2001). In the district council elections Sinn Fein won 51.6 per cent of the nationalist vote, compared with the SDLP's 48.4 per cent. In the 2002 elections in the Irish Republic, Sinn Fein won five seats in *Dail Eireann*.

Sinn Fein has demonstrated an increasing ability to capture the support of middle-class Catholics, as exemplified by its gaining a seat in South Belfast in the 2003 Assembly elections. However it has been the party's ability to mobilize support among the young, the less educated and the manual working class that has provided its electoral strength (McAllister, 2004). Sinn Fein's support base is stronger among less devout Catholics; its support among Protestants is negligible (at 1 per cent) although the SDLP, which tends to draw support from practising Catholics, also has little Protestant support, at 3 per cent (ibid.)

Successful implementation of the GFA might offer the prospect of the cross-community politics once envisaged by the SDLP. The alternative for the party would be to attempt to retain its position as the main recipient of nationalist votes through the promotion of a green agenda. This would involve vigorous activity in support of the GFA's micro changes and a stance on populist issues such as Orange parades, which would satisfy the party's own members. SDLP supporters were keen to see the party's nationalist rival join the government of Northern Ireland. According to one survey, 68 per cent supported the inclusion of Sinn Fein, even if the IRA did not decommission its weapons; only 15 per cent believed it worthwhile to form an executive without Sinn Fein (*Irish Times*, 27 April 1999). The difficulty with the SDLP adopting a green agenda is that it would fail to check Sinn Fein's advance and would further legitimize the latter's approach. The nationalist electorate appears to be turning increasingly to what it sees as the stoutest defender of its bloc interests.

The SDLP also has to decide whether to position itself as a major recipient of Alliance Party and 'soft' Ulster Unionist Party vote transfers. Unionist support has, on occasions such as Joe Hendron's defeat of Gerry Adams in West Belfast in the 1992 British general election, proved invaluable, but it has remained exceptional. There is some evidence of cross-community vote transfers in the 1998 Assembly elections. Staged amid the euphoric aftermath of the GFA, the elections indicated an increase in the willingness of pro-GFA electors to vote on a cross-community basis. According to Kelly and Doyle (2000) there was a 5 per cent increase in pro-GFA unionist transfers to the SDLP, Evans and O'Leary (1999) state that 10 per cent of lower preference votes were transferred across the community divide, and Sinnott (1998) found that 36 per cent of final UUP vote transfers went to the SDLP in constituencies where an Alliance Party candidate no longer remained in the contest. Obviously, under the first-past-the-post Westminster election system the possibility of lower preference transfers does not exist, but for district council or Assembly elections the SDLP could position itself as a repository for moderate, pro-GFA unionist or Alliance Party transfers. Even among the ruling body of the UUP there is an avowed willingness to bridge electoral divisions. Fifteen per cent of UUC members say that they 'definitely' or 'might' consider transferring lower preference votes to the SDLP, with a further 26 per cent describing such a prospect as a 'slight possibility' (Tonge and Evans, 2000).

Yet voting across the divide remains uncommon. Over 96 per cent of Sinn Fein terminal vote transfers (i.e. where another Sinn Fein candidate was not available) went to the SDLP in the 2003 Assembly elections. With SDLP members being elected on lower, often final, counts, there were fewer terminal transfers of its votes outside the party. In one constituency, West Belfast, 99 per cent of SDLP terminal transfers went to Sinn Fein, perhaps unsurprisingly given that the rival candidate was from the DUP. SDLP gains relative to Sinn Fein, through tentative breaches of the sectarian divide, were always likely to be outweighed by the increasing trend for DLP voters to transfer their lower preference votes to Sinn Fein. Whereas in the past the strength of Sinn Fein's association with the IRA had caused a substantial body of SDLP supporters to transfer votes to the centrist, avowedly non-sectarian Alliance Party, the new moderation of Sinn Fein meant this was no longer the case. Sinn Fein's position as the main repository of SDLP vote transfers is unlikely to change, given the continuing demise of Northern Ireland's political centre.

Sinn Fein's strengthened position has led to a cooling of the party's interest in electoral pacts with the SDLP. Whilst such pacts had tactical (electoral gains) and strategic (legitimation) value in the past, Sinn Fein's new dominance has diminished the utility to republicans of electoral alliances. Not everyone welcomed the electoral battle for the nationalist vote: while almost 50 per cent of Sinn Fein supporters argued that there should be an electoral pact between their party and the SDLP, fewer than one third of SDLP supporters were prepared to reciprocate (*Belfast Telegraph*, 18 May 2001). SDLP members were divided on the merits of such an alliance, with 47 per cent in favour and 36 per cent against.

Nationalist convergence part two: the changing agenda of Sinn Fein

The changes in Sinn Fein during recent decades have been dramatic. During the 1970s the party served as a vastly inferior adjunct to the IRA. Its main political offering during this period was the romantic federal socialism of its *Eire Nua* policy, under which Ireland would be governed by four largely autonomous parliaments, one in each of its ancient provinces. Unionists could enjoy a majority in an Ulster parliament, where they would have greater political rights than those awarded by unionists to nationalists coerced into the British northern province. Nonetheless, in a federal Ireland with the union removed, unionists' political aspirations would be limited.

Sinn Fein emerged as a serious force in the 1980s, following the electoral mobilization of the nationalist constituency during the republican hunger strikes of 1981, in which ten prisoners died. Federalism had been dropped by 1983 and abstention from the Irish parliament was abandoned in 1986, the latter leading to the formation of the tiny Republican Sinn Fein Party, which was committed to what it insisted were 'true' republican principles. By 1988 'ourselves alone' had been replaced as a political approach by an interest in pan-nationalism, as illustrated by Sinn Fein's engagement in dialogue with the SDLP. The party's 1992 policy document, *Towards a Lasting Peace*, revealed two fundamental changes in the party's approach. First, it did not demand immediate British withdrawal from Northern Ireland; rather Britain should act as a persuader to unionists for a united Ireland. Second, some cognizance of the position of unionists was evident. Sinn Fein no longer believed that unionists were merely deluded Irish citizens who would 'come quietly' if their British prop was withdrawn. Developing publicly the hitherto secretive Adams exit route from armed struggle, Sinn Fein now preferred to use the language of Irish self-determination rather than 'Brits out'. Although this form of self-determination was heavily qualified in the Downing Street Declaration, issued in 1993 by the British and Irish governments, the IRA ceasefire of 1994 indicated a shift away from violence.

The balance of forces within the movement in the mid 1990s nonetheless ensured that armed struggle could not be abandoned at that stage, although the IRA's 'spectaculars', notably the bombings in Canary Wharf and Manchester in 1996, were designed to force the inclusion of Sinn Fein in talks, rather than to achieve overall objectives.

The common interpretation among journalists and academics was that the IRA's military campaign was in dire trouble (Harnden, 1999; Moloney, 2002; English, 2003). Yet in terms of financial damage to the British government the IRA had achieved far more in the first half of the 1990s than it had in the previous two decades. Hence it was not surprising that the first ceasefire, followed by Sinn Fein's exclusion from talks, produced disquiet in the republican movement. The 1996 IRA convention was the last triumph for hardliners in the movement. That convention inserted a clause into the IRA constitution stating that 'the IRA would not decommission any of its weapons until the aims and objectives of the IRA had been achieved'. This move, according to 'dissidents', was 'designed to constrain and impede the political and military compromises that were clearly on the agenda of the Provisional leadership' (*Sovereign Nation*, vol. 4, no. 5, 2001, p. 1). However in October 1997, one month after Sinn Fein signed up to the Mitchell principles of non-violence, a narrow majority at an extra-ordinary IRA convention granted a 'special dispensation' to the IRA leadership to deal with the issue of arms. The subsequent resignation of a member of the convention and the formation of the dissident Real IRA consolidated the majority of those who wished to steer the Provisionals away from violence. 'Not an ounce, not a bullet' slogan-izing was replaced by three acts of Provisional IRA arms decommission-ing in 2001–3. The Omagh bombing by the Real IRA was condemned by the Provisionals as indicative of the futility of militarism when conducted without reference to the political context (*An Phoblacht*, 21 August 1998), although for dissidents the context of continued British rule and republican compromise provided sufficient justification.

The 1997 slogan 'No return to Stormont' gave way to support for the GFA in 1998 and Sinn Fein's entry to the Northern Ireland Assembly in 1999. At the party's *ard fheis* in 1998, Sinn Fein delegates voted overwhelmingly (by 97 per cent to 3 per cent) to change the party's constitution to allow entry to the Assembly. Whilst expectant of backing from the membership for entry to Stormont the Sinn Fein leaders had taken no part in the negotiations on the formation of the Assembly, opposing its creation but acknowledging its inevitability as part of any deal (Hennessey, 2000). The Provisional movement had been borne of opposition to entry to Stormont, which in 1970 had been viewed as merely a vehicle of unionist hegemony. The 1998 power-sharing version, with Sinn Fein participating, was seen as a funda-mentally different entity. Provisional republicanism lacked the fixed principles of traditional republicanism. The old southern leadership of the Provisional movement had grafted the politics of 1916–19 onto northern defenderism, but by the 1990s the two wings of republican-ism had largely disengaged.

Now committed to its peace strategy and support for the GFA, Sinn Fein had been transformed from the embryonic electoral force of the early 1980s, when its *ard fheis* had instructed all candidates to declare unequivocal support for the IRA's armed struggle. With that phase of conflict over, the party, while emphasizing its continuing republican objectives, offered a participatory form of politics that contrasted sharply with its previous support for the armed destruction of the state. The party's firm insistence on full implementation of an agreement that kept Northern Ireland in the United Kingdom appeared at odds with traditional republican dogma, even if the party's tactics exposed divisions within unionism. Sinn Fein at least kept the border issue alive by calling for a fixed date for simultaneous north–south polls on Irish unity. Over two decades earlier the party had called for a boycott of a border poll in the north. In the review of the GFA in 2004, the party urged the repeal of the Northern Ireland Act 2000, which gave the British government the powers to suspend devolution. The party's insistence on full restoration of the GFA, with places for Sinn Fein ministers in a Northern Ireland administration, meant that it rejected the idea of a 'gentle' return of devolution via the creation of committees rather than full ministries. Contrary to its earlier insistence that there was no Stormont way, Sinn Fein now insisted that there was only a Stormont way.

According to republican critics of Sinn Fein's changed approach, the party's electoral success could not disguise its failure to achieve its objective of a united Ireland, now displaced by participation in a Northern Ireland state that had previously been held as illegitimate (McIntyre, 2001). While Sinn Fein's manifesto asserted that the GFA 'transcends partition' (Sinn Fein, 2001, p. 6), this claim was belied by the agreement's assertion that Northern Ireland would remain part of the United Kingdom for as long as the people of Northern Ireland so chose. As such the agreement was clearly partitionist, or at least in the short to medium term. Electoral imperatives appeared to have supplanted ideological purity, as exemplified by Sinn Fein's decision to enter Stormont in the absence of any realistic prospect of a united Ireland, or even joint British–Irish authority (Hazleton, 2001). At the heart of Sinn Fein's approach was its desire to consolidate its position as the largest nationalist party, but its defining objective could not be fulfilled via Stormont. Prime Minister Blair ruled out a united Ireland, insisting that:

> My agenda is not a united Ireland and I wonder just how many see it as a realistic possibility for the foreseeable future? Northern Ireland will remain part of the United Kingdom as long as a majority here wish ... I believe in the United Kingdom. I value the Union ... Northern Ireland is part of the United Kingdom because that is the wish of the majority of the people who live here. It will remain part of the UK for as long as that remains the case ... Unionists have nothing to fear from a new Labour Government. A political settlement is not a slippery slope to a united Ireland. The Government will not be persuaders for unity. (quoted in Tonge, 2002, p. 179)

Palpably the aims and objectives of the IRA were nowhere near realization. Sinn Fein's decision to sign up to the Mitchell Principles of non-violence in September 1997 was followed by an extraordinary IRA convention one month later. By a narrow majority, this granted a special dispensation to the Provisional leadership to deal with the issue of arms, effectively allowing the leadership to proceed (eventually) with decommissioning. Dissidents claimed that this was at odds with the IRA constitution and left to form the Real IRA (RIRA), with a political outlet in the 32 County Sovereignty Committee. The RIRA bomb explosion in Omagh in August 1998, killing 29 and forcing the organization to call a ceasefire, stopped large-scale defections. Moreover, the organization lacked an urban base and had been penetrated by informers (Mooney and O'Toole, 2003). The existence of the RIRA, despite being beset by internal division, and the equally tiny Continuity IRA (CIRA) indicated that a form of republican armed struggle might endure, against overwhelming odds and maintained by a very low level of violence. Sinn Fein derided these ultras for attempting to continue what it had supported for 25 years. Implicit in this U-turn was the argument that, as the Provisional IRA had lost, no other group could possibly win or even attempt to do so, with Martin McGuinness dismissing the 'micro-groups' as 'militarily useless' (BBC Northern Ireland Newsline, 17 September 2003).

Having abandoned their armed struggle far short of the achievement of their purpose, Provisional republicans cared not to dwell on the criticism by Bernadette Sands-McKevitt – sister of the IRA hunger striker Bobby Sands and member of the 'dissident' 32 County Sovereignty Committee – that 'Bobby did not die for cross-border bodies with executive powers. He did not die for nationalists to be equal citizens within the British state' (quoted in Hennessey, 2000, p. 112). It had been argued for some time that a lowering of republican horizons would result from the promotion of electoral politics at the expense of traditional, abstentionist and militarist republicanism (Ryan, 1994). Sinn Fein's promotion of the politics of identity, pluralist in concept and tone, offered a new, non-holistic form of republicanism in which there would be equal respect for nationalist and unionist mandates (Bean, 1995). The party maintained discipline through a hierarchical approach, albeit one that often took care, through consultation and planning, to keep its members on-side. Republicanism was increasingly diverted into cultural expressions of Irishness, partly illustrated by the nature of the hunger strike commemorations in 2001 (Breen, 2001). The growth of Sinn Fein relative to the SDLP and the overall rise in nationalist voters masked a slight tailing off of enthusiasm for the political process among nationalists. In 2003 the reduced turnout (by 9 per cent) in constituencies in which a majority of nationalist candidates were returned was double the reduction in majority unionist areas. However this can be partly explained by tighter electoral procedures, and the turnout in nationalist majority areas, at 68 per cent, still exceeded that in unionist areas by 8 per cent.

The difficulty for republican critics of Sinn Fein's new approach was in advancing a coherent alternative strategy. The 32 County Sovereignty Committee urged republicans to 'seriously consider whether their allegiance is to one particular party or to the goal of a 32 county sovereign island' (Rory Dougan, quoted in the *Independent*, 25 October 2001, p. 2). Yet Sinn Fein's continued insistence on eventual British withdrawal and Irish unity reassured many republicans. Furthermore republican ultras appeared to be devoid of a serious political outlet. Republican Sinn Fein, which at times seemed to be as obsessed with criticizing the 'partitionist' Irish parliament (accepted for decades by the citizens of the Irish Republic) as it was with condemning British sovereignty in Northern Ireland, urged West Belfast nationalists voting in the 2001 British general election to spoil their ballot papers in support of political status for the Continuity IRA prisoner Tommy Crossan. While the number of spoilt ballots, 1500, was high, this was dwarfed by the support for Gerry Adams, who captured two thirds of the votes cast. Provisional Sinn Fein's diminished association with armed struggle gave it electoral mileage. During 2001 the election campaign the IRA had issued a statement confirming that a third examination of its arms dumps had been conducted and that four meetings between the IRA and the International Commission on Disarmament (ICD) had taken place since March 2001. In a separate statement the ICD expressed its satisfaction with the inspection and declared that the IRA had fully honoured its commitments.

Sinn Fein's approach lay in its desire to become not merely the largest nationalist party but also the largest of all parties in Northern Ireland (Adams, 2001). In 2003 it became the second largest party in the Assembly, along with the UUP. Sinn Fein stresses the party's continuing green credentials and calls for additional all-Ireland political and electoral arrangements, including the advancement of all-Ireland bodies, the right of those elected in parliamentary contests in Northern Ireland to participate in the Irish parliament, and for Northern Ireland citizens to be given the right to participate in presidential elections and referendums in the Irish Republic. It has demanded further changes in policing, including full implementation of the recommendations in the Patten Report. Its electoral strategy, emphasizing support for the GFA, was always likely to pay dividends among an electoral base that strongly favoured the accord and was desirous of robust political representatives.

The changes within Sinn Fein need to be placed in a historical context. There have been no other fundamental republican principles during its nearly century-long existence than a commitment to work towards an independent, sovereign and united Ireland. Even this commitment was questionable at the outset, as the first leader of Sinn Fein, Arthur Griffith, advocated a system of dual monarchy in Britain and Ireland (Feeney, 2002). Republican ultras may be correct in asserting that the absorbtion of republicans into the existing political systems on the island has diluted republicanism. The difficulty has been to advance an alternative, given that any military option is undertaken against overwhelming British superiority. The failure to achieve a united, sovereign, independent Ireland splintered the movement, resulting in the split over whether to accept the Anglo-Irish Treaty (a fracture partly caused by partition but primarily by disagreement over whether sufficient independence had been given to the 26 counties of the Republic) and the subsequent civil war. De Valera's entry into *Dail Eireann* with Fianna Fail in 1926 threw scorn on the notion that abstention was a fundamental republican principle. Sinn Fein, in its various guises, revived the idea of abstention as a republican shibboleth. Sixty years after De Valera's decision, however, Sinn Fein's president, Gerry Adams, presided over a decisive (429 votes to 161) move at the party's *ard fheis* away from abstentionism, which had, like earlier Sinn Fein policies such as federalism, been elevated from a tactic to a principle.

Even prior to its transformation in the 1990s, the Provisonal republican movement had always been a curious hybrid of republican fundamentalism, urban sectarianism, reaction to British mismanagement and response to the structural conditions experienced by nationalists (Bishop and Mallie, 1988; McIntyre, 1995, 2001; Patterson, 1997; Moloney 2002; English, 2003). The Provisionals were partly a product of the sectarian attacks on nationalists in 1969, although this is imperfect history as such attacks temporarily declined in 1970, when the republican movement began to grow. The Provisional IRA expanded quickly after a series of disastrous 'security' measures by the British armed forces, including curfew, internment and the army's actions on Bloody Sunday in Derry. McIntyre (1995, 2001) argues that the Provisionals were essentially a responsive force with no particular ideological compass. Yet the leadership of the republican movement had proclaimed allegiance to the Irish Republic established under the first *Dail Eirean* of 1919, even if the grassroots supporters had little interest in doctrinal orthodoxy. The northern-based leadership, which controlled the movement from the early 1980s, wasted little time in ditching fundamentalism.

The republican movement's political journey has now reached the point where it is engaged in what has been described as radical transformist egalitarianism (Todd, 1999), although the extent of Sinn Fein's egalitarian principles is open to debate. In office, Sinn Fein implemented private finance initiatives, unwelcome arrangements which the party blamed upon British legislation (Coates, 2004). Even leaving aside the question of whether Sinn Fein's policies are radical or egalitarian, in what sense are the party's principles transformist? The party's rigid insistence on full implementation of the GFA is transformist in respect of the internal politics of Northern Ireland, but it is also a tacit acknowledgement of the legitimacy of the northern state, and as such it is non-transformist in terms of constitutional politics. The transition from 'ourselves alone' to 'equal treatment for our mandate' has been the most striking transformation in republican politics (Breen, 2001, p. 7).

Conclusion

Nationalist politics have taken a new form. The traditional fault
line between the constitutional, participatory and civic nationalism
espoused by the SDLP, and the extraconstitutional, often violent,
ethnic republicanism offered by Sinn Fein and the IRA, has largely
vanished as Sinn Fein and the IRA have moved away from armed
struggle and tacitly accepted the SDLP's 'unity by consent' formula.
Structural differences between the two parties have assumed greater
importance than ideological distinctions. Sinn Fein's position as the
only significant all-Ireland party, consolidated by electoral successes
north and south of the border, has made the SDLP look like a narrow,
sectional, northern nationalist party, which has accentuated the party's
problems of an ageing membership, low recruitment and loss of electoral (and moral) superiority. The SDLP's electoral losses have not
been sufficiently compensated by a political realignment that would
allowed transfers from pro-GFA unionist electors.

Sinn Fein is reliant on a vague, unsubstantiated 'inevitability' thesis,
rather than a specific strategy to achieve its goal of a united Ireland.
Nonetheless its verbal commitment to ending partition – when added
to the lack of alternative outlets for its critics and the modest interest
in unification among nationalists – means that it is still viewed as a
republican party. In the future its vigorous participatory politics and
its civil-rights-based agenda are likely to yield further gains at the
expense of rivals throughout Ireland.

6

The Big Tent at Stormont: The Northern Ireland Assembly

The fragility of the Good Friday Agreement meant that the institutions it created failed to take root in the years immediately after its signature. The Northern Ireland Act 1998 laid down the legislative powers of the Northern Ireland Assembly, conferred in December 1999. The Assembly was awarded full legislative and executive authority in respect of matters that had previously been the remit of the six Northern Ireland government departments. The secretary of state for Northern Ireland remained responsible for Northern Ireland Office matters that had not been devolved to the Assembly, including policing, security policy, the prison service and criminal justice. Although it sat just one full day (Tuesday) and one afternoon (Monday) each week, the Assembly made some progress towards establishing itself as a meaningful legislative and scrutinizing body. The part-time nature of the Assembly was emphasized by the fact that 55 per cent of MLAs were also local councillors (Carmichael and Knox, 2003). The executive, an uneasy collection of republican, nationalist, unionist and loyalist forces, often appeared to be a less than coherent body and at times was disrupted by bloc rivalries.

The overblown size of the Assembly, with 108 members, was the ultimate example of how Northern Ireland had moved from ' "democratic deficit" to surfeit mode' (Carmichael and Knox, 2003, p. 4), with its electors also represented by 582 councillors, 18 Westminster MPs (albeit including four abstentionists) and three MEPs. Despite the huge number of elected representatives, much of the governance of public services continued to be conducted by non-elected quangos, such as the health and social service boards, hospital trusts and education and library boards. There was a considerable element of 'feeling the way' in the early stages of the Assembly, while MLAs with little or no experience of government or legislative scrutiny attempted to adapt. Assembly procedures altered considerably in the early stage of its existence, with 44 amendments being made in the first two years by the Assembly Committee on Procedures. The vulnerability of the new political institutions was emphasized by the suspension of Assembly proceedings on a number of occasions in 2000 and 2001, followed by a prolonged, indefinite suspension in October 2002.

This chapter explores how the Assembly functioned and suggests that, in contrast to the often dysfunctional executive, it had positive features. Nonetheless its work was overshadowed by perpetual crises.

Institutionalized crisis and made-up the rules? Assembly problems in 1998–2002

From the outset the Assembly was devoid of a secure pro-GFA majority. The first elections to the Assembly, in June 1998, reflected the near-even split on the GFA among unionists. Parallel consent mechanisms were built on the assumption of a solid pro-GFA majority in both communities. Devoid of such a majority the Assembly failed to function effectively, but it was at the executive level that the lack of unionist support for the GFA had the most impact. The 2003 contest confirmed unionists' increased disillusionment with the deal, necessitating the renegotiation, at the minimum, of power-sharing arrangements (Table 6.1).

The selection of pro-GFA UUP candidates for the 1998 Assembly elections represented a rare triumph of party discipline for the UUP. However the precarious balance between the pro- and anti-GFA unionists tilted towards the anti-GFA wing in subsequent years, with the defection of Peter Weir to the DUP after his expulsion from the UUP in November 2001, and the suspension of Pauline Armitage during the same month. Aside from Armitage and Weir, support for Trimble among UUP MLAs was strong. Only Derek Hussey broke ranks and voted for the DUP's motion to exclude Sinn Fein from government when devolution was restored in May 2000. This contrasted with the narrow support by the UUC for the decision to re-enter government with Sinn Fein. The 53 per cent to 47 per cent majority on the UUC in favour of Trimble's position highlighted the split in the party, a division

Table 6.1 *Composition of the Northern Ireland Assembly, 1998–2003 (number of seats)*

1998–2002		2003–	
Pro-GFA unionist parties		Pro-GFA unionist parties	
Ulster Unionist Party[1]	26	Ulster Unionist Party[5]	24
Progressive Unionist Party	2	Progressive Unionist Party	1
Anti-GFA unionist parties		Anti-GFA unionist parties	
Democratic Unionist Party	20	Democratic Unionist Party	33
Northern Ireland Unionist Party[2]	3	UK Unionist	1
United Unionist Assembly Party[3]	3	Nationalist parties (pro-GFA)	
		Sinn Fein	24
Independent Unionist[4]	3	SDLP	18
UK Unionist	1	Other (pro-GFA)	
Nationalist parties (pro-GFA)		Alliance	6
SDLP	24	Independent	1
Sinn Fein	18		
Other (pro-GFA)			
Alliance	6		
Women's Coalition	2		

Notes:
[1] Peter Weir was expelled and joined the Democratic Unionist Party.
[2] Elected as UK Unionist Party; resigned and formed the Northern Ireland Unionist Party, with effect from 15 January 1999.
[3] Elected as independent candidates; formed United Unionist Assembly Party, with effect from 21 September 1998.
[4] Total includes Roger Hutchinson, who was expelled from the Northern Ireland Unionist Party in December 1999.
[5] The UUP won 27 seats in the 2003 election, but three anti-GFA UUP MLAs (Nora Beare, Jeffrey Donaldson and Arlene Foster) defected to the DUP in January 2004.

that was not reflected among the MLAs. The argument of UUP 'dissidents' such as Jeffrey Donaldson that it was 'simply not possible to run a political party on a basis that suppresses 40 per cent plus' carried less weight with the UUP Assembly group (*Belfast Telegraph*, 30 November 2001). When the DUP overtook the UUP in the 2003 Assembly elections the unrest within the UUP took a decisive turn. Donaldson, Arlene Foster and Nora Beare left to join the DUP in January 2004, a development matched by the defection from the party by some constituency associations. Barring a wholesale rewriting of the rules, an effort that would be doomed to failure, restoration of power sharing would be at the behest of the DUP, a party that had pledged not to do business with Sinn Fein whilst the IRA continued to exist.

In the first phase of the Assembly the DUP sought the expulsion of Sinn Fein from government by means of petitions of concern, but it failed to receive cross-community support. Paisley's party could see no reason why it should sit in government with Sinn Fein when the *taoiseach* had ruled out a similar prospect in the Irish Republic, due to 'insuperable constitutional difficulties', and until Sinn Fein chose to 'resolve its relationship with the IRA' (*Sunday Independent*, 20 November 2002). In July 2002 the secretary of state for Northern Ireland promised a rigorous assessment of the state of play with paramilitary ceasefires and indicated his future willingness to exclude parties associated with active paramilitary groups from the executive, this following rioting in parts of Belfast and alleged IRA training activity in Colombia. The statement, which amounted to a 'yellow card' for paramilitary groups and their political associates, was a minimal response to the public disquiet of unionist leaders, attempting to pacify a unionist community in psychological retreat. Following allegations of an IRA spy ring at Stormont and a police raid on Sinn Fein's office there in October 2002, the British government sought SDLP assistance in excluding Sinn Fein. When this was not forthcoming the UUP made clear it would no longer participate in government and the executive and Assembly duly collapsed, their future uncertain.

Although it was alleged IRA activity that had brought down the institutions the GFA had been a fragile child since birth. The decommissioning of weapons by the IRA, long seen as inevitable in informed republican circles, was sufficiently protracted to place the devolved institutions in jeopardy. Republicans realised that the public had supported the 'moral' basis of the agreement, rather than a literal reading of the deal. seventy-nine per cent believed the IRA's political allies should be expelled from the executive if decommissioning did not occur (*Daily Telegraph*, 14 October 2001). The events of 11 September 2001 in the US hastened the process of decommissioning, but they were not a catalyst. The decommissioning of IRA weapons was, for republicans, an unwelcome but inevitable denouement of Sinn Fein's peace strategy. Protracted crises en route to devolution were a product of unionist impatience and doubt among the republican leaders about whether decommissioning could be sold to the remaining hardliners. In order to allow more time for progress on decommissioning, the secretary of state suspended the devolved government twice in 2001, once in August and again in September. The suspensions were technicalities, designed to buy more time. In October that year, exasperated by the apparent lack of movement by the IRA on decommissioning, David Trimble, having already resigned as first minister in July, engaged in successful brinkmanship by withdrawing the UUP ministers from the executive. Within a week the IRA announced that it had decommissioned a quantity of weapons. A second act of decommissioning, in which a 'varied and substantial quantity of ammunition' had been put beyond use, was announced in April 2002 (ICD statement, 8 April 2002). The symbolic nature of the decommissioning row was emphasized by the British government's willingness, made public on December 2001, to extend the date for final decommissioning to 2007. The Good Friday Agreement had indicated that all weapons should be put beyond use by 2000.

Despite the IRA's move, the DUP and other anti-GFA unionists were nearly successful in their attempt to prevent the reinstatement of David Trimble as first minister in November 2001. The DUP met with General John de Chastelain, head of the International Commission on Decommissioning, shortly after the IRA announced that it had placed some weapons beyond use. The party declared itself 'astounded that David Trimble had recommended that his party re-enter the Executive Committee ... on the basis of an unspecified event where an unspecified number of weapons of an unspecified type were put beyond use in an unspecified way at an unspecified location' (*Daily Telegraph*, 27 October 2001). The UUP's Pauline Armitage supported the DUP's position, on the basis that her party was 'really leaving decommissioning to the IRA – they are calling the tune' (*Irish Independent*, 2 November 2001). Perhaps even more worrying for Trimble was that a poll had found that only 29 per cent of Protestants believed a statement by De Chastelain that a significant act of decommissioning had been carried out by the IRA (*Irish Independent*, 2 November 2001).

There was a failed attempt to re-elect Trimble at the beginning of the following month. Although he secured 70.6 per cent of the overall vote in the Assembly, unionist MLAs rejected his reinstatement by 30 votes to 29, leaving Trimble 0.8 per cent short of the unionist majority required by the parallel consent rules. However the redesignation of three Alliance MLAs, on the basis of a promise of a 'procedural review' of the GFA (which yielded nothing), secured Trimble's re-election four days later. Thirty-two unionists, allied to three Alliance Party MLAs and a single Women's Coalition redesignation, secured victory. Under the original Assembly rules, redesignation was permitted only once in the lifetime of an Assembly and 30 days' notice was required. It was far from apparent that the latter rule had been observed.

The Northern Ireland Act 1998 appeared to place an obligation on the secretary of state to call a fresh Assembly election in the event of a failure to elect the first minister and deputy first minister within six weeks of the Assembly having sat. The re-election of Trimble had taken place on 6 November, two days after the apparent six-week deadline, given that devolved government had been restored, after its third suspension, on 23 September 2001. The DUP pursued this matter through the courts, its case initially being rejected by the Belfast High Court and eventually taken to the House of Lords (*Robinson* v. *Secretary of State for Northern Ireland and ORS*, 2002). Whilst the party's case that there was an obligation to call a fresh election was accepted, the courts declared that it was the prerogative of the secretary of state to decide when such an election should be held. This decision was upheld by the Law Lords by a margin of three to two, which must have come as a huge relief to the secretary of state, John Reid, given the likelihood of election gains being made by anti-GFA unionists. The British government solved the problem of 'wrong result' Assembly elections in spring 2003 by using the intriguing democratic device of suspending the contest. By then, the Assembly had collapsed and belated elections in November did not immediately revive its prospects.

Reid's interpretation of Sections 16 and 32 of the Northern Ireland Act 1998, upheld by the majority of Law Lords, was that an immediate election was not mandatory. The rigidity involved in a mandatory election was contrary to the agreement's fundamental purpose of creating the most favourable constitutional environment for cross-community government, a situation that demanded flexibility. The secretary of state was entitled to take into account the fact that the Assembly had succeeded in electing a first minister and deputy first minister. This decision was curious, in that it rewarded the secretary of state for acting arbitrarily in proceeding with the second attempt to secure the election of the first minister and deputy first minister on 6 November.

The main basis for the verdict in Reid's favour appeared to be that the six-week deadline had originally been set to prevent prevarication over elections for the two ministerial posts. Lord Bingham argued that the application of a six-week deadline would have 'precluded the possibility of negotiation and compromise to find a political solution to an essentially political problem, contrary ... to British political tradition'. (*Robinson* v. *Secretary of State for Northern Ireland*: www. publications.parliament.uk/pa/ld200102, pp. 1–9.) More acceptably, he noted that the Act was not explicit on what should occur in the event of a failure to elect a first minister and deputy first minister within the specified deadline. Section 32 of the 1998 Act states that 'if the Assembly passes a resolution that it should be dissolved the Secretary of State shall propose a date for the poll for the election of the next Assembly'. Despite its failure to elect a first minister and deputy first minister, the Assembly had passed no such resolution, arguably the secretary of state's only legal card. In their dissenting judgements, Lords Hutton (later embroiled in another controversy) and Millhouse offered an argument that was grounded more securely in what the Northern Ireland Act 1998 actually stated, rather than the vague notion of 'British political tradition', which appeared to place the secretary of state as *the* interpreter of the Act and the Good Friday Agreement. The dissenting Law Lords pointed out that the Assembly, a creature of statute, had not been given any power to elect a first and deputy first minister after six weeks of devolved government had taken place. Allied to the revision to the date for full paramilitary weapons decommissioning, the episode highlighted the elasticity of deadlines attached to the political process, or put more simply, the making up of rules according to expediency.

The plan to revive the Assembly and elections the following year involved the establishment of a four-person independent monitoring body with the power to exclude parties linked, through their association with paramilitary groups, to breaches of ceasefire. The proposal for the establishment of the body was rushed through parliament in a single day in September 2003. Predictably, Sinn Fein claimed that the establishment of the body lay outside the terms of the GFA. A majority of unionists at Westminster voted against the measure, principally on the ground that one of the body's members would be a representative of the Irish government. These unionists – all of the DUP MPs and three of the UUP MPs – argued that the involvement of the Dublin government in strand one of the GFA breached the terms of the deal.

Modelling Assembly relationships

The Assembly offered several different prospects. One was a loose pan-nationalist alliance between the SDLP and Sinn Fein, encouraged by the parallel consent rules. This could have resulted in the zero-sum-game, sectarian politics discussed in other parts of this book, and was a negative model of segmental consociation in which ethnic blocs would be frozen. In this (unproven) scenario, political institutions would freeze ethnic bloc rivalries. Indeed the consociational model of democracy imposed by the GFA was held responsible for the development of even more vigorous ethnic bloc rivalries (see for example Dixon, 2001; Taylor, 2001). Yet the ethnic bloc divisions had preceded, and existed independently of, Assembly arrangements. The Assembly did not preclude their dismantling, nor reinforce the divisions, but it did acknowledge ethnic divisions. Nor did a consociational arrangement exacerbate ethnic politics. It has been demonstrated that the 'greening of the SDLP' occurred after the collapse of the experiment in consociationalism in 1974 (Evans *et al.*, 2000). Sinn Fein MLAs saw the bloc politics of pan-nationalism, insofar as it existed, as a construct of the peace process rather than as part of its outcome.

An alternative prospect was the emergence of a centrist UUP–SDLP coalition, designed to isolate the ethnic bloc 'extremists' of Sinn Fein and the DUP. This coalition could, in one formulation of the model, have worked with the existing centre parties: the Alliance Party and the NIWC. Alternatively the cross-community rules of the Assembly and executive could have resulted in the existing centre being overlooked when the SDLP and UUP formed an elite centrist coalition of their own. The declining original centre ground, represented by the Alliance Party, could have been displaced by a cooperative relationship between the centripetal forces of unionism and nationalism. Cooperation between the middle-class, centre-leaning SDLP and UUP (notwithstanding the latter party's significant internal divisions, particularly outside the Assembly) appeared a possibility, involving incremental cross-community political deals between moderate pro-GFA forces. This centrist coalition would be a loose alliance, predominant only at the executive level via a formal coalition of the offices of the first minister and deputy first minister, as will be discussed in the next chapter. For SDLP and UUP MLAs, effective cooperation had a logic based on survival. If both parties combined to make a success of legislation, this ought to be noticed by the electorate and could prevent electoral shifts to Sinn Fein and the DUP. In fact in October 2002 one UUP MLA, Duncan Shipley-Dalton, did call for an electoral pact between his party and the SDLP to prevent a possible collapse of the Assembly (*Fortnight*, October 2002, p. 18).

The third model was one of far-reaching, radical coalitions of interests, developed through rainbow alliances in which parties would coalesce around certain issues, possibly on a class basis in the case of Sinn Fein and the PUP. There would be genuine scope for informal cross-community cooperation between former antagonists, particularly Sinn Fein and the PUP, most notably on issues of education, health and social services and, to a lesser extent, housing. The two parties had similar views on how the Assembly should work. Equally, both were keen to build devolution from below, developing models of republican–loyalist cooperation on local councils and devolving the powers of the Civic Forum to the local level. The validity of the radical alliance model is examined below.

Getting along just fine? Republican and loyalist cooperation in the Assembly

There was a considerable array of forces ranged against any coalition of the new centre. The DUP and various other anti-GFA unionists were perpetual critics of the UUP and SDLP. Sinn Fein and the PUP, formerly bitter enemies, often cooperated amicably, and the PUP's Billy Hutchinson even described Martin McGuinness as 'undoubtedly the best Minister in the Executive' (speech at Argyle Business Centre, Shankill, 30 November 2001). Another PUP member, Eddie Kinner, claimed that the praise heaped upon McGuinness was justified 'because he is implementing all our policies' (interview, 28 November 2002). The most optimistic scenario was that cooperation at the Assembly level between republicans and loyalists would enable the institution to develop into a genuine forum for working-class representation, with a probable spillover effect on society. However the problems besetting the institutions denied them credibility as political entities.

There were two Sinn Fein MLAs on nine of the ten departmental committees and one on the Regional Development Committee. Sinn Fein members chaired the Finance and Enterprise committees, whilst on the loyalist side the Progressive Unionist Party, which was equally anxious to prevent the formation of a UUP–SDLP alliance, was represented on two departmental committees. Sinn Fein was also represented on each of the six standing committees of the Assembly, joined by the PUP on the Committee of the Centre and the Audit Committee. Sinn Fein had neither supported nor opposed the establishment of the

Assembly and had taken no part in the negotiations leading up to strand 1 of the GFA (Hennessey, 2000). Despite the party's abstentionism, its MLAs were highly participatory.

Zero-sum-game, loyalist–republican sectarian politics were rare, although there was hardly a flowering of class politics, in which former polar opposites would emphasize commonalities and promote a new radicalism. On the Social Development Committee, Sinn Fein's Michelle Gildernew argued that the PUP, represented by Billy Hutchinson, concerned itself with 'maintaining territory' for its supporters in respect of regeneration projects in North Belfast (interview with Michelle Gildernew, 28 June 2000). Within the Assembly itself the Sinn Fein MLAs saw themselves as closer to the PUP than to their fellow nationalists in the SDLP. Most attributed this to the similarities in class background between themselves and the PUP MLAs. The Sinn Fein MLAs conceded, however, that there were important political differences within the SDLP, with one arguing that the SDLP was more heterogeneous than was sometimes perceived and therefore it was important that Sinn Fein did 'not treat it as a monolith' (interview with Mitchel McLaughlin, 28 June 2000).

Insofar as a pan-nationalist alliance existed it lay purely in the reluctance of Sinn Fein to argue that the SDLP was uninterested in the equality agenda and its view that the SDLP had 'bottled' the negotiations on strand two of the GFA, diminishing its all-Ireland dimension (interview with Pat Doherty, MLA, 27 June 2000). Other Sinn Fein MLAs claimed that the biggest obstacle to pan-nationalist unity was the SDLP's weakness on the equality agenda (interviews with Alex Maskey, Sinn Fein MLA, West Belfast, 20 May 2000; Mary Nelis, Sinn Fein MLA, Foyle, 28 June 2000). The failure of the SDLP to support Sinn Fein's proposals for a women's department and a minister for children came in for particular criticism. Sinn Fein MLAs were also sceptical of the leftist agenda of the PUP. In an earlier era Gerry Adams (1995, pp. 127–8) had insisted that 'Those who profess to be "Northern Ireland Socialists" are involved in mere parochialism of the municipal gasworks and waterworks variety'. Sinn Fein's Assembly priorities – an expansionist housing programme; the removal of selection in education and the establishment of a strategic framework for the expansion of public services – were in accord with the PUP's agenda. Understandably, Sinn Fein's control of the Education Ministry and presence on the Higher Education Committee prompted a belief that the party would shape the education agenda. The PUP was not represented on either committee.

Cooperation between republicans and loyalists in the Assembly was assisted by their mutual concern to prevent the attempts by others (mainly the DUP) to expel them because of their links with active paramilitary organizations. Indeed almost three quarters of PUP members (74.1 per cent) believed that Sinn Fein should be allowed to participate in the Northern Ireland Assembly (McAuley and Tonge, 2003). For Sinn Fein there was no electoral damage to be had from associating with loyalists as it had no rival to 'outgreen' its approach. In the loyalist community the presence of a large anti-GFA electoral rival and the move by the UDA away from support of the GFA ensured that public cooperation with republicans remained difficult for the PUP. Furthermore cooperation at the Assembly level between republicans and loyalists did not have a spillover effect, given the problems at interface areas, although both parties and their paramilitary associates displayed an ability to 'keep the lid on' such problems.

However there was a clear limit to the extent of the cooperation between republicans and loyalists. The PUP MLAs disparaged what they perceived as a Sinn Fein attempt to 'narrow the ground of unionism by the use of in your face street politics' (ibid.). David Ervine spoke of being 'sucked out of the process by Sinn Fein's actions' (NI Assembly Official Report [Hansard], 24 January 2000). Sinn Fein MLAs conceded little on questions of national identity, accusing the PUP of being confused about what constituted their Britishness. The unionist promotion of Ulster-Scots in the Culture Arts and Leisure Committee and more widely in the Assembly was seen as evidence of such insecurity. Furthermore there were differences between republicans and loyalists on important social and moral questions, reflecting the different religious affiliations of party members and supporters. This became apparent when the Assembly debated the sensitive issue of abortion in 2001. Sinn Fein did not support abortion on demand. Indeed Mitchel McLaughlin stated that the majority of his constituents, as Catholics, were opposed to abortion. McLaughlin was in favour of referring the issue to an Assembly committee, but made clear that this should not be construed as backing the extension of the 1967 Abortion Act to Northern Ireland. Nonetheless the issue of abortion divided Sinn Fein (unlike the PUP, which was clearly 'pro-choice'), and two Sinn Fein MLAs described their party's position as 'ambiguous'.

Naturally, PUP members remained hostile to Sinn Fein's wider political agenda and considered that Sinn Fein was acting out of narrow sectarian interests. An example was the row that developed after ministers McGuinness and De Brun ordered their civil servants not to fly the Union flag as part of the Coronation Day celebrations. The PUP saw this as yet another example of Sinn Fein's antagonistic approach, and of playing to its own ethnic gallery. As one PUP executive member put it:

> Most people could live with Sinn Fein Assembly members as Assembly members representing their constituency, but when they took executive positions, they represented everyone. So, whenever they went into a position in the executive and did what they did about the flags and then were prepared to sit on committees with RUC members ... Well it was clear they won't represent unionists, so therefore they won't perform their executive role. (McAuley and Tonge, 2003, p. 189)

The Assembly as a legislature

In common with other legislatures, the Northern Ireland Assembly had institutional procedures for legislation and scrutiny (Table 6.2). The Assembly followed the Westminster model, in that a bill was introduced prior to its referral to a committee for scrutiny. This contrasts with the procedure for the Scottish Parliament, based on the European Parliament model, in which bills are placed before a committee prior to being presented to all members (although any member of the Scottish Parliament can attend a committee meeting). The committee stage of the Northern Ireland Assembly differed from that in Westminster in terms of the lack of an in-built government majority and existence on each committee of a reconsideration stage, but otherwise it followed the Westminster model.

The further consideration stage was where the final debate took place, given that the bill had been modified by this point. Assent at the final stage was normally a formality and the Assembly passed or rejected the bill without amendment. In the 2001–2 legislative session the average time for a bill to pass from the first stage to the conclusion of the consideration stage was four months and six days, the longest period being seven months 12 days; the shortest three months and

Table 6.2 *Stages of the legislative process in the Northern Ireland Assembly*

Prelegislative	Department consults with the relevant committee, which scrutinizes the policy issues Minister publishes a statement that the bill is within the legislative competence of the committee
Introduction	Bill introduced to the Assembly
First stage	Copy of the bill sent to the Northern Ireland Human Rights Commission
Second stage	Assembly debates and votes on the general principles of the bill
Committee stage	Clause-by-clause examination of the bill, concluding with a report
Consideration stage	Amendments to the bill proposed/examined and voted upon
Further consideration stage	Further amendments proposed/examined
Final stage	Final debate prior to approval, preceded by checks for legislative/legal/human rights competence
Royal assent	Crown approval
Reconsideration	Occurs only if the Judicial Committee of the Privy Council decides that an aspect of the bill is not within the legislative competence of the Assembly

seven days. Ministers could request, normally at first reading, to speed a bill through the Assembly by means of the accelerated passage procedure. Under this procedure the two budget bills each took only seven days to pass from the first stage to the conclusion of the consideration stage. In addition to bills sponsored by departments it was possible for legislation to be introduced by Assembly members. In 1999–2001 only one private member's bill was introduced, rising to two in the 2001–2 session. Private members' bills were subject to the same legislative procedure as executive bills.

All legislative included a procedure to ensure that bills complied with the human rights standards outlined in the European Convention of Human Rights. The Assembly's legal advisers also considered international standards on human rights. However the Northern Ireland Human Rights Commission offered the view that a separate human rights committee should scrutinize each bill and have the power to investigate human rights issues (see http://www.ni-assembly. gov.uk/procedures/reports/report1–01r.htm, pp. 57–8). According to the chair of the Human Rights Commission, Brice Dickson, the work of a specialized committee would complement rather than replace the existing scrutiny of bills by standing committees (ibid., p. 62). The Committee on Procedures rejected this idea, arguing that it would be better to embed awareness of human rights across the full range of committees, rather than make such issues the domain of a small number of MLAs on a specialized committee. Provision was made for the establishment of an *ad hoc* Committee on Equality in 1999, but the committee was never convened.

Assembly committees: scrutineers and legislators

Perhaps the most notable success of the GFA strand 1 institutional arrangements in the immediate post-GFA era lay in the workings of Assembly committees. Away from the grandstanding of the Assembly floor, business was conducted amicably among all the parties. Given the quality of the committees' work it was perhaps surprising that only a minority of meetings were open to the public. Between December 1999 and June 2002, 933 departmental committee meetings were held, of which only 256 were fully open to the public (www.ni-assembly. gov.uk/highereduc/press/cel45–01.htm). There appeared to be little reason to exclude the public, and indeed there was considerable variation in public access across committees. Whilst other committee meetings often remained closed, 60 of the 94 meetings of the Employment and Learning Committee, until its suspension in October 2002, had open access. Statutory committees examined the legislative proposals of departments and assisted with the formulation of policy. The departmental committees that existed at the time of suspension in 2002 are shown in Table 6.3.

There were also six standing committees whose tasks were to oversee the smooth functioning of the Assembly, ensure the satisfactory operation of financial procedures and scrutinize the office of the first minister and deputy first minister:

Table 6.3 *Northern Ireland Assembly committees prior to suspension in 2002*

	Committee chair	Deputy chair
Agriculture and Rural Development	Ian Paisley (DUP)	George Savage (DUP)
Culture, Arts and Leisure	Eamon O'Neil (SDLP)	Mick Murphy (SF)
Education	Danny Kennedy (UUP)	Sammy Wilson (DUP)
Employment and Learning	Esmond Birnie (UUP)	Mervyn Carrick (DUP)
Enterprise, Trade and Investment	Pat Doherty (SF)	Sean Neeson (APNI)
Environment	William McCrea (DUP)	Patricia Lewsley (SDLP)
Finance and Personnel	Francie Malloy (SF)	Roy Beggs (UUP)
Health, Social Services and Public Safety	Joe Hendron (SDLP)	Tommy Gallagher (SDLP)
Regional Development	Alan McFarland (UUP)	Alban Maginness (SDLP)
Social Development	Fred Cobain (UUP)	Gerry Kelly (SF)

- Committee on Procedures (11 members)
- Business Committee (13 members)
- Committee of the Centre (17 members)
- Public Accounts Committee (11 members)
- Committee on Standards and Privileges (11 members)
- Audit Committee (5 members)

Ad hoc committees were set up to explore particular issues, rather than to scrutinize departments. Such committees had specific, time-bound terms of reference and normally reported within a few months of their establishment. Between 2000 and 2002, eight *ad hoc* committees were set up to consider the subjects of flags, financial investigations, life sentences, proceeds of crime, criminal injuries compensation, criminal justice reform, disqualification legislation and draft access to justice.

Ad hoc committees often dealt with particularly controversial matters, although some disputes seemed arcane to outsiders. The wrangles were perhaps the least edifying aspect of the committees' work. The Flags Committee dealt with the issue of which flags should be flown on public buildings in Northern Ireland. Party submissions followed predictable lines. The UUP and DUP argued that the Union flag must be flown as a clear expression of the constitutional position of Northern Ireland within the United Kingdom. The UUP insisted that the Irish tricolour ought not to be flown, as this would imply that the

GFA had introduced joint sovereignty. The DUP contended that the GFA had effectively brought about joint sovereignty anyway, but the removal of the Union flag would be a further step down the road to Dublin. The SDLP argued that the present constitutional position of Northern Ireland did not legitimize the flying of the Union flag. Sinn Fein declared that the Union flag had been used by unionists as 'a symbol of political dominance and a tool of sectarian coat trailing' (www.ni-assembly.gov.uk/adhocs/flags/reports/adhoc1–00r.htm, 15 September 2002). The Alliance Party urged the use of shared symbols, such as the European flag and a new Northern Ireland flag. In the event the unionist perspective triumphed, in that the Union flag would be flown on certain days of the year. In 2001 the Assembly reconvened over the decision to allow the display of Easter lilies in the Assembly building as part of the annual commemoration of the 1916 Easter Rising by republicans. The DUP's attempt to overturn the decision, via a petition of concern, failed due to the absence of cross-community support. These episodes highlighted how symbolic issues could displace substantial ones.

Committee chairs and deputy chairs were chosen under the D'Hondt allocation procedure, according to party strength in the Assembly, and were not drawn from the same party as the departmental minister. Unlike at Westminster, the choice of committee members was not based on their expertise in particular policy areas, which made their success (sectarian battles on *ad hoc* committees apart) perhaps all the more surprising. However, the committees did have the power to appoint special advisers. The unicameral basis of the Assembly meant that the scrutiny of bills was confined to its committees and, to a lesser extent, the floor of the Assembly. The committees drew on good practice elsewhere. For example the Committee on Procedures visited the Scottish parliament and *Dail Eireann* to examine legislative and scrutiny procedures.

The legislative process was similar to that at Westminster, apart from the way in which the committee stage was managed, the existence of a reconsideration stage and the lack of an in-built government majority in a committee system where the normal rules of government and opposition did not apply. Membership of committees was determined according to party strength in the Assembly. Such membership was more backbench-oriented than the Scottish system, in which ministers could be members of committees. Following prelegislative scrutiny, the Northern Ireland Assembly committees presented reports on bills and suggested amendments that could usefully be made by ministers at the consideration stage. Liaison between departments and committees improved and consultations with the committees prior to the introduction of a bill became the norm. This was extended, in instances such as the Railway Safety Bill introduced by the Department for Regional Development in 2001–2, to the placement of draft bills before the relevant committee, with Assembly committees possessing the power to initiate legislation. Statutory committees could initiate legislation but not amend it, a situation that appeared anomalous.

From December 1999 to the end of the 2000–1 session, 21 bills progressed through the Assembly, of which 17 went through the committee stage. The Committee for Finance and Personnel was by far the most active and considered eight bills in contrast to the one bill considered by most committees in the first year of their existence. However none of the committees was idle producing a total of 67 reports in the first two years of their existence.

The pace of legislation was rapid. During the 2000–1 session the average time taken to process a bill in the Assembly was 16 weeks, less than in the Westminster and Scottish parliaments. The committee stage was initially allocated 30 calendar days, but this proved inadequate and extensions were sought in over 50 per cent of cases. The allocated time was much too short in cases where a committee had to consider more than one bill during the same period. The 30 calendar days were increased to 30 working days, although this was still too short a time for the scrutiny of some bills. The executive proposed a reduction in the time between bill stages from five days to four, but this was rejected by the Committee of Procedure as unrealistic, given the time needed for amendments to be considered. Eventually, the average length of the committee stage grew to nine weeks.

Perhaps contrary to popular perception, the Assembly was an efficient, functional body in terms of scrutinizing and passing legislation between 2000 and 2002. Nonetheless deficiencies in the legislative and scrutiny processes were identified by the Committee on Procedures. Chaired by Sinn Fein's Conor Murphy, the committee operated on a largely consensual basis. Its main aim in the first two years of the Assembly was to establish an acceptable system of pre-bill consultation between departments and committees. The Committee on Procedures was particularly concerned that Section 13 of the Northern Ireland Act 1998 and the initial standing orders of the Assembly provided for a single bill amendment stage, reducing the opportunity for detailed scrutiny of legislation. A second amendment stage, the further consideration stage, was introduced in July 2000, although this provoked concern that initial Assembly decisions (at the first consideration stage) would be reversed. Debate at the further consideration stage was normally confined to amendments to the bill so as to prevent repetition of earlier scrutiny.

Not all legislation was subject to further consideration; for example this was not required when no amendments had been tabled at the consideration stage. Budget bills were given accelerated passage as they provided legal endorsement of the agreed sums allocated to departments and programmes from the consolidated fund. Accelerated passage bills were not put through the committee stage, subject to confirmation by the Committee for Finance and Personnel that there had been sufficient consultation. Other bills could also be given accelerated passage, although at first the opposition of a solitary Assembly member was enough to prevent this. The requirement for accelerated passage was subsequently diluted from unanimity to cross-community consent. The Committee on Procedures was anxious to stress that Assembly committee scrutiny was not a barrier to the passage of legislation. In order to achieve continuity, the committee introduced the automatic carry-over of legislation from one Assembly session to the next.

The Committee of the Centre (the largest committee, with 17 members) was responsible for checking that legislation complied with equality requirements. Under the Good Friday Agreement it was envisaged that a dedicated department of equality would be created to engage in cross-departmental audits of legislation. Instead an equality unit was established within the office of the first minister and deputy first minister. This could be seen as empire building by that office, but it should be noted that none of the parties opposed the absence of a dedicated department of equality. The Committee of the Centre began inauspiciously when the chair, Gregory Campbell of the DUP, refused to acknowledge the Sinn Fein members present (Wilford, 2001b). The DUP continued to chair and vice-chair the committee.

An obvious question about the committee system is the extent to which party loyalty precluded genuine scrutiny. It was unlikely that a Sinn Fein committee member would make a stinging criticism of a Sinn Fein minister; likewise the DUP with its ministers. Furthermore committee recommendations could be overridden by a minister. An early example was the decision by Bairbre de Brun, the minister for health, to locate maternity services in (nationalist) west Belfast when the Health Committee favoured South Belfast. Of course, some ministerial decisions required cross-community assent, but any decisions not designated as 'key' were vulnerable to unilateral ministerial action at the expense of department–committee partnerships.

Public and party support for the Northern Ireland Assembly

Despite its inflated size, erratic performance and vulnerability, in 2000–2 the Northern Ireland Assembly was a moderately popular institution among the region's voters. Even among anti-GFA Protestants, 57 per cent thought that the Assembly had achieved something, 5 per cent believed it had achieved a lot (MacGinty, 2003). Furthermore, as Table 6.4 shows, only 24 per cent of anti-GFA Protestants thought that the Assembly had done a bad job. The most common response was neutral, neither ringing endorsement nor scathing condemnation. Given the erosion of Protestant confidence in the GFA more generally (down to 33 per cent among unionists by October 2002), it was evident that the problems with the agreement lay outside the Assembly (BBC Northern Ireland Hearts and Minds Poll, 17 October 2002 www.news.bbc.co.uk/1/hi/northern_ireland/2335861.stm).

When attempts to revive the Assembly were undertaken after its collapse in 2002, it was evident that its restoration would not be a consequence of public clamour. Only 31 per cent of the population

Table 6.4 *Protestant's views on whether the Northern Ireland Assembly and executive did a good job in the day-to-day running of Northern Ireland (per cent)*

	Voted against GFA	Did not vote on GFA	Voted in favour of GFA	All Protestants
Did a good job	18	13	54	30
Neither good nor bad	55	57	38	49
Did a bad job	24	13	7	15
Don't know	4	16	1	6

Source: Data from MacGinty (2003).

chose 'the return from suspension of the power-sharing Assembly' as their preferred model for government in Northern Ireland, this being a minority option for both unionists and nationalists. Return of the Assembly was the most popular option for 39 per cent of nationalists; among unionists direct rule by Westminster commanded the support of 42 per cent, compared with only 23 per cent backing for the Assembly (www.news.bbc.co.uk/1/hi/northern_ireland/2335861.stm, 15 November 2002). Only 21 per cent of the population wished to see the return of the Assembly without preconditions, although, much more hearteningly for most of the political classes, only 11 per cent stated that they never wanted the Assembly to return (www.news. bbc. co.uk/1/hi/northern_ireland/2335861.stm, 15 November 2002). The overall message of indifference but not antagonism towards the Assembly is reinforced by the findings presented Table 6.5, which shows that only a minority of anti-GFA Protestants would be pleased if the Assembly was suspended for a number of years. There were strong intercommunal differences in respect of those who would be 'disappointed' if the Assembly was not restored: about 66 per cent of Catholics compared with 42 per cent of Protestants (MacGinty, 2003).

Surveys by the author of the memberships of three parties that supported the Good Friday Agreement – the SDLP, the UUP and the Alliance Party – revealed support for the Assembly. This suggests that, away from constitutional or conflict resolution issues, interethnic bloc rivalries may have been relatively unimportant. Party members were mere foot-soldiers in the construction of the GFA institutions, which were established by the party leaders in an elite accommodation and members were not consulted until after the deal had been done. No party balloted its members on whether to accept the agreement,

Table 6.5   *Protestants' views on the Northern Ireland Assembly being suspended for a number of years*

	Voted against GFA	*Did not vote on GFA*	*Voted in favour of GFA*	*All Protestants*
Pleased	27	8	4	14
Disappointed	27	26	71	42
Neither	40	50	23	36
Don't know	6	16	3	7

Source: Data from MacGinty (2003).

although Sinn Fein's decision to enter Stormont was overwhelmingly ratified by party delegates at the party's *ard fheis* (annual conference) in May 1998. Indeed a majority of SDLP and Alliance Party members believed they had little or no decision-making influence in their respective parties, a belief that cannot simply be attributed to false modesty.

Despite their differences in terms of national identity and constitutional ambitions, there remained a possibility that the Northern Ireland parties could develop commonalities on policy issues across the community divide, backed by party members outside the Assembly, an essential prerequisite. At the general level there is little evidence that this happened. Unionists were unconvinced that nationalists required their 'equality' agenda. Fewer than 2 per cent of UUP members subscribed to the proposition that nationalists were second-class citizens in Northern Ireland, but 36 per cent believed that unionists were second-class citizens. It was perhaps always thus. Rose's (1971) pioneering study found that an overwhelming majority (three quarters) of unionists thought that Catholics had not suffered discrimination under the old Stormont government of 1921–72, a view that, unsurprisingly, was rejected by an almost equal majority on the other side of the sectarian divide.

Despite these differences, post-GFA there was cross-community recognition of the potential of devolved institutions to achieve positive social and economic results. Notwithstanding a sizeable UUP integrationist tendency, there was a broad cross-party consensus that devolution was a good thing. This may have owed something to the devolutionary arrangements of the GFA being seen – as successive secretaries of state for Northern Ireland insisted – as the 'only show in town', with rival solutions attracting insufficient consensus. A slight majority in the UUP and 45 per cent of Alliance Party members supported the idea of giving more powers to local councils. However the notion of building devolution from below, by giving more power to local councils rather than the Assembly, found support among only one third of UUP members and only 13 per cent of Alliance Party members. Judging by the evidence offered by these parties it appears that the Assembly was viewed as an appropriate repository of power in Northern Ireland.

Furthermore party members were optimistic about the possibilities created by devolved government. Two thirds of Alliance Party members believed that the GFA would create unity among unionists and nationalists. Over half of UUP members believed that the GFA

Table 6.6   *Party members' views on whether a devolved Northern Ireland Assembly would improve local services (per cent)*

	Strongly agree	Agree	Neither agree nor disagree	Disagree	Strongly disagree
SDLP	9.3	42.8	36.9	7.4	1.5
UUP	24.7	48.1	13.6	9.5	4.1
APNI	20.9	54.3	20.9	2.9	0.9

would lead to real power sharing and cooperation between the two traditions, with two thirds of SDLP members adopting a similarly positive view. Despite the earlier greening of the SDLP, over two thirds of its members thought that power sharing was more important to the party than Irish unity. Most encouragingly for supporters of devolved institutions, members of the SDLP, UUP and Alliance Party agreed that the new Assembly would improve local services (Table 6.6). A majority in all parties also believed that north–south bodies would lead to greater cooperation between the two parts of Ireland.

Among voters, however, optimism was limited, with 50 per cent believing there was little or no cooperation among Assembly parties in respect of Northern Ireland's problems (Northern Ireland Life and Times Survey 2001).

There were considerable divisions on the policy questions that would confront a restored devolved government, but these were not necessarily based on a zero-sum-game sectarian division. The deployment of weighted majority voting or parallel consent on education, health or transport issues could be superfluous, as intrabloc division could be of greater importance than sectarian cross-community rivalries. A petition of concern from 30 of the 108 MLAs would be sufficient to trigger the parallel consent requirement. This meant that no party was alone capable of demanding cross-community support, a device that might exacerbate sectarian politics on issues without such a flavour.

Of course the non-sectarian flavour to highly contentious issues would not have diminished the difficulties for the Assembly and executive in providing good governance. Prior to its suspension the Assembly was grappling with vexed questions on education that divided social classes as much as religious communities, as reflected in divisions among party members. The abolition of university tuition fees was supported by a majority of members of the SDLP, the Alliance Party and the UUP, but there was a significant dissenting minority within each party. Among electors the charging of university tuition fees was opposed by 43 per cent of Protestants and 51 per cent of Catholics (Northern Ireland Life and Times Survey 2001).

The possible abolition of the eleven-plus examination also caused considerable intraparty division. Under Sinn Fein's control of the Education Ministry there was the prospect of a rainbow coalition emerging, embracing most nationalists, many unionists and the loyalists of the PUP. Support for abolition of the eleven-plus varied according to class and income. A majority of UUP members were more conservative and favoured the retention of selection via the eleven-plus, although nearly one in five would have liked to see its abolition. Alliance Party members were evenly divided. The electorate was also divided on the issue, but not automatically along sectarian lines. Substantial numbers of supporters and opponents of grammar schools could be found in both communities. Thirty-five per cent of Protestants thought that the system of separate secondary and grammar schools was unfair, compared with 51 per cent of Catholics (Northern Ireland Life and Times Survey 2001). When asked whether the entire system, including the eleven-plus, should be changed, there was a majority in favour in both communities (ibid.). Following the publication of the Costello Report (DENI 2004) the Department for Education in Northern Ireland announced that the transfer test (eleven-plus) would be abolished after 2008. There would, however, be a system of 'voluntary' grammar schools. This prompted concern among critics that there would be 'selection by mortgage' rather than through the eleven-plus.

Among UUP members there was also disagreement on the question of integrated education. When asked whether such a system was preferable to that of denominational schools, 44 per cent agreed it was, but 34.7 per cent disagreed. Much greater agreement was found among Alliance Party members, with 92.8 per cent preferring integrated education.

Despite the often non-sectarian basis of the afore-mentioned divisions, institutional structures and traditional enmity meant that disagreement could acquire a sectarian flavour. Within the Assembly, the UUP's concern about the possible abolition of grammar schools in Northern Ireland and the broad hostility to the Sinn Fein education minister among unionist MLAs, meant that cross-community consent to change was unlikely to be forthcoming. In this respect parallel

consent rules, although well-intentioned, could have served to exacerbate essentially non-sectarian divisions. The designation of parties
within the Assembly as unionist, nationalist or 'other', the weighted
majority or parallel consent rules, and use of the D'Hondt mechanism
for allocating executive places and Assembly chairs obliged the parties
to share devolved power. However the matters that were devolved were
those in which sectarian difficulties were largely absent. Direct rule, or
the deployment of quangos such as the Parades Commission, was the
norm for more controversial matters. The modes of enforced power
sharing were based on the assumption that given the chance, one ethnic
bloc might dominate the other on socioeconomic issues, an assumption that was in turn based on the workings of the pre-1972 Stormont
'Protestant parliament' model, but currently had less relevance because
intraparty divisions were greater.

The possibility raised by the lack of coherent, ethnically based belief
systems on post-conflict issues was that sectarian voting patterns
might be erased. It was suggested that the new political dispensation in
Northern Ireland might lead to a thawing of ethnic bloc voting
patterns among pro-GFA voters (Evans and O'Leary, 1999; Mitchell,
2000). The arrival of the 'electoral spring' was likely to be later for
party members, given the reasonable assumption that they were more
committed to their party than were mere supporters.

Conclusion

The performance of Northern Ireland's political institutions in the
early post-GFA years needs to be disaggregated. Only 13 per cent of
voters believed that the Assembly almost never worked in the best
interests of the Northern Ireland population and only 15 per cent
believed that MLAs from different parties never cooperated with each
other (Northern Ireland Life and Times Survey, 2001, www.ark.ac.uk/
nilt2001/Politcal_Attitudes). There were intercommunal differences
over the performance and role of the Assembly, but these were less
strong than those over the full GFA package. Catholics were more
enamoured than Protestants with the Assembly and wanted it to have
more powers, such as the ability to raise taxes, although neither
community claimed to have extensive knowledge of its functions
(MacGinty and Wilford, 2002).

In terms of developing an effective committee system and initiating legislation the Assembly worked reasonably well until its suspension in 2002. It embedded the idea of power sharing and was supported across the community divide, yet it institutionalized divisions through the communal registration of MLAs. This communalism was condemned as sectarian by critics, who overlooked the pre-existing ethnic division that provided the very foundation (local ethnic majoritarianism) of the country over which the Assembly governed. Registering concern over sectarian politics in Northern Ireland could be seen as the political equivalent of protesting that night follows day. Nonetheless any restored Assembly should consider abandoning communal registration and demanding a straightforward consensus of a minimum of 65 per cent. Of course this would leave the new Assembly vulnerable to anti-GFA forces, but should these be in the ascendancy the Assembly might not be restored anyway.

Many unionist MLAs voiced opposition to aspects of the new security agenda associated with the GFA, but these were outside their control and most were implemented, including many of the Patten policing reforms and all prisoner releases. The main theoretical criticism of the GFA, common to consociational settlements, was that intra-ethnic group bidding, rather than cross-community healing, would result. There was a perception among unionists that their bloc was faring poorly relative to the other, requiring strong corrective politics. Ethnic bloc politics undoubtedly remained, but were less apparent in the Assembly and its committees than in the executive and, arguably, society at large. Ethnic-bloc party competition owed more to pre-existing intrabloc electoral rivalries than the particular nature of the devolved settlement in Northern Ireland.

Insufficient consensus on issues devolved to the Northern Ireland Assembly (most of the non-constitutional and criminal issues) arose from genuine (and healthy) intraparty divisions, rather than interbloc rivalry. Unionist or nationalist ideologies played little part in determining the stance of MLAs and party members on most devolved matters. Indeed there was no coherent, ethnically based belief system among the parties in both blocs in respect of non-constitutional and non-reserved matters. Hence the weighted-majority or parallel-consent voting rules ought to prove largely superfluous in a restored Assembly, rarely needing deployment. The extent of intraparty unity among MLAs might prove more important than traditional bloc rivalries. In the Assembly party cohesion was very strong, apart from in the

UUP (which nonetheless maintained more of a semblance of unity inside the Assembly than outside) and the disintegrating UKUP.

The failure of the GFA to persuade a sufficiently large majority of unionists of its merits led to the demise of the Assembly. However the collapse of the institution also followed controversies over decommissioning and IRA activity, which had been beyond its remit. The development of non-bloc politics in any revised version could be contingent on two factors: the willingness of Assembly bloc parties to forgo petitions of concern that would demand parallel consent, as such petitions could encourage bloc voting; and even more problematically, permitting MLAs to have independence of thought, rather than making heavy use of the party whip system. Should these problems be resolved, a very big task, there might be the prospect of divisive politics on a wide range of issues over which a devolved Northern Ireland assembly *does* have control, but with differences being brought about by the diverse beliefs of party members rather than shaped by particular unionist or nationalist visions.

7

Never the Sum of its Parts? The Executive

The most problematic element of institution building was the executive committee, or cabinet, which at times appeared to be an incoherent and divided body, and even dysfunctional in the immediate post-GFA years. One analysis of the performance of government institutions during post-GFA reconstruction in Northern Ireland graded their performance as 'good' (Wolff, 2002a, p. 110). Overall, this high grade was justified, but the executive performed more patchily than the Assembly. Of course higher demands and perhaps unrealistic expectations were made of the executive. Historical enemies were required to exercise common, judicious governance within a political framework that acknowledged the depth of their divisions. Moreover two of the members had been elected on the basis of their opposition to the new political dispensation. The executive had no experience of government *per se*, let alone governance in a far-reaching, ideologically divided administration, some of whose members had previously questioned Northern Ireland's right to exist. In combination these factors amount to a formidable plea of mitigation in respect of the shortcomings of the executive.

The narrowness of the pro-GFA unionist majority, DUP hostility to the GFA and allegations of IRA activity undermined both the Assembly and the executive. Despite its hostility to the GFA, the DUP, a party that avowedly supported devolved power sharing, saw no contradiction in occupying seats on the executive. Simultaneously the party contributed to the instability of the GFA by rotating its executive ministers, boycotting the interlinked North–South Ministerial Council (NSMC) and seeking the expulsion of Sinn Fein from government by means of petitions of concern. The DUP also declined to engage in ministerial subcommittee discussions with Sinn Fein

(Wilford, 2001a). The DUP's boycott led to its exclusion by the executive from the confederal British–Irish Council. Although Sinn Fein repeatedly called for full implementation of all aspects of the GFA, it too occasionally played the 'boycott game', as evidenced by the refusal of the health minister, Bairbre de Brun, to attend a joint ministerial committee meeting in October 2000.

The consequence was an Executive that was never the sum of its parts. Undermining episodic hints at coherent government and notable performances by individual ministers from all the governing parties (Sinn Fein, the SDLP, UUP and DUP) was an undercurrent of hostility. The problems of the executive can be summarized thus: the lack of a formal system of government and opposition meant that scrutiny of executive action was confined largely to committees; it was difficult to remove incompetent ministers; ministers would 'play' to the gallery of their party's MLAs; ministers in the executive did not support the interlinked institutions established under the Good Friday Agreement (the DUP) or some institutions of the state (Sinn Fein, on policing); there was little sense of collective responsibility; and key financial decisions rested with Whitehall and Westminster, given the constraints of the Barnett formula.

The DUP acted rationally in terms of its political marketing. Its voters disliked the GFA, particularly, the sharing of power with 'Sinn Fein/IRA'. These voters overlooked the securing of the union under the deal, concentrating only on what they saw as its distasteful elements: 'terrorists' in government, prisoners freed, decimation of the police force, and 'interference' by Dublin in the internal affairs of Northern Ireland. The DUP justified its presence in government against such an unacceptable backdrop as being warranted by its mandate and merited by its support for devolved power sharing (minus Sinn Fein), as well as being necessary to prevent further UUP concessions to nationalists. Equally, the party was aware of the electoral dangers of abstention from the executive, decreased visibility being a major concern (as it was to Sinn Fein). To avoid the charge of negativity the DUP merely insisted that it would 'renegotiate' the agreement, presumably to exclude Sinn Fein, however unrealistic the prospect.

After its 2003 Assembly election victory the party appeared to revive the idea of rolling devolution, with committee structures rather than a full executive, and with powers to be transferred when the IRA dissolved. Clearly there would be a limit to the tactic of refusing to share power with Sinn Fein, given that the Provisional IRA's war was over. However allegations of continuing IRA activity fuelled the 'moral' basis of the DUP's opposition to fully inclusive government. DUP executive meetings were sometimes preceded by prayers for the demise of the GFA (Bruce, 2000). Given that the Provisional IRA's war had effectively ended more than nine years earlier and mindful of Sinn Fein's mandate, there appeared to be limited value in refusing to cut a deal with its republican rival when the prospect of Assembly restoration could benefit both parties at the polls. There were signs that, notwithstanding the stricture of Paisley at the 2002 party conference that any member doing a deal with Sinn Fein would be expelled, elements within the DUP wanted to come to an arrangement with Sinn Fein. In September 2003 the deputy leader, Peter Robinson, hinted at his willingness to adopt a pragmatic approach in order to revive the executive, although whether any reconstituted body would gel was open to question:

> Parties don't have to love each other. They can hate each other, just as they do, I have to say, in Great Britain and they can still do business, even though they have massive differences in terms of their ideology. The DUP can work within a system that has any other representatives in it. It doesn't require us to have any relationship with the other parties in order to be able to do business for the people we represent. (interview on BBC News 24, 21 September 2003)

Executive formation

The allocation of ministries was determined by party strength in the Assembly under the D'Hondt formula (which was first used to ensure fair representation for Flemings and Walloons in Belgium over a century earlier). This was governed by the formula $S/(1 + M)$ where S was the number of seats held by a party in the Assembly and M was the number of ministries held. In the event of two parties holding an identical number of seats, the party with the higher percentage of first preference votes had the next choice of ministerial portfolio.

The first attempt to form an executive, in July 1999, was inauspicious as the body lasted just ten minutes. The British government attempted to facilitate the creation of an executive in advance of the IRA decommissioning its weapons by outlining a twin-track approach (government formation, quickly followed by decommissioning) in its document *The Way Forward*. The UUP executive rejected the document on 14 July and the party failed to put in an appearance at Stormont when the D'Hondt procedure was triggered the following day (Tonge, 2000). Under standing orders, the speaker was obliged to wait five minutes for the absent UUP to arrive and make its nominations. Although the DUP was present it declined to make nominations. Consequently an executive of six SDLP and four Sinn Fein members was formed, but given the requirement for a unionist presence the new executive was immediately ruled invalid, an inauspicious start to Northern Ireland's new political dispensation. In November 1999 the UUP moved from Trimble's 1998 conference position that the party would not enter government with Sinn Fein without prior IRA decommissioning. The UUC voted by 58 per cent to 42 per cent to join a fully inclusive executive, but with the proviso that Trimble would quit as first minister if decommissioning did not occur. The proviso indicated that the new government was seen as conditional and, if necessary, impermanent – an insecure foundation.

When a proper executive was formed in December 1999, Sinn Fein's Assembly representation was sufficient for the party to be awarded two ministries (Education, and Health, Social Services and Public Safety) under the D'Hondt mechanism of ensuring cross-community representation on the executive. The choice of the education portfolio came as a surprise to many, although the SDLP had some prior knowledge of the move. Sinn Fein thus controlled the two ministries that most directly affected the lives of Northern Ireland's citizens. Apart from providing the first minister, the UUP covered more marginal concerns, including the uncoveted culture, arts and leisure portfolio. With the SDLP filling the post of deputy first minister and taking the finance portfolio, it was arguable that nationalists had claimed most of the key aspects of Northern Ireland government.

The first few years of the Assembly and executive were marked by the tendency of the UUP and SDLP to try to act as an unofficial, loose coalition of the centre, most notably in the attempt to centralize power within the office of the first minister and deputy first minister, held by David Trimble (UUP) and the SDLP's Seamus Mallon, and then by Trimble and Mark Durkan (SDLP). The office was created on the basis of equal status for both ministers and Trimble and Mallon, and then Trimble and Durkan, appeared anxious to promote their status, relative to that held by the executive committee, beyond one of 'first among equals'.

The bolstering of the office of first and deputy first minister could be seen as a response to the lack of power afforded to the office in the first instance. The ministers were inhibited by the lack of patronage accruing to their office. Executive committee members and posts, along with committee chairs and deputy chairs, were chosen by parties under the D'Hondt formula, rather than through the normal system of first minister selection. Furthermore ministers could only be removed by a cross-community majority vote. It was possible to remove a minister (for a minimum of 12 months) under this provision if the individual was a member of the minority party in a dual-party bloc system. For example if UUP and SDLP Assembly members had voted for the removal of either a DUP or a Sinn Fein minister it may have been possible for such action to be taken. However under D'Hondt the replacement would have to be drawn from the party of the 'offending' minister. Generally, however, ministers and committee chairs were insulated from censure. Sanctions were party-based, rather than located in the office of the first and deputy first minster. A UUP first minister, for example, could exert influence on the party to replace an under-performing UUP minister, but could not exercise a personal sanction.

Financial constraints

The Executive amounted to a non-congenial collective, neither cabinet nor coalition. As Laver (2000) declared, the 'Executive Committee looks more like a holding company for a collection of ministers with different party affiliations than a collective decision making body'. In 2000 the two Sinn Fein ministers took the first minister to court over his ban on their attending the North–South Council; in 2001 the DUP attempted to take the first minister and deputy first minister to court over the withholding of executive documents. In May 2001 the first minister announced he would resign if the IRA failed to begin decommissioning its weapons, a move that was denounced as an electoral tactic by the DUP and Sinn Fein but ultimately reaped dividends, as Trimble was later re-elected and IRA decommissioning commenced. Meanwhile the DUP derided the programme for government, a statutory obligation of the executive of which it formed part, praising merely the contribution of its own members. The DUP also opposed the executive's first budget and Sinn Fein attempted to have it amended in the Assembly, even though the party's ministers had signed up to it. Cohesive was not the first adjective that came to mind when describing the executive.

Nonetheless some individual performers sufficiently impressed in their fiefdoms to offer a longer-term prospect of progress in developing coherent governance in Northern Ireland. Brid Rodgers, agriculture minister at the time of the foot and mouth crisis in 2001, proved competent. Although the DUP rotated its ministers (in July 2000 Gregory Campbell and Maurice Morrow replaced Nigel Dodds and Peter Robinson) the ministerial performance of all its representatives was impressive. They participated in the devising of strategic pro-grammes and were concerned to ensure budget maximization and positive agendas. Cross-party unity was achieved on the executive when devising programmes for government in 2000 and 2001. The executive soon realized that only through a sustained period of devolution could priorities be developed within the financial constraints of a budget determined by the oft-criticized Barnett formula, a method that allo-cated resources on the basis of population rather than social need. The Barnett formula pushed up expenditure by applying population-based percentages, in Northern Ireland's case 3.4 per cent, to gains in spending programmes in England (Heald, 2001). This fixed ratio meant that there was no 'peace dividend', as monies were not trans-ferred from savings on security costs.

Although the Barnett formula was criticized as out of date even by its architect, the Labour government made clear that it would remain in place until a new needs assessment formula was introduced (Barnett, 2001). Expenditure would still predominantly be determined by population size and ratio of population compared with that of England. The options for increasing expenditure on local services were therefore highly constrained. One option would have been to raise local rates, which were little more than half of the average council tax bill in England (Heald, 2001). The financing of services in North-ern Ireland was also hindered by a growing population, which even with regular updating meant that the finance minister would have to play 'catch-up' on allocations that depended on population ratio. Furthermore there was greater, indeed near-total, dependence on state education (fewer than 1 per cent of Northern Ireland's schoolchildren are educated privately) and health services, unlike in England, causing a larger drain on the public purse.

The finance minister, Mark Durkan, was not engaging in special pleading when he informed the Assembly on 12 December 2000 that the executive did 'not have sufficient resources to take forward all the policy initiatives that the region needs', given the underinvestment in the region's infrastructure under direct rule in previous decades. Without tax-varying power being given to the Assembly, a move supported by the Alliance Party, the SDLP and Sinn Fein, the executive was stymied as a significant investor in the province. Yet the British Treasury was unlikely to be sympathetic to Northern Ireland's plight, given that, according to one calculation, overall spending per head (as distinct from the financing of services) was 39 per cent higher than in England (Wilson, 2001). In terms of increased Treasury spending at least, Northern Ireland had enjoyed a good war. Despite the construction boom in Belfast and elsewhere, however, internal economic growth was no greater than elsewhere in the United Kingdom, whatever the peace dividend of the 1990s (Wilson, 2001).

The Best Report (2001) highlighted the dependency of the Northern Ireland economy upon public sector employment, with scant indigenous industry and little technological development, shortcomings that had been acknowledged earlier by the Department of Economic Development (DED, 1999). Indeed Birnie and Hitchens (2001) note that many of the economic problems faced by the post-1999 devolved government, particularly its dependency and lack of management and entrepreneurialism, were similar to those confronting the pre-1972 administration. The enterprise minister, Sir Reg Empey, accepted the critique and promised structural overhauls, including the merger of economic development agencies and centralized control of economic development, yet the problem of a dependency culture remained. Under its circumscribed economic circumstances, the executive's role at times appeared more managerial than strategic. The executive did enjoy some financial largesse beyond allocations by the finance minister to individual departments. In an attempt to establish 'joined-up government', £372 million was allocated in 2001–4 to broad, cross-departmental programmes, such as social inclusion and service modernization, under the executive programme funds (Wilford, 2001b).

Despite its financial constraints the executive underspent by £75 million in 2000–1 and by £48 million in 2001–2, partly due to the uncertainty surrounding devolved government (www.ni-assembly.gov. uk/finance/press/cfp1–01.htm, 25 September 2001). In his 2001 budget the chancellor provided an extra £19.3 million of finance, whilst in 2002 the Labour government considerably eased the executive's financial constraints by offering a £125 million loan and promising further sums, to be repaid at a low rate of 5.4 per cent over 25 years (*Guardian*, 3 November 2002). This generosity facilitated an increase in departmental allocations of 7 per cent for 2002–3.

Under pressure from the Treasury the executive increasingly relied on the private finance initiative (PFI, which hitherto had been less apparent in Northern Ireland than elsewhere in the United Kingdom) to fund capital projects. By mid 2002 there were 25 such projects, valued at £192.9 million. The PFI was formally opposed by Sinn Fein, but this opposition was tempered by the 'challenge of recognizing its [the PFI's] existence' and that PFI public service provision was 'preferable to no public service provision at all' (Sinn Fein, 2003a, pp. 6–7). That Sinn Fein's criticism of the PFI was muted is perhaps not surprising: its education minister in the Northern Ireland executive had announced £70 million worth of PFI projects in March 2001, to the chagrin of teachers' unions (Wilson, 2001, pp. 47–50).

Executive controversies

In its early years the executive was involved in a number of controversies. Sinn Fein controlled the Health Ministry, which accounted for 40 per cent of the executive's expenditure, and controlled education (up to higher level), which accounted for 22 per cent of public expenditure (Carmichael and Knox, 2003). The Sinn Fein health minister, Bairbre de Brun, was accused of favouring nationalist areas in terms of health provision. Her decision to locate maternity services in West Belfast was ruled unlawful because she had failed to consult properly with the Assembly. De Brun also announced a plan to abolish GP fundholding. The 'Delivering Better Services' white paper issued by the Department of Health, Social Services and Public Safety (2002) nonetheless received a cautious cross-party welcome, not least because it offered the prospect of streamlining the overelaborate health management structures. The health minister was also confronted with the problem of a £20 million deficit among health trusts by 2001, although the finance minister's budget promised partial alleviation. De Brun proved a cautious minister, whatever the radicalism of Sinn Fein's overall agenda. She rejected the idea of free health care for the elderly as too expensive, despite supporting the idea in principle, but did oversee the introduction of a children's commissioner.

Ministerial performance in respect of health was not judged solely on merit. By 2001 almost half of Protestants believed that the health service had deteriorated since the Assembly was established (Northern Ireland Life and Times Survey, 2001). The relative lack of criticism among Catholics (only 28 per cent believed services had deteriorated) suggested that 'their' minister was backed, whereas Protestants were more hostile to a Sinn Fein minister, a measure of cheerleading or criticism, depending on which party the minister belonged to.

The higher education minister, the SDLP's Sean Farren, ran into difficulties over his failure to recommend the abolition of university tuition fees. The Education Committee argued that fees should only be repayable when income, after graduation, reached £25 000 per annum, a much more generous threshold than in Scotland, with which comparisons were made. Initially, SDLP MLAs agreed with the Education Committee report, although they later backed 'their' minister in lowering the £25 000 threshold (Wilford, 2001b, p. 12–27). The executive's dilemma over the fees issue reflected public disagreement between those who argued that some students should contribute to tuition costs (44 per cent) and those who were entirely opposed to the idea (46 per cent), with little difference across the communities (Northern Ireland Life and Times Survey, 2001).

Perhaps the most contentious issue dealt with by the Assembly was education. The awarding of an extra £14.5 million to the Education Department in 2002 bolstered what was already seen as a successful education system, in which state schools thrived and provided 99 per cent of the intake of Northern Ireland's universities. However the division between the academically selective grammar schools and other secondary schools remained stark. The Sinn Fein education minister, Martin McGuinness, announced his plans to abolish the eleven-plus examination, success in which resulted in a grammar school education, and to introduce comprehensive education for 11–18 year olds by 2004, an optimistically early target. The Burns Report (2001) on post-primary education in Northern Ireland supported the education minister's ambitions. Its recommendations included abolition of the eleven-plus, which was to be replaced by parental choice of school according to the profile of the pupil and the educational establishment. Clusters of collaborative schools would be created in a system of collegiates. Eventually the abolition of the eleven-plus was announced not by Sinn Fein but by a British 'direct ruler' in 2004. Prior to the publication of the Burns Report the Assembly Education Committee had drawn its own conclusions. Having received 33 written submissions and visited Germany and Scotland to examine post-primary schooling, the committee had recommended the abolition of the eleven-plus and the development of a core curriculum until the age of 13 or 14, based on academic, vocational and technical subjects. As education minister, McGuinness could at least claim to have instigated a process of change. He also banned the publication of school league tables and attempted to change the ethos of education policy to quality of delivery rather than individual performance measurement.

The proposals by the education minister and those in the Burns Report, which were followed by similar recommendations in the Costello Report, were strongly opposed by the unionist parties, apart from the PUP. Whilst critical of the eleven-plus, the UUP opposed its removal as this would 'result in a drift towards all schools effectively becoming comprehensives'. In the long-term it favoured parental choice, 'guided by primary and post-primary school assessment of what is in the pupil's best interests' (UUP, 2002, p. 4). The party argued that selection by postcode, with inevitable oversubscription in some schools, would result from the introduction of a comprehensive system, and pointed out that the British government was moving away from this form of educational provision. The party leader, David Trimble, told his party conference in 2002 that 'Burns is not the answer'. Trimble was addressing a sympathetic audience: 62 per cent of the UUC favoured retention of the eleven-plus. However nationalist and other parties favoured its abolition. Meanwhile the Northern Ireland citizens were divided on whether the system of grammar and secondary schools was unfair, with 42 per cent arguing it was and 39 per cent that it was not (Northern Ireland Life and Times Survey, 2001). A slender majority (51 per cent) of Catholics believed that the grammar–secondary system was unfair, compared with only 35 per cent of Protestants, indicating a slightly more egalitarian attitude among Catholics.

Although it was widely expected that there would be an 'anti-McGuinness' faction among unionists in respect of educational change, this was not borne out. Sinn Fein's control of the Education Ministry did not elicit widespread mistrust among Protestants, only 19 per cent of whom believed that education had worsened since devolution. Across the entire population, the proportion of those who believed education had improved (24 per cent) was double that of those who thought it had worsened, with the large majority (43 per cent) believing that things had remained the same (ibid.) McGuinness's egalitarian approach was welcomed by working-class unionists, who felt they had suffered from an inferior education.

McGuinness was the subject of a no-confidence motion by the DUP in May 2001 after admitting, to the surprise of no one, that he had been a member of the IRA in Derry during the 1970s. This attempt by one executive 'partner party' to remove another's serving minister highlighted the lack of cohesion in the Northern Ireland government. With SDLP MLAs siding with Sinn Fein and few UUP MPs bothering to join forces with the DUP, the motion was defeated by 45 votes to 31. Whatever the people's opinion of McGuinness as a minister, the fact that 43 per cent of the population felt that education had neither worsened nor improved reflected the wider view that the new political dispensation had yet to have a major impact (ibid.) Protestants were almost equally divided on whether the government spent more than was fair on schools for Catholics, despite there being no evidence that McGuinness had introduced a partisan funding regime (ibid.)

DUP ministers were also embroiled in controversy. A proposal by the social development minister, Maurice Morrow, to ban Sunday betting was overturned by the Assembly. In contrast the DUP transport minister's introduction of free travel on public transport for pensioners from October 2001 was a popular if very expensive move. The real problem, however, was not the cost of public transport but the very poor infrastructure. As a result of increased Assembly spending, Northern Ireland's public transport company ordered new stock, the first purchase of trains (other than for the Dublin–Belfast line) since the 1960s. A low point in executive–Assembly relations came in 2000 when the executive decided to increase the regional rate by 8 per cent. Although Sinn Fein's two ministers supported the executive's decision, the entire Sinn Fein Assembly party opposed the measure. Again, this highlighted the lack of cohesion in the system of government and legislature.

As with health issues, perceptions of the state of the economy under the executive were to an extent divided on religious lines, with 32 per cent of Catholics but just 19 per cent of Protestants believing that the economy had grown better, although in both communities the predominant perception was that the economy had stayed the same as in the predevolution era. This perception of continuity of performance rather than improvement appears apposite, given that devolution had still to bed down fully when it was abruptly suspended in 2002. Overall it was apparent that Catholics had greater faith than Protestants in the executive and Assembly. Fifty nine per cent believed they acted in Northern Ireland's best interests 'always' or 'most of the time', compared with only 40 per cent of Protestants (ibid.) There was a similar differential in respect of belief that the parties cooperated in solving Northern Ireland's problems: a majority of Catholics thought that this occurred 'a great deal' or 'a fair amount', but only a minority of Protestants shared this view (ibid.)

Quasi-presidency? The office of first and deputy first minister

Committee members were anxious to ensure that the emerging 'quasi-presidency' of the first and deputy first ministers did not become too powerful. The Trimble–Mallon and Trimble–Durkan duopolies were nonetheless powerful. Elected by cross-community consent (Sinn Fein abstained in the Trimble–Mallon election) the first and deputy first ministers were the only ministerial post-holders who enjoyed the legitimacy of an Assembly mandate. The Good Friday Agreement did not make provision for the office of the first and deputy first minister to be subject to committee scrutiny and it was the task of Assembly members, particularly those outside the emergent UUP–SDLP axis, to rein back the powers of the two leading ministers. Although a large number of Assembly ministers would have preferred more committees to scrutinize the work of the office, the UUP and SDLP MLAs combined to ensure that a single committee, the Committee of the Centre, was charged with this task.

Any bill emanating from the office of the first and deputy first minister was referred for scrutiny to the Committee of the Centre. Under the initial arrangements the committee could only scrutinize such legislation if an Assembly motion demanded that it be done. The office of first and deputy first minister received considerable criticism for its excessive size. In what appeared to critics to be a clear case of empire building, its number of staff had grown to 424 by 2002, more than twice the number (190) working in the office of the British prime minister. Although the staffing level did appear excessive, the comparison was superficial. The first minister's office operated as a fully functioning government department, covering a wide (perhaps too wide) range of responsibilities. It contained units dealing with the executive committee, economic policy, community relations, equality, information services, policy innovation, liaison with European and international bodies, liaison with the North–South Ministerial Council and the British–Irish Council, public appointments, victims, standards in public office, freedom of information, planning, women's issues and the appointment of the Assembly ombudsman.

The first and deputy first minister's office had overall responsibility for negotiating Northern Ireland's block grant, although this was broadly determined by the oft-criticized Barnett formula. The office also dealt with EU grants. Moreover it was involved in the determination of strategic priorities for the executive, and as such it was far more than a 'dignified' aspect of government machinery, acting instead as the main repository of power. The first minister and deputy first minister (who constitutionally were of equal status) were more than *primus inter pares*, even though they lacked the power of appointment that is normally associated with a prime minister. The authority of the first and deputy first minister's office was strengthened by the occasional lack of collective responsibility in the executive. Indeed the increased size of the office can be partly attributed to the absence of collective ministerial responsibility. As the leader of the Alliance Party, David Ford, put it, 'it looks like there's very little collective responsibility and that only one department really matters' (*Irish News*, 10 August 2002).

Conclusion

The idea of devolution enjoyed broad public support in Northern Ireland, although Catholics were more enthusiastic about the Assembly and executive than were Protestants. The executive functioned well in terms of individual ministerial performance, but rarely appeared to be a cohesive entity. Encouraged by the fate of the earlier Sunningdale Agreement, the DUP representatives did not commit themselves to the agreement that had given its ministers power. Meanwhile the UUP ministers' attempts to isolate themselves from the increasing unrest in their party and among electors collapsed in mid 2002. Even its moderate executive team grew sceptical about the GFA, fearful of electoral punishment if the party was seen as being too close to Sinn Fein. This fear led to the UUP making greater political demands of opponents with whom they were supposed to be working in a collective body. Alleged IRA activity further undermined confidence in the disparate coalition. For Protestants and Catholics, the failure of the executive to bring about the full decommissioning of paramilitary weapons remained the biggest bugbear, with 84 per cent and 55 per cent respectively citing the issue as the reason for their dissatisfaction with the implementation of the GFA (Irwin, 2003, p. 1). For some unionists the dysfunctional nature of the executive indicated a need to revive majoritarianism in the Assembly if effective government was to take place. Under this formula a system of government and opposition, or a new means of executive selection, rather than collective, consociational power sharing was desirable. This missed the essential point that the executive of 1999–2002 was plagued by outside demands, most notably a demand for IRA surrender beyond the literal terms of the GFA, rather than hindered by domestic issues, which individual ministers were actually tackling creditably. The 2003 elections produced an ironic result, in that it boosted Sinn Fein and the DUP but seemingly reduced the prospect of devolved power sharing and their reacquisition of the ministries in which they had performed competently on an individual (not collective) basis from 1999 to 2002. Impressive individual fiefdomhood had not been transformed into collective government.

Republican analysis indicated that part of the problem lay in the focus upon sanctions on Sinn Fein, amid societal unrest in which loyalist pipe bombings and shootings were the substantial components of paramilitary activity. Sanctions might be more useful as a double-edged sword. The failure of unionists to rejoin the political institutions could be followed by a shift towards binationalism by the British and Irish governments, in a decisive move towards joint authority, and ultimately joint sovereignty. This might more accurately reflect the wishes of the people of the island than periodic failed attempts to persuade unionists to share power on a durable basis with nationalists.

8
Cross-Border and Confederal Dimensions

Much of the focus on the complex architecture of the Good Friday Agreement rested on strand one, the Northern Ireland Assembly and executive and controversial non-constitutional aspects. The unacceptability to nationalists of an internal settlement ensured that strand two of the deal would involve some executive role for Dublin via all-island bodies. The North–South Ministerial Council (NSMC), established by the GFA, brought together ministers from the Northern Ireland executive and the Irish government for consultation, cooperation and the implementation of policies on an all-island, cross-border basis. The suspension of the institutions of the GFA in October 2002 rendered uncertain the future of the north–south bodies created under the NSMC, although these parties participating in the NSMC continued to nominate representatives to the all-island boards, normally to serve three-year terms. The implementation bodies continued their programmes, but did not develop new ones.

Fearful of the development of strand two, the UUP attempted to change the all-island element of the deal into a wider package of relationships within the British Isles, linking the Northern Ireland Assembly to other devolved institutions in the United Kingdom. The British–Irish Council was established under strand three of the GFA to 'promote the harmonious and mutually beneficial development of the totality of relationships among the peoples of these islands' (GFA, p. 14). Although the British–Irish Council offered some reassurance to unionists that the new political arrangements were part of a broader restructuring of the United Kingdom, rather than heralding its break-up, the real business of strand three was the establishment of the British–Irish Intergovernmental Conference. This subsumed the Anglo-Irish Intergovernmental Council and the intergovernmental conferences created under the 1985 agreement. With a number of powers still excluded or reserved, rather than devolved from Westminster, it was thought that the Anglo-Irish axis might be of great significance, a supposition confirmed by the role played by the conference in the wrangling over the implementation of the GFA. This chapter explores the development of the cross-border and confederal elements of the GFA, arguing that the potential of the former was unrealized and the remit of the latter was far from clear.

North–south cooperation

For its advocates, north–south cooperation offered 'a route out of the dead-end conflict over territorial sovereignty' and a move away from the 'mutually unattainable bargaining positions' of an independent united Ireland and an exclusively British Northern Ireland (Anderson, 1998: 114). The institutional approach to north–south cooperation needed to be accompanied by participatory approaches to the construction of an all-island society, although it was possible that a Northern Irish society would emerge instead as contests over sovereignty diminished.

North–South cooperation was formalized by the NSMC, supported by a joint secretariat based in Armagh and staffed by over 600 civil servants from Northern Ireland and the Irish Republic. The remit of the NSMC was to identify and agree at least six matters for cooperation where existing bodies would remain the mechanisms for cooperation in each separate jurisdiction. The NSMC also had to identify and agree six areas where new all-island bodies would implement policy. These bodies were established under a supplementary agreement between the British and Irish governments in March 1999.

The remit of the NSMC and its accountability mechanisms were more clearly defined than those of the previous all-island body, the Council of Ireland, established under the 1973 Sunningdale Agreement. The mere title of that council alarmed unionists. The proper functioning of the 1998 version was clearly dependent on its approval by the Northern Ireland Assembly. The NSMC had executive authority but was not capable of bypassing the restraints of northern unionists. Indeed, although the NSMC was brought into being by British–Irish intergovernmental legislation, its areas of cross-border executive authority were determined by an agreement between the Northern Ireland executive and the government of the Irish Republic (O'Leary, 2001). The North–South Council could not stand apart from the Northern Ireland Assembly, a constraint designed to lure republicans into the Assembly; and equally the Assembly could not function without the all-island dimension of the NSMC. Whilst this looked like a useful safeguard it overestimated the commitment of the DUP and anti-GFA wing of the UUP to an assembly that included Sinn Fein. Unionist opponents of the GFA regarded cross-border institutions as expendable, as part of a process of derailing the agreement. The linking of the GFA's constitutions, although necessary, weakened the deal, making it easier to undermine.

The areas of north–south cooperation suggested in the GFA were agriculture, education, transport, environment, waterways, social security/welfare, tourism, EU programmes, inland fisheries, aquaculture and marine matters, health, and urban and rural development. The highlighting of transport as an area of north–south cooperation under the GFA proved problematic, given the DUP's control of that ministry in the north, and the party refused to participate in the NSMC.

The six implementation bodies agreed to were inland waterways, food safety, trade and business development, special EU programmes, language, and aquaculture and marine matters. Of these bodies the most important is the Special European Union Programmes Body (SPEUPB). The North–South Language Body comprises two separate agencies, *Foras na Gaeilge*, which is responsible for promoting the Irish language on an all-island basis, and *Tha Boord o Ulster-Scotch*, the Ulster-Scots agency. Based in Dublin and Belfast respectively, each has a subsidiary office in the other jurisdiction. Aquaculture and marine matters fall mainly under the remit of the Foyle, Carlingford and Irish Lights Commission, covering fisheries, loughs and lighthouse projects. Inland waterways are overseen by Waterways Ireland, whilst cross-border scientific cooperation on food safety and standards falls under the remit of the Food Safety Promotion Board. Finally, the Trade and Business Development Body, operating under the title InterTrade Ireland, oversees aspects of cross-border business. The north–south bodies employ over 600 people. With the exception of the SPEUPB and Waterways Ireland, the north–south bodies are headed by boards appointed by the NSMC.

The inaugural meeting of the NSMC in December 1999 was an impressive affair, visibly ending a north–south cold war that started in the 1920s and extended beyond the thaw marked by the Lemass–O'Neill talks of the 1960s until the signing of the Good Friday Agreement. The NSMC brought together all factions on the island, with the conspicuous exception of hardline unionists, as the DUP boycotted the meeting. It was clear from the outset that the NSMC would be used as a vehicle of unionist resistance to irritations elsewhere during the implementation stage of the GFA. The NSMC was used as a blunt instrument by David Trimble to exert pressure on Sinn Fein to force the IRA to decommission its weapons. In October 2000 the first minister prevented the two Sinn Fein ministers from attending NSMC meetings. This meant that north–south cooperation in the education and health spheres had to proceed informally, via bilateral meetings between Sinn Fein and the Irish government, until a challenge by Sinn Fein in the courts resulted in the first minister's action being ruled unlawful

The presence of 15 ministers from the Irish government at the NSMC inaugural meeting, including the *taoiseach* and *tanaiste*, plus six northern nationalist ministers, compared with only four unionist representatives, impressed those who saw the GFA as capable of reshaping relations on the island and creating momentum towards a united Ireland. However any impression of a nationalist victory was misleading, in that whilst the NSMC roll call was A-list, its range of competences was decidedly C-list. Indeed even Sinn Fein (2003c), whilst claiming that the north–south bodies were 'organisational paths to advance all-Ireland development', acknowledged that the twelve areas of cooperation contained in the NSMC were 'modest remits'. The establishment of six all-island executive bodies was poor reward for the republicans' 30 years of armed struggle, overlooked partly by the obsession of others with the removal of the IRA and its weapons. Paragraph 12 on page 12 of the agreement constituted a real setback, however, as it removed the validity of the 'dynamic' and 'transition' arguments of Sinn Fein, a party that in other aspects preferred a literal reading of the GFA. It read:

Any further development of these arrangements to be by agreement in the Council and with the *specific endorsement of the Northern Ireland Assembly* and Oireachtas, subject to the extent of the competences and responsibility of the two Administrations. (emphasis added)

Barring a miraculous transformation of unionist opinion, the agreement offered no prospect of the long-term extension of its all-island dimension. Furthermore one of the architects of the pan-nationalist alliance that fostered the peace process, Martin Mansergh, conceded that 'there is no evidence, let alone inevitability, from international experience, that limited cross-border co-operation necessarily leads to political unification' (quoted in *Saoirse*, October 2000, p. 1). At best the cross-border bodies would act as institutional facilitators of the development of economic cross-borderism, but this role was subordinate to the future political resistance of unionism. Nonetheless the claim that the NSMC 'satisfactorily linked northern nationalists to their preferred nation-state' was true, given the willingness of Catholics to back the GFA (O'Leary, 2001, p. 61). For republicans, however, there remained the difficulty of portraying the linkages as dynamic and transformative, set against the textual requirements of the GFA.

The NSMC met in plenary format three times between 1999 and 2002. While the plenary sessions enjoyed a high profile, much cross-border business was undertaken in sectoral meetings, covering each of the 12 areas of cross-border cooperation (six through new bodies, six through existing bodies) agreed by the NSMC in its initial work. Thirty-four sectoral meetings had taken place by the end of 2002: eight each for the SPEUB and the Foyle Carlingford and Irish Lights Commission; five each for the Food Safety Promotion Board and Waterways Ireland, and four each for the language and education agencies. The GFA also allowed the development of institutional format meetings and the fostering of cross-sectoral linkages, including in relation to the EU and for dispute resolution. The first institutional format meeting took place in December 2001, which, in a more hopeful sign for republicans, considered the expansion of north–south cooperation to other areas of work outside the present remit of the NSMC.

Sectoral meetings oversaw the extent of cooperation. The relevant ministers from both sides of the border normally attended. For example the northern and southern health ministers were usually present at Health and Food Safety sectoral meetings, overseeing the Food Safety Promotion Board, a north–south implementation body and presiding over health policy discussions, a north–south cooperative area. Education sectoral meetings prioritized special needs education, underachievement, teacher mobility, qualification standardization and school exchanges. Talks on educational change, notably the abolition of league tables and transfer (eleven plus) tests, were confined to the north, rather than coming under the remit of the all-island council.

The early sectoral meetings were predictably exploratory and consultative, with the relevant ministers hearing reports on progress to date from the chief executive of each board. Priority action areas were identified across the island; for example in the case of health these were accident and emergency services, emergency planning, high technology equipment cooperation, cancer research and health promotion. There were also a number of research project allocations to the academic community on an all-island basis. The sectoral meetings emphasized the economic and social logic of cross-border cooperation, with the language agencies going further by stressing their cultural pluralist credentials through their role 'promoting greater respect, understanding and tolerance in relation to cultural and linguistic diversity' (www. northsouthminsterialcouncil.org/communiques/langjc210600.htm).

The suspension of the executive and Assembly from February to May 2000 delayed the second wave of sectoral meetings, which normally rotated between north and south. The controversy over representation on the NSMC when the first minister attempted to bar Sinn Fein ministers added to the delays and uncertainty. Moreover in some sectors there was a natural tendency for slippage on the dates of meetings. For example the third health and food safety meeting was scheduled for October 2000 but did not take place until October 2001 (see Joint Communiques of North–South Ministerial Council, 4 July 2000, 16 November 2001, www.northsouthministerialcouncil. org/communiques/foodjc161101.htm).

However the plenary meetings amounted to more than mere symbolism. The meeting in June 2002 considered barriers to cross-border mobility and the NSMC endorsed 42 of the 50 proposals outlined by consultants for cross-border action to remove such obstacles. The NSMC also encouraged planning for road infrastructure to be developed on an all-island basis; supported cross-border health insurance provision; facilitated social security cooperation between the two administrations; assisted mutual recognition of professional and educational qualifications and joint accreditation of vocational training courses; developed mutual recognition of periods of service in the public sectors of both administrations; encouraged movement towards the standardization of telecommunication charges throughout the island; and promoted the removal of insurance levies on individuals travelling across jurisdictions.

The NSMC adopted an incremental approach to the removal of obstacles to cross-border mobility in four categories. Category one merely noted that work to redress the problem was already occurring; category two offered an enhanced information dissemination strategy, but this appeared to amount to little more than putting information on a website; category three referred the issue to a subject-specific working group to put forward implementation proposals; and category four referred the issue to officials from the British and Irish administrations for further scrutiny. A cynical view was that the categorization amounted to much prevarication about nothing; an optimist would argue that little else could be expected in the fledgling stage of the NSMC. A fifth category was established for issues where no action on cross-border development would be taken due to the 'level of effort or expense required' (www.northsouthministerialcouncil.org/ pubs/obstacles_to_cross_bord . . . /category5.ht). The eight proposals allotted to this category included cross-border schemes for home loans, housing, mortgage applications and tax relief.

The budget for cross-border initiatives was considerable, with the Community Support Frameworks of Ireland and Northern Ireland committing a minimum of €400 million to cross-border cooperation (www.northsouthministerialcouncil.org/communiques/spjc160600.htm).

Confederal elements

Devoid of legislative power, the activities of the British–Irish Council were overshadowed by the crises of the executive and Assembly in Northern Ireland and the cross-border symbolism of the NSMC. Cross-national commonalities were developed more through the UK-based Joint Ministerial Committee on Devolution, chaired by the prime minister, than by the British–Irish Council. Nonetheless the council broadened the scope of the GFA, offered a confederal element and enjoyed greater permanence and less controversy than other elements of the GFA. The council was designed to promote harmony and mutually beneficial relationships among the peoples of the United Kingdom and Ireland. It linked representative institutions throughout the United Kingdom and Ireland and was supported by a secretariat of the British and Irish governments. The first ministers of the various countries, or their equivalent, formed part of the delegation. Northern Ireland delegates at the 2002 summit were the first minister and deputy first minister, plus three other ministers, one each from the UUP, SDLP and Sinn Fein. The suspension of the Northern Ireland Assembly meant that it was not represented at the council meeting in Scotland in Autumn 2002, attended by 19 delegates. Thus the architect of the council, the first minister of Northern Ireland, was absent from the institution he largely established. Without pressure from the UUP this confederal element of the GFA would not have appeared. It attracted minimal interest from other parties to the GFA negotiations (Hennessey, 2000) and was seen by the British government as a harmless institution.

Transport was identified as the key priority area to be addressed by the British–Irish Council (Table 8.1). This meant that the Northern Ireland executive would determine the agenda and convene meetings on the issue. The choice of transport was not unreasonable given the province's poor infrastructure, particularly in respect of railways, but it was unclear how the council could influence the executive minister responsible for rectifying the problem. The council agreed to prioritize knowledge exchanges, particularly in respect of public–private partnerships, regional air links and road safety.

The main non-transport-related input from Northern Ireland ministers was on the growing problem of drugs. At the March 2002 sectoral summit in Dublin on the misuse of drugs the health minister, Bairbre de Brun, urged greater community involvement in tackling the problem. In previous years the approach of republicans to the issue could be described as robust and unorthodox.

Unlike the institutions established under strands one and two of the GFA, the British–Irish Council has no statutory power. It is grounded in voluntarism and remains a forum for the exchange of ideas and

Table 8.1   *Priorities of the British–Irish Council*

Priority area	Lead administration
Transport	Northern Ireland
Drugs	Republic of Ireland
Environment	United Kingdom
Social inclusion	Scotland and Wales
Knowledge economy	Jersey
Tourism	Guernsey
Telemedicine	Isle of Man

formulation of best practice. The council permits bilateral and multi-lateral agreements between members, without reference to the institution in its entirety. In common with the NSMC, the council meets in summit and according to sector. Four summit meetings were held between 1999 and 2002, although it was originally envisaged that these would be held twice yearly. The inaugural session in London in December 1999 was followed by a meeting in Dublin on the misuse of drugs in 2001 and sessions on the knowledge economy (held in Jersey) and social inclusion (held in Scotland) in 2002. Four meetings of sectoral ministers took place during the same period, covering transport, the environment (twice) and drugs. The council can also choose to meet on a cross-sectoral basis.

Although the establishment of the British–Irish Council, at the behest of the UUP, was seen as a means of anchoring an evolved Northern Ireland to the British Isles, it could be credibly argued that its creation has weakened the concept of a United Kingdom (Meehan, 2001). Scottish political elites have countenanced direct business with the Irish government, thus bypassing British institutions. Whether genuine confederalism or patchy, possibly divisive bilateralism will emerge is still open to question. Thus far the council has perhaps been a less binding confederation than the Nordic Council, with which comparison is invited. The other potential weakness of the council is that it is elite dominated, lacking a grassroots, bottom-up approach to confederal arrangements. As such it risks being ignored by the peoples it is attempting to bind. A further (minor) confederal element is the British–Irish Parliamentary Body. Established in 1990, this was designed to facilitate dialogue and cooperation between members of the British and Irish parliaments. The body was expanded in 2001 to accommodate members of other institutions represented in the council.

The revision of Articles 2 and 3 of the Irish constitution arguably raised the prospect of a confederal Ireland. The old dream of absorbing one million unionist dissidents was replaced by recognition of the diversity of traditions on the island. Hence a united island could, if it were ever realized politically, take the form of a loose confederation, with autonomy for unionists. This idea was scarcely new and it had long been offered by the diehards of Republican Sinn Fein. The difference in thinking between militant republicans and the Irish government is in terms of whether a six-county northern state has the right to exist. The Irish Government is no longer ambiguous in supporting the right of Northern Ireland to remain in the United Kingdom.

Political contexts and contests

Even among Protestants there was majority support (52–36 per cent) in 2000 in favour of the idea that the Northern Ireland Assembly should 'better integrate the economies North and South' (Murphy and Totten, 2000, p. 298). However in 2003, 68 per cent of Protestants stated that dissatisfaction with the (hitherto benign) NSMC had become part of their general dissatisfaction with the GFA, a higher level of discontent than that recorded for the Assembly and the executive (Irwin, 2003, p. 73).

The contest between nationalist and unionist forces on the island was predictable. Unionists preferred cross-border cooperation to be limited and worked in the pre-GFA negotiations for all-island bodies to be ringfenced. Nonetheless the UUP was supportive of certain aspects of all-Ireland cooperation. In the case of health care, for example, an area of very limited all-island cooperation, the party declared itself 'open to the possibility of partnership arrangements with acute hospitals in border areas' and to the development of cross-border, supraregional services (UUP, 2002). Conversely nationalists wanted the all-island bodies to be dynamic and a means of transition to a united Ireland. These seemingly irreconcilable demands are contained in the GFA.

Non-participation in the North–South Ministerial Council was not a viable long-term option for the UUP. Given the party's need for nationalists and republicans to make devolved (strand one) government work, the UUP had little option but to participate in strand two, the all-Ireland institutions. Furthermore the agreement made clear that participation in the British–Irish Council was mandatory for ministers in the executive, with unspecified 'alternative arrangements' to be made in the event of non-compliance. This mandatory requirement did not unduly trouble the DUP, whose executive ministers declined to participate in what the party viewed as a trojan horse for Irish unity. The DUP was also dismissive of the British–Irish Council as a vehicle for curtailing the powers of the North–South Council. The UUP leader, David Trimble, was prepared to use withdrawal from the North–South Council as a bargaining tool. The net result was that the council was not immune from the periodic crises that afflicted the northern Assembly in the first five years after the signing of the GFA, although the problems in the Assembly received far greater attention.

Sinn Fein adopted an optimistic, neofunctionalist approach, arguing (publicly at least) that increased economic cooperation would lead to closer political union between the two parts of the island. Potentially, the party held leverage in both Northern Ireland and the Irish Republic, given its position as a growing electoral force in both countries. Sinn Fein showed little interest in strand three of the GFA, the British-Irish Council, on which it was of course not represented. Some party members nonetheless argued that the presence of nationalists in the Scottish Parliament and Welsh Assembly offered the possibility of a coalition of nationalist forces. At the 2004 Sinn Fein *ard fheis* a motion was put forward for a 'tactical alliance with the Scottish and Welsh parliaments' in order to work towards independence (Sinn Fein, 2004). It was argued that a 'concerted policy between the three Celtic nations presents a formidable challenge to English rule and will facilitate the break up of the so-called United Kingdom', making Irish unity easier to achieve (ibid.). However the motion was heavily defeated.

Although overshadowed by even more controversial aspects of the GFA, the establishment of cross-border bodies was always likely to be contentious for the unionist community. Many UUP members still hankered after an internal settlement, with 44 per cent preferring devolved power sharing *without* cross-border bodies, compared with the 36 per cent who favoured devolved power sharing *with* cross-border bodies. Among Protestants there was little antipathy to cross-border cooperation, provided this was outside the political sphere, as Table 8.2 indicates.

Table 8.2 *Attitudes towards cross-border cooperation between Northern Ireland and the Irish Republic, by area of cooperation (per cent)*

	Strongly support		Support		Neither support nor oppose		Oppose		Strongly Oppose	
	Prot.	RC	Prot.	RC	Prot.	RC	Prot.	RC	Prot.	RC
Tourism	34	53	38	36	13	7	5	0	6	0
Transport	26	52	38	34	17	9	9	1	6	0
Agriculture	24	49	33	35	21	11	10	1	6	0
Health	24	50	28	32	22	12	14	2	8	1
Security	25	50	24	32	18	11	14	1	8	43
Political future of N. Ireland	8	43	14	32	15	21	4	23	1	27

Source: Adapted from MacCarthaigh and Totten (2001), pp. 339–40.

The establishment of the North–South Ministerial Council and the development of all-island implementation bodies were clearly economic *and* political acts as Fianna Fail made clear in the Irish Republic:

> The setting up of democratically mandated North–South institutions with executive powers is essential, both for practical reasons to serve common interests North and South against the backdrop of the European Single Market and for reasons of identity as a reflection of the Irish dimension. (Fianna Fail, 1995, pp. 9–10)

Almost 75 per cent of Protestants opposed political cooperation, but on average only 17 per cent opposed cross-border cooperation in the other areas cited in Table 8.2. Clearly there was little opposition among unionists to all-island economic cooperation, other than amongst a core of hardliners who were opposed to any form of Irish unity, economic or political. Furthermore the level of support for non-political cooperation, averaging 59 per cent among Protestants, suggests that cross-border concords were not viewed as part of a threatening, unity-by-stealth project. Other possible variables – age and sex – were not significant determinants of attitude. There is no evidence of a huge groundswell of support by younger people for a breaking down of barriers on the island. The attitude of under-35s towards cross-border cooperation was very similar to those of their elders: considerable enthusiasm among Catholics; milder support among Protestants.

There remained a sceptical unionist constituency that regarded the cross-border dimension of the GFA as part of a process of British withdrawal by instalments. Its position was articulated by the deputy leader of the DUP, Peter Robinson:

> So there will be no big surrender, just dozens of little ones. No event so momentous in itself to provoke community unrest. One thing is certain – once the line of all-Ireland executive authority has been crossed (in whatever form and to whatever extent) it is only the slipperyness of the slope that will determine when we arrive in a united Ireland, as the destination will have been irreversibly set on that fateful day. (Peter Robinson, quoted in McAuley, 2002, p. 114)

Whilst the DUP advocates friendly relations between north and south, with Paisley meeting the *taoiseach* in 2004, it continues to call for a purely internal settlement, whatever the unacceptability of this to northern nationalists. The DUP argues from a 'realist' perspective on interstate cooperation, suggesting that cross-borderism impinges on sovereignty and will eventually lead to absorbtion. This view is not only opposed by pro-GFA UUP supporters but is also disdained by the PUP, which supports modest all-Ireland relationships, confined to the economic sphere. All shades of unionist oppose the nationalist neofunctionalist idea of 'creeping' integration. Republicans and unionists share the same assumption of the viability and superiority of the nation state as a means of territorial (and societal) organization, despite the growth of global transnationalism and the partial erosion of national sovereignty by the EU.

Europeanism and cross-borderism

Functionalist ideas on the necessity of cross-border, interstate cooperation are based upon the premise that borders will wither as citizens cooperate across territorial boundaries (Tannam, 1996). However this bottom-up, civil society approach to cross-border cooperation has so far failed to develop fully across the Irish border. Travel has increased and north–south trade has improved slightly, but people's sense of identity has, if anything, polarized, with Northern Ireland Protestants' sense of Britishness becoming even greater in recent decades. Far from the border withering, it has become an even bigger marker of national identity. The essential problem with the functionalist approach to cross-border cooperation is that it assumes a symmetry of ideas across borders. However, whilst the citizens of the Irish Republic have no formal objection to, but little interest in and possibly some fear of developing economic and social relations with the north, the unionist population has considerable objections to 'north–southery'.

The asymmetry of pressure from below led to the development of the neofunctionalist approach of the Good Friday Agreement. Political elites from north and south combined to create a set of top-down institutions that encouraged economic (and political) cooperation across the border. This process was aided by funding, which encouraged business leaders to increase their limited-cross border trade. This cooperation has been formalized in certain policy areas by the north–south GFA bodies, and it is likely to continue outside those forums. While 'north–southery' may once have been seen as threatening Northern Ireland's constitutional position, the formalization of this under the GFA has allowed northern business and political elites to take a more relaxed view. The EU may thus have kick-started a move towards a postnationalist Ireland, in which the earlier exclusivism of national identity and British and Irish nation states will be replaced by a more confederal British–Irish relationship, existing within the broader context of a Europe of regions (Kearney, 1997). It is not immediately apparent that cross-border cooperation will reshape national identities. However the emergence of the hybrid 'Northern Irish' identity as the primary one for over a quarter of the population in the north might indicate a reconfiguring of identity among those who accept the interdependence of both parts of the island (Northern Ireland Life and Times Survey, 2001).

The largest providers of funds for cross-border initiatives have been the International Fund for Ireland (IFI) and the EU. The IFI was established in 1986, after the Anglo-Irish Agreement. The majority of the IFI funds have been provided by the United States and have gone primarily to areas most afflicted by the conflict. It enjoys high public awareness, with three quarters of the population being aware of its existence. In contrast fewer than half of the population claim to be aware of the (admittedly more recent) huge EU peace fund programme (Irvin and Byrne, 2002). During the early 1990s Northern Ireland benefited from EU funding as a result of its 'objective one' status, which entitled the region to the maximum allocation of EU structural funds. This was not renewed for the 2000–6 aid programme, but substantial compensatory aid was awarded. Institutional links have grown, with the European Commission maintaining a permanent office in Belfast and the Northern Ireland executive operating a Brussels office. Each of Northern Ireland's 26 local councils has a European liaison officer. Policy in respect of overall UK–EU relations is still formulated at Westminster. However until 2002 the implementation of EU policy directives became increasingly a matter for the Northern Ireland executive. The executive formally approved the Community Support Framework (which includes a north–south chapter) and had the task of applying horizontal principles to all EU programmes, including accountability, equal opportunities, the targeting of social needs and environmental sustainability. EU policies also affected 80 per cent of 'programme for government' legislation produced by the Northern Ireland executive (McQuade and Fagan, 2002, p. 172).

The European Policy Coordination Unit (EPCU), established within the office of the first and deputy first minister, was set up to provide cohesive Northern Ireland responses to EU legislation. Direct influence on EU legislation by Northern Ireland appeared to be minimal, being at best filtered through the Westminster government, mainly via the Foreign and Commonwealth Office and Cabinet Office European Secretariat, to which the EPCU could send representatives. The EPCU provided assistance for Northern Ireland ministers at UK-wide ministerial committee meetings on European policy. Under devolved government, it also administered the EU programme for peace and reconciliation (see below). Given the importance of EU legislation to Northern Ireland, the lack of a dedicated minister of EU affairs might be seen as surprising, but the absence of such a minister indicates the extent to which Westminster (although not prescriptive in respect of a designated post within the Northern Ireland executive) dominated the filtering process in terms of representation. Prior to its suspension in 2002 the Northern Ireland Assembly intended to create a standing committee on EU affairs to broaden EU legislative input, representation and scrutiny beyond the executive. Although the beneficiary of much EU funding, Northern Ireland did not establish full representative channels as a regional government in the immediate post-GFA years. The development of executive representation was hindered by the fragility of Northern Ireland's political institutions. Relations with the EU mirrored those with the UK, being based on dependency rather than autonomy and full representation. The UK government was still seen by 51 per cent of the population as having the greatest influence on how Northern Ireland was run, compared with the 28 per cent who viewed the Northern Ireland assembly as the main influence and the 7 per cent and 4 per cent respectively who saw local councils and the EU as the primary influences (Gilland and Kennedy, 2002).

EU funding for Northern Ireland is provided via the Community Support Framework. This is based on two programmes: the Programme for Building Sustainable Prosperity, which accounts for two thirds of funding, and the Programme for Peace and Reconciliation, which provides the remaining third. The EU has distributed large sums for reconciliation, regional development and cross-border cooperation, notably via the Peace, Interreg, Leader, Equal and Urban programmes. The Peace and Interreg programmes committed themselves to disbursing €1.33 billion (£830 million) of funds across the island between 1995 and 2006 (www.northsouthministerialcouncil.org/ communiques/spjc091002.htm). The Peace I programme (Special Support for Peace and Reconciliation in Northern Ireland and the Border Counties) ran from 1995 to 1999 and was followed by Peace II, which had an even larger budget. The Peace II funds were distributed by 26 local strategy partnerships, six county council border task forces and 15 intermediary funding bodies. Together these bodies formulated an integrated area development plan. By mid 2003 nearly half of the total funding had been committed (but not disbursed) to 1500 different projects, at a rate of €2 million per week (House of Commons, Northern Ireland Affairs Committee, 21 May 2003; evidence from Ian Pearson, minister for finance and personnel).

An important question begged of the institutional arrangements established under the GFA was how they would shape existing cross-border provisions exercised under the auspices of the EU. The agreement made provisions for consideration of the implementation of EU programmes by the NSMC, and made clear that the views of the NSMC were to be relayed to relevant EU meetings. The creation of the NSMC and cross-border bodies affected the European programme for cross-border cooperation, Interreg, in two main ways (Laffan and Payne, 2002). First, they increased the number of actors involved in the implementation of Interreg. Second, the existing cross-border networks, which in combination acted as a border corridor group, assumed greater importance, with an input into the administrative closure of the Peace I and Interreg II programmes and the development of the Interreg III programme.

The Special European Union Programme Body (SEUPB) is the paymaster and managing agent for the Peace II programme, as it is for Interreg IIIA, the cross-border element of the Interreg programme. The SEUPB is guided in its progress by the Structural Funds Plan for Northern Ireland and the National Development Plan for the Irish Republic (2000–6), which contain a common chapter of agreed text covering all-island development. The SEUPB has developed an implementation plan for the ideas outlined in the common chapter. This input has prevented a purely top-down implementation of EU programmes. The three existing networks covered 18 border corridor group councils, including unionist-controlled bodies, which, despite political reservations, acknowledged the economic rationale of cross-border development (ibid.)

The establishment of the SEUPB as an all-island implementation body gave extra impetus to the European dimension of transnational cooperation. The SEUPB was also mandated to negotiate with the European Commission on the Peace II programme and acted as a cross-border programme leader, with a minimum budget of €75 million. Peace II was a huge investment programme, providing over €600 million of funding for Northern Ireland and the border region from 2000–4 of which eighty per cent was allocated to Northern Ireland. The Interreg III, Equal, Leader + and Urban II programmes contributed further substantial sums as Table 8.3 indicates.

Even accounting for the high level of demand (2700 project applications were received in 2002 alone) the level of EU funding is huge. There are five priority areas: economic renewal, social integration, inclusion and reconciliation, local regeneration and development, and regional and cross-border development, the extensiveness of which encourages a large number of funding bids. Nine per cent of programme funds are allocated for administration. A joint Northern Ireland–Irish

Table 8.3 *EU Structural Fund programmes 2000–4 (£ million)*

	EU funds	*Combined EU and matching total (includes additional sources)*
Northern Ireland		
Peace II	274.0	366.0
Leader +	10.0	15.0
Equal	8.0	10.0
Interreg IIIA	52.0	69.5
Urban II	7.0	9.0
Total	351.0	469.5
Border region/Ireland: funds		
Peace II	106.0	141.0
Leader +	47.9	73.7
Equal	33.9	7.0
Interreg IIIA	53.6	71.8
Urban II	5.3	11.4
Total	246.7	344.9

Source: www.northsouthministerialcouncil.org/communiques/spjc301001.htm, June 2003.

Republic monitoring committee oversees the contribution made by structural funds to the Common Chapter of aims for the Structural Funds Plan for Northern Ireland. The committee also assesses the impact of structural funds upon the National Development Plan of the Irish Republic

The establishment of the SEUPB has led to a revision of the established practices for EU programmes, with the Dublin government adopting a more relaxed, hands-off approach than the more regulatory stance adopted by the Department of Finance and Personnel in Northern Ireland (Laffan and Payne, 2002). The bulk of the Peace II programme money is filtered to 26 local strategy partnerships (LSPs), which have evolved from the district partnership model of Peace I but have a broader range of deliverers. Whereas Peace I partnerships operated within the boundaries of the 26 district councils, the Peace II deliverers interact across areas. One half of the members of LSPs comprise councils and agencies, the other half consisting of representatives from business, trade unions, the voluntary sector and other interested parties. A Regional Partnership Board oversees the activities of LSPs.

Based in Belfast, with regional offices in Monaghan and Omagh, the SEUPB has assumed responsibility for a large number of EU initiatives under European Structural Funds and the Peace Programme. It also promotes cross-border cooperation in the implementation of the National Development Plan for Ireland and the Northern Ireland Structural Funds Plan. At its first quarterly sectoral meeting in Dublin in June 2000, ministers acknowledged that the SEUPB had a political basis as well as an economic one, its establishment reflecting the commitment to reconciliation and peace offered by the EU and placing the cross-border dimension of the GFA within a European context (www. northsouthministerialcouncil.org/communiques/spjc160600.htm).

The SEUPB has established a Peace II monitoring committee, covering a range of community interests, to oversee details of the negotiations for the programme and its subsequent implementation. In terms of allocation of monies, Northern Ireland departments are responsible for 39 per cent, intermediate funding bodies 34 per cent and LSPs the remaining 27 per cent (Meehan, 2000, p. 42).

As can be seen from the above discussion, the extent of EU support for cross-border cooperation is very substantial and incorporates a plethora of activities. The placement of these all-island activities under the auspices of the NSMC and an executive cross-border body has more than mere symbolic importance: it also represents a substantial withering of the border under the GFA.

Scrutinizing EU programmes

The prolonged suspension of the Northern Ireland Assembly from October 2002 raised questions of how the EU's Peace II programme could be adequately scrutinized. The Northern Ireland Department of Finance and Personnel was responsible to the European Commission for Peace II, via Whitehall. A Peace II monitoring committee was established in November 2000, chaired by the Northern Ireland finance minister, and a committee was set up in January 2001 to establish how border corridor groups could contribute to spending decisions in respect of the EU Structural Funds. The Northern Ireland Affairs Committee at Westminster conducts some scrutiny, seeking evidence from relevant ministers and civil servants. The minister for the Department of Finance and Personnel is accountable for reporting progress to the UK parliament.

The British government has acknowledged difficulties with implementing Peace II (House of Commons, Northern Ireland Affairs Committee, 21 May 2003; evidence from Ian Pearson). These problems are due to (1) the sheer scope of the programme, particularly the organizational demands of setting up new delivery bodies; (2) the complexity of the Structural Fund regulations; (3) the need to satisfy the rival bids of prospective user groups, whose own members, for example those in the local strategy partnerships, are often unpaid novices; (4) the requirement to ensure continuity between Peace I and Peace II; and (5) the necessity of developing an adequate model of accountability for a transnational initiative. Prior to its suspension the Northern Ireland executive indicated that the same mix of delivery mechanisms would operate for Peace II, that is, local bodies, intermediary funding groups and central departments (Northern Ireland Executive Information Service, December 2000).

Taken together, these problems resulted in underspending in the opening year of Peace II, with substantial delays in negotiating and implementing the programme, although these were exacerbated by the fact that several local strategy partnerships complained about the 15 per cent ceiling on administration spending in their individual budgets. Two years after the programme was implemented, only one claim, for €0.5 million, had reached the European Commission (Northern Ireland Affairs Committee, 21 May 2003). The SEUPB blamed inactivity by the Agriculture, Culture and Enterprise, and Training and Industry Departments for the slow pace of implementation, a criticism accepted by the government.

The problem of accountability is particularly acute. Progress on Peace II is reported via three Whitehall departments rather than a single channel. For the user groups, there is a duplication of auditing procedures, with some organizations being audited by up to eight different bodies, a situation that is acknowledged as 'horrendous' by the relevant minister, who advocates acceptance of national auditing standards rather than EU procedures (House of Commons, Northern Ireland Affairs Committee, 21 May 2003; evidence from Ian Pearson). Each Structural Fund has its own audit trail, as established by the European Commission, leading to duplication and wastefulness.

The politics of EU intervention

The utility of external aid is disputed across the communal divide. Unionists contest the idea that external support has helped to reduce the level of violence, Sinn Fein believes the opposite, and – perhaps surprisingly given their fondness for external referents – SDLP supporters are fairly evenly divided on the matter (Ulster Marketing Survey, August 1997, cited in Irvin and Byrne, 2002). The political role of the EU, if it can be divorced from its aid programmes, remains a source of controversy. Whilst the SDLP has always embraced the possibility of an EU contribution to the debate on Northern Ireland's constitutional future, unionist parties have been sceptical. The pragmatic wing of the UUP has consistently welcomed economic contributions from binational and supranational institutions, but resisted the possible territorial implications. Whilst embracing the cross-border cooperation promoted by the GFA, the UUP has argued that such cooperation was already a reality and did not need to be revamped by substantial all-island political incrementalism (Alcock, 2001). As such, the pro-GFA section of the UUP has promoted the all-island aspect of the GFA and limited EU cross-border activity to its supporters as merely formal acceptance of *de facto* economic reality. For nationalists the GFA is important as the promoter of a unitary economic island, shifting cooperation away from an internal UK basis towards an all-Ireland one.

Sinn Fein's policy on the EU, like so many other aspects of its party doctrine, has been radically overhauled. Until 1999 the party favoured withdrawal from the EU, but then endorsed a policy of 'critical engagement' and abandoned the idea of withdrawal as no longer feasible (Sinn Fein, 1999). It also endorsed many aspects of the provisions offered by the EU Structural Funds. In 2001 the party opposed the Nice Treaty in a successful campaign of opposition in the first referendum (overturned later by the seemingly inevitable second referendum that followed an 'incorrect' initial vote). In 2003 it endorsed the eventual adoption of the euro in Northern Ireland as 'a crucial part of the process of economic unification' (Sinn Fein, 2003b).

For Sinn Fein, the European dimension has provided a useful context in which to dilute its original claim to unfettered Irish sovereignty. The zero-sum-game approach of Irish versus British has been reconfigured to allow a broader set of intergovernmental relationships, a pooling of sovereignty within the EU and a reconciliation of the peoples of Ireland within a European framework. Critics view this as a wishful withering of the border. Indeed Sinn Fein does remain committed to the construction of an Irish nation state and Irish unity, but within the context of an increasingly integrated Europe. As evidence of the new realism the chair of the party has referred to the 'dominance of the EU on the island of Ireland' (quoted in Cox, 1998, pp. 73–84).

Of the four main parties in Northern Ireland, only the SDLP has adopted a post-nationalist position, denying traditional concepts of the nation state and sovereignty. Although Northern Ireland's three Euro MPs (one each from the DUP, UUP and SDLP, elected on a far higher turnout than elsewhere in the United Kingdom) cooperate extensively to secure EU assistance, the preferred conception of the EU held by the UUP, DUP and Sinn Fein is broadly one of a 'non-interfering' body presiding over a Europe of essentially independent states. Scepticism within the DUP has occasionally assumed an (unpersuasive) religious dimension, in which the EU is portrayed as a 'Catholic club'. Such a view has been encouraged by occasional polemical bursts by Ian Paisley, his description of the EU as 'Babylon the Great, the mother of harlots and abomination of the Earth' ranking among the more colourful (quoted in Moloney and Pollok, 1986, p. 405).

Within the SDLP there is conflict between its support for intergovernmental, binational initiatives, which according to the British and Irish governments do nothing to undermine sovereignty in either jurisdiction, and its belief that such arrangements, when allied to the growth of a Europe of regions, are a means of withering borders. The SDLP has long advocated the all-Ireland framework established under the GFA. Although the party's concept of an 'agreed Ireland' is primarily political, it also has economic referents, such as increased north–south trade. Some tension is discernible in the party's ability to oscillate between the binationalism (facilitated by pan-nationalism) at the heart of the GFA and its support for the neofunctionalist (post-nationalist) processes of European integration, based on spillover from the economic to the political sphere, which ultimately could render binationalism redundant (McGovern, 1997).

The SDLP's advocacy of EU involvement has been forceful. The party's submission to the Brooke–Mayhew talks of 1992, *Agreeing New Political Structures*, suggested that the EU had been successful in overcoming divisions. As such it was appropriate to have a repre-sentative from the European Commission in a six-person ruling executive in Northern Ireland, scrutinized by an Assembly modelled on the European Parliament and linked to the North–South Council of Ministers. Subsequently the party was forced to water down its enthusiasm for the EU, but it still sees all-Ireland structures as part of a desirable weakening of the 'redundant' nation state in favour of pooled sovereignty in a Europe of regions. The party's support for European integration is grounded in electoral as well as political logic. Catholics in Northern Ireland have been much less sceptical about the EU than have Protestants. By a majority of five to one, Catholics believe that UK membership of the EU is a good thing, compared with only two-to-one support among Protestants (Greaves, 2002). Catho-lics also favour EU expansion and supported the Maastricht Treaty by a two-to-one majority, whilst Protestants were narrowly opposed (Kennedy, 1994).

The application of post-nationalist ideas to Northern Ireland can be found in a variety of postmodern accounts (cf. Delanty, 1996; Kearney, 1997; McCall, 1999). These accounts reject traditional borders in favour of a multiplicity of 'sovereign' institutions at the regional, national and, above all, European levels. Traditional political commu-nities will no longer exist, making redundant the historical narratives and myth-making that accompany such bodies. Ancient hostilities will be swept away by globalization, supranational institutions and rejection of a universal truth. The antihistorical basis of postmodern accounts rests uneasily against the reliance on history and continuing interest in territorial sovereignty among Northern Ireland's political actors (McGough, 2003). The 'dreary steeples' of a localized political wrangle remain in view, far from being swept away by transnational economic and political forces. Historical narratives remain paramount, although knowledge of and interest in the other side's narrative may have increased.

The promotion of cross-border linkages by the EU has been the most significant aspect of economic unity. A neo-Marxist account suggests that a reconfiguration of states is occurring broadly in line with the requirements of capital (Goodman, 1996a, 1996b). Transnational borders and territorial integrity have become less relevant in a global economy. There is a role for a supranational institution such as the EU in promoting regional economic development, although this may create unevenness between economic and political development. Whilst a Europe of regions may emerge in economic terms, the slower pace of political change will ensure that a federal Europe remains a distant prospect. The death of the nation state is much exaggerated, but a process of reconfiguration by economic forces is apparent. What has yet to be satisfactorily measured is the extent to which top-down, EU-promoted economic cooperation can foster a transnational community throughout Ireland. Support for the 'old solution' of nation statehood remains substantial. A slight fall in unionist support for Northern Ireland remaining in the United Kingdom has been countered by a slight rise in the desire of Catholics for a united Ireland.

Cross-border economic prospects

An obvious question in respect of all-island economic arrangements is whether they can bring tangible benefits. The growth of the 'Celtic tiger' during the 1990s did not persuade unionists of the logic of all-island economic cooperation. Indeed they continued to deny that the lack of cross-border trade was abnormal. Thus it was claimed that the idea of an island economy could be a useful marketing concept, but in substantive terms it could only make a minor contribution to economic competitiveness (Bradley and Birnie, 2001). Indeed trade between Northern Ireland and the Irish Republic remained low, although the 1990s saw a steady increase in the percentage share of Northern Ireland's manufacturing exports to the Republic, rising from 7 per cent of total sales in 1991–92 to 9 per cent by the end of the decade, whilst sales to mainland Britain fell by 3 per cent to 34 per cent during the same period (ibid., p. 66). These figures offer tentative evidence of a gradual shift towards an all-island economy, in which the markets of the Irish Republic will assume greater importance for northern businesses. The small size of Northern Ireland's population makes it incidental to the marketing strategies of many companies in the Irish Republic, an export-driven economy in which overseas sales account for more than 50 per cent of GDP. At the time of the GFA, north–south business accounted for only 5 per cent of Northern Ireland's GDP and less than 2 per cent of the Republic's GDP (ibid., p. 68). The adoption the euro in the Irish Republic in 2002 introduced a possible currency barrier to trade.

The extent of North–South trade may appear small, but it is not dissimilar to that between neighbouring countries in other parts of Europe (Scott and O'Reilly, 1992). Business leaders in north and south have discussed the possibility of a 'Belfast–Dublin trade corridor', facilitating economic growth in what is already the most prosperous sector of the island. However this idea has been met by scepticism among academics (Bew *et al.*, 1997). There appears to be a mismatch between the types of industry located either side of the border. Where there are matches, these are predominantly in the commercial sector and are often subsidiaries of multinational companies, for which the border has diminished in salience anyway.

The assumption thus far is that there are institutional (top-down) and commercial barriers to the development of a thriving all-island economy. A further difficulty, apart from the obvious unionist scepticism, lies with the workforce, which has been slow to respond to the possibilities of cross-border economic change. In some sectors, notably agriculture, this is a legacy of close relations between the state and employee representatives. Greer (1994, p. 412) cites the example of a closed agricultural policy community in Northern Ireland, characterized by a cordial parental relationship in which the key to relations between the Northern Ireland state and the Ulster Farmers' Union was the 'common belief in, and commitment to, the union with Britain'. A rival farmers' organization with greater nationalist representation was subsequently formed and state–union ties have been severely weakened. Nonetheless trade unions in Northern Ireland still tend to be inward looking, and although ties with union partners in the Irish Republic are increasing, they remain very underdeveloped. Therefore attempts to harmonize labour market representation from below are exceptional. Equally the lack of cross-border training and educational provision, with different regimes prevailing either side of the border, inhibits the scope for labour transfers across the border.

Conclusion

The cross-border dimension of the Good Friday Agreement was modest. Its limitations were a consequence of unionist hostility to anything other that a tightly ringfenced all-island dimension and the relative uninterest and lack of attention to detail shown by Sinn Fein in the pre-GFA negotiations on strand two of the deal. Sinn Fein subsequently displayed far greater interest in cross-border arrangements as part of its optimistic promotion (not shared privately by some in the party) of north–south bodies as a means of transition to Irish unity.

The main impetus to cross-border activity has been provided by the EU, rather than the GFA. Membership of the EU by the United Kingdom and the Irish Republic has ensured that conflict resolution in Northern Ireland has a European dimension, added to the bilateral territorial management that has been evident since the Sunningdale Agreement in 1973. Thus far the EU's contribution has been primarily economic rather than political, an approach feeding into post-GFA structural arrangements through the Special European Union Programmes Body, the most important of the all-island bodies created.

The economic cooperation and removal of barriers between states across the EU have been mirrored in cross-border linkages between Northern Ireland and the Irish Republic. The GFA accelerated the process of functional cooperation and heightened its political importance, but without diminishing national loyalties. The gradual shift towards an all-Ireland economy has not been accompanied by significant movement towards an all-island polity.

9

Civil Society and the Problem of Sectarianism

Supporters of the Good Friday Agreement believed that it offered the prospect of an end to the Troubles and gradual normalization of Northern Ireland's polarized society. The death toll dropped dramatically, although this was a consequence of paramilitary ceasefires rather than the agreement itself. By the time of the agreement's prolonged suspension in 2002, the Provisional IRA and UVF had to all intents and purposes been 'stood down', at least with regard to their respective aims of ending or maintaining the union. The agreement was, however, quickly followed by the worst atrocity of the Troubles: the killing of 29 people in Omagh by a Real IRA bomb.

The GFA said very little on the problem of sectarianism in Northern Ireland. Although it established a variety of commissions to deal with inequality and perceived injustice, its primary focus was on the constitutional accommodation of political elites. The unstated assumption was that resolution of the constitutional conflict would result in the normalization of society and the eventual eradication of societal sectarianism. This was ambitious, given that 23 per cent of the population claimed to have family or close friends who had been injured in a sectarian incident (Cairns *et al.*, 2003, p. 39).

There were also wider theoretical and practical problems associated with the process of normalization. First, anti-consociationalists argued that the institutions created by the GFA were solidifying the communal division (Taylor, 2001; Wilford, 2001a). Second, the homogeneity of religious support for and membership of the major political parties (pre- and post-GFA) made it electorally unwise to make appeals across the divide or to the diminishing centre ground. Third, the conclusion of an elite-driven constitutional deal, although complex, would be easier to attain than the erosion of embedded sectarianism, which would require a multifaceted, multiorganizational approach to bringing about attitudinal change. Fourth, defining sectarianism was not easy and sectarianism was often erroneously conflated with legitimate political ambition or pluralism. Was the desire for a united Ireland and rejection of Northern Ireland as illegitimate in any way sectarian? Was the desire to send one's child to a religiously exclusive school sectarian? Did acknowledgement of religious difference constitute acceptance of residual sectarianism? Eighty-five cent of people believed that religion would 'always make a difference to the way people feel about each other in Northern Ireland', with a figure of over 80 per cent being recorded for each of the two main religions (Northern Ireland Life and Times Survey 2001, www.ark.ac.uk/nilt2001/Community_Relations).

Finally, the desire to 'rid' Northern Ireland of sectarianism was set against the sectarian basis of its foundation and maintenance. The basis of consent and the state's border rested on rejection of the expressed wishes of a majority of the island's population and was based on a crude religious headcount, designed to ensure a unionist majority within a given space. Hence it is scarcely surprising that Northern Ireland society was subsequently plagued by sectarianism and there remained a hollowness to anti-sectarian campaigns. Majoritarianism, which followed the sectarian carving out of Northern Ireland from a hitherto undivided land and its foisting on a largely reluctant people, had run its course by the 1970s, having palpably disadvantaged the minority population. Its replacement, consociationalism, offered internal equality of treatment, but the sectarian foundation remained.

Given the above problems and the continuing unionist political–religious links, civic unionists will have an uphill task convincing nationalist opponents that their claim is one of legitimate territorial and political self-determination. Civic republicans, whilst pointing to the libertarian and egalitarian concerns of republicanism and (not unreasonably) denying responsibility for what emerged in the Irish Free State and Republic, have that green, ethnic and religiously exclusive legacy to overcome in pitching an appeal to unionists.

Division and the Good Friday Agreement

The major criticisms of the theoretical and practical bases of the GFA are that it denies a common humanity and legitimizes sectarianism.

An alternative view is that the consociational ideas in the agreement should be seen as facilitating an improved society. Elite accommodation has diminished the political contest. As republicans have become enmeshed in the state, the death toll from political violence has diminished markedly. For example in 2002 there were six deaths from paramilitary violence, compared with 100 in 1992. Economic boom and near equality have displaced relative impoverishment and disadvantage for the nationalist community. Increased sectarianism, rather than political rebellion, appears to be the new curse, although the pattern is uncertain. A summer of sectarian violence in 2002 was followed by a much quieter 2003. However a majority of Belfast residents believe that intercommunity relations have deteriorated since the paramilitary ceasefires; for example the percentage of residents of North Belfast working in mixed-religion workplaces in that area fell from 75 per cent to 33 per cent during the 1990s (www.irl-news, 26 July 2002). At the same time expressions of community identity increased. By the end of the 1990s there had been a sharp increase in the number of annual Orange Order parades, rising from under 2000 in the mid 1980s to 3200 (www.irl-news, 26 July 2002). Between 1999 and 2002 there was also an increase in the number of those in both communities who preferred segregated housing, workplaces and schools (*Guardian*, 10 July 2002; NILT, 2002).

Two explanations can be offered for the perceived rise in sectarianism. The first is to do with unionists' perceptions of the GFA. Despite the placement of (northern) consent at the heart of the agreement, a sizeable proportion of the unionist population fails to perceive that it has won the constitutional war. Sinn Fein's presence at Stormont, anathema to diehard republicans, failed to assuage unionist doubters who feared that the agreement's ultimate destination lay in the demise of the province. In the meantime, many in the Protestant population fear economic loss relative to their Catholic counterparts as a result of the 'equality agenda'.

The second and perhaps more convincing explanation lies in the depoliticization process that has accompanied elite accommodation. Cultural and sectarian conflicts have replaced political and constitutional questions, or economic rivalries, rendering unionism and nationalism devoid of their traditional ideological compasses. Identity has become the framework within which the peace process is being developed. Zero-sum-game contests of support for a united Ireland versus maintenance of Northern Ireland's place in the United Kingdom

Table 9.1 *Paramilitary violence, January 1998 to July 2002*

Deaths	101
Shootings	1089
Bombings	744
Punishment shootings/beatings	1193

Source: Adapted from Police Service of Northern Ireland (2002).

no longer motivate the actions of either community. As the 'war' has subsided, the major role of the Provisional IRA appears to be policing its own community, a role also adopted by the UVF in its community. The Ulster Defence Association/Ulster Freedom Fighters have continued to engage in sectarian conflict, their ceasefire being ruled invalid in 2001, whilst republican dissidents have attempted to continue the old war. The consequence of increased sectarianism and the desire by paramilitary groups to maintain their status within their communities, plus the flickering embers of the old conflict being fanned by the actions of republican ultras, has been an imperfect peace, as Table 9.1 shows.

To what extent is the Good Friday Agreement culpable of promoting sectarian rivalry? The verdict is mixed. At the asssembly level, the designation of MLAs as unionist, nationalist or other is a necessary factor in the achievement of power sharing, unless a voting threshold (around 60–70 per cent) to ensure a strong overall (cross-community) majority is introduced for legislation. The use of unionist and nationalist labels merely amounts to recognition of pre-existing ideological (as distinct from religious) divisions, and an attempt to harness these within a framework of incremental cooperation. Nonetheless for critics the labelling approach appears to deny a common humanity. This exaggerates the impact of labelling: placing parties in broad ideological camps is hardly a Northern Ireland phenomenon (consider, for example, the European Parliament). However, labelling is reductionist, a criticism made by the main centrist party, the Alliance Party, which has always rejected sectoral designations. It may also be unnecessary for most of the legislation processed by a devolved assembly. Under the GFA, unionism and nationalism are seen as ideologies to be accommodated, rather than overcome. The device may accentuate ethnic bloc politics and offer few incentives for moderation.

The GFA also celebrates the cultural diversity of Northern Ireland. As noted in Chapter 2, the sectoral autonomy promoted in the agreement is not great; hence the promotion of cultural diversity is not strong, although it is implicit in the agreement. To suggest that the agreement's anodyne sections on promoting linguistic diversity are responsible for exacerbating sectarian rioting is to stretch a point. The agreement's reference to ethnic communities as 'part of the cultural wealth of the island of Ireland' (p. 20) recognizes the previous failure to achieve parity of esteem for different ethnic identities. It makes no reference, however, to expressions of ethnonational or ethnoreligious identity that are unpalatable to the other community, be they sectarian Orange parades or segregated schooling. The agreement offers the prospect of a more robust legal framework for the eradication of discrimination. However it also supports diversity, autonomy and the promotion of difference, from which renewed sectarianism could arise.

What is sectarianism?

Perhaps the most difficult aspect of formulating any kind of antisectarian policy is determining what constitutes sectarianism, a term that is freely used and frequently misapplied. Coulter (1999a) argues that the concept of sectarianism should be confined to the realm of religion. As he rightly argues, 'commentators frequently use the term "sectarian" to denote forms of belief and conduct which are clearly secular and which would be more accurately characterised with the categories of "ethnicity" and "nationalism"' (ibid., p. 12). By restricting its categorization in this way, sectarianism can be described as religious bigotry, the promotion of one's religion or religious background at the expense of an alternative. This definition avoids the (frequent) misuse of the term sectarian to describe republicanism, which draws its support base from individuals baptized as Catholics but has no other formal connection. When defending the existence of Northern Ireland, unionists avoid the charge of sectarianism and argue purely in terms of the right of supporters of the union to determine their own future.

The creation of Northern Ireland might be described as a piece of gerrymandering based on sectarianism. However the province was not founded strictly on the basis of a Protestant majority, but on a unionist one that happened to be Protestant. The situation among unionists is complicated by the presence in the ranks of the UUP of a religious–cultural organization that excludes Catholics. If the Ancient Order of Hibernians held voting rights in Sinn Fein or the SDLP, one could safely assume that this would add to the sectarian label that tends to be attached to those parties. The unionist position is further complicated by the fact that the DUP is led by a politician who is stridently opposed to the Roman Catholic Church and whose politics are a derivative of his religion.

The other problematic conceptual distinction is that between sectarianism and racism. The link between religion and national identity, commonly Catholic Irish and Protestant British, has sometimes blurred the distinction between religious sectarianism and ethnic ill-feeling. The hostility felt by many unionists towards nationalists was a product of antipathy towards the ethno-religious identity of the Catholic Irish and was reinforced until recent years by asymmetrical power relations (McVeigh, 1998). The conflation is apparent in the casual dismissal of nationalists as Fenians, which refers primarily to the republican aspirations of those designated as members of the 'other' community but might also be seen as an anti-Catholic jibe. Similarly the label *taig* is used to describe Catholics, but is also a common derogatory term for nationalists. Catholic denunciations of 'Orangies' might be seen as purely religious sectarianism, but this label is sometimes applied to the broader unionist community, particularly in interface areas.

The labelling of actions as sectarian can be even more problematic. Cultural, social, religious and political divisions do exist in Northern Ireland, but these may be a consequence of ethnic division rather than sectarianism. Some divisions can be seen as normal features of a liberal, pluralistic society. Educational segregation, for example, is normal elsewhere in the United Kingdom, as Roman Catholic parents have the option (exercised less outside Northern Ireland, but still common) of educating their children in Catholic schools. Denominational schools are justified by the Church as providing a basic right to a Catholic education and can be seen as the baseline of a liberal, tolerant society. Critics suggest that separate schooling from the age of five, on the basis of religious denomination, institutionalizes division, from which it is too late to recover by the time education becomes mixed at university level. Non-denominational schools attract few Catholics.

Religious educational division reflects the importance of religious affiliation and worship in Northern Ireland society. Weekly church attendance by Catholics is the highest in Western Europe and nearly half of the Protestant population also attends church on a regular basis (McGarry and O'Leary, 1995). Although not part of the ethno-political conflict, theological disputes between fundamentalist Protestants of the Free Presbyterian Church (who are over-represented in the DUP, given the size of the Church) and the Roman Catholic Church are important to protagonists, if of little interest to many in Northern Ireland. Although the Northern Ireland problem is not essentially ethnoreligious (for a rival argument see Bruce, 1986), intercommunal identification and hostilities arising from denominational affiliation clearly contribute to societal dysfunction.

At integrated schools, Protestants and Catholics are educated at the same establishment in a religious balance that does not exceed 60–40 for either religion. Such schools have been advocated by some as a means of diminishing sectarian division (Lambkin, 1996). The debate on faith versus integrated schools can divide liberals and multi-culturalists. Some defend faith schools as examples of diversity and pluralism; others, possibly less religiously oriented, are not persuaded of the continuing value of church schools. Politically there is no prospect of a move away from state facilitation of denominational schools, even if this were desirable. The widespread development of integrated education would have to be preceded by one or more of the following.

First, there might be further growth in secularism. Between the 1991 and 2001 censuses the proportion of the population who claimed they had no religion or refused to state their religion rose from 7.3 per cent to 13.9 per cent. Second, there could be more support from the Roman Catholic Church for integrated education. The Catholic Church is not formally opposed to the practice, but might reasonably be regarded as lukewarm. Third, the growth of integrated education would perhaps have to follow a diminution of residential segregation, allowing easier access to multidenominational schools. However such segregation is, if anything, increasing. Finally, a substantial attitudinal change among parents might be required. In 1997 only one in 43 pupils attended integrated schools (Coulter, 1999a, p. 25).

Irrespective of the type of school attended, Northern Ireland's schoolchildren have been subject to a curriculum with common elements since 1990. These common elements include education for mutual understanding (EMU) and cultural heritage, which is designed to improve knowledge of both communities, in order that differences might be better understood and respected. Information and knowledge deficits are seen as key problems. In a cogent critique, Rolston (1998) points out several problems with this approach. First, it is reductionist in locating division within the field of psychology, putting blame on the attitudes of individuals rather than structures. Second, multi-culturalism tends to screen out 'unacceptable' historical events or political theories, such as British colonial involvement in Ireland, as part of a process of depoliticization. Third, multiculturalism relies on a relativist approach, presenting all – or at least some – actions as being of equal legitimacy or wrongdoing. Finally, programmes such as EMU promote the two-traditions idea in assuming the permanence of their existence and prioritizing knowledge of their features. A similarly persuasive critique is offered by Rooney (1998).

Social class and communal division

One of the most famous statements on British politics is that class is everything, with all else being 'embellishment and detail' (Pulzer, 1967, p. 98), but this is clearly not applicable to Northern Ireland. Rose's (1971) pioneering work indicated that class identity was subordinate to national and religious identification, and this was confirmed more recently by McGarry and O'Leary (1995). Even if one measurement of class sentiment – the negligible support for class-oriented parties such as the Workers' Party – might be seen by critics as somewhat reductionist, the fact that a majority of people identify more with their nationality and religion than their social class is indisputable. This is not to state that there is an unawareness of class; indeed Hayes and McAllister (1995) found a greater ability among Northern Ireland citizens to locate their class position than citizens elsewhere in the United Kingdom. Thus far, however, awareness of social structure has often been divorced from identification with class.

Coulter (1999b) offers a realistic account of the lack of impact that social class has had in Northern Ireland as a primary means of identification. However he correctly notes that social class, not religion, is the main determinant of life chances. Northern Ireland's grammar schools and two universities are filled by middle-class students from both sides of the communal divide, whilst working-class pupils are more likely to leave school early and take unskilled and manual jobs. Although the Northern Ireland education system is not blighted by the state–private school divide that afflicts education in England, its claim to meritocracy, through the brutal and class-affected eleven-plus examination, is at best only partially borne out. Class unity has been overridden by the intercommunity conflict of the past, which further polarized the working classes. The loyalist and republican working classes suffered considerably during the conflict. The predominantly working-class (and admittedly densely populated) areas of North and West Belfast endured 1088 deaths between 1969 and 1989, compared with a mere eight in affluent North Down (ibid., p. 83). Despite the mutual suffering, Coulter acknowledges that it 'is "the Sash" or "the Soldiers' Song" rather than the Internationale that brings tears to the eyes of working class men as the end of licensing hours beckons' (ibid., p. 95).

The underlying weakness of class-based analyses is that, at their core and despite their denial, they assume that primary identification with country or religion is somehow mistaken or retarded. Such analyses are correct in stating that the working classes share similar problems as a result of structural conditions. However the division of the working class is seen as something imposed from above, rather than an aspect of working-class choice. This deterministic approach patronizes the working classes it aims to defend, assuming they are somehow dupes of British imperial masters, the Orange Order, the Catholic Church or Irish historical myth. The idea that the working classes could themselves decide that Irish self-determination or union with Great Britain are causes worth fighting for is seen as irrational emotivism, rather than as political acts of liberation. Class-based analyses also assume that commonalities must inevitably flow from a shared structural position. Yet there is no particular reason why similar class status should automatically lead to the articulation of a shared set of political interests. Class may remain intangible, carrying no formal rights of entry, unlike, for example, entrance to the Catholic Church, which is reinforced by a sacramental programme, a particular education and distinctive processes of socialization. From a republican viewpoint, class-based approaches lament division between the working classes whilst supporting the retention of a territorial border and northern enclave that was never favoured by the majority of working-class people in Ireland.

None of this is to deny the possibility of class-based approaches forming part of the new Northern Irish politics. Rather it constitutes a plea for greater understanding of the dynamics and motivations of working-class politics. National and religious loyalties are not imposed on a helpless underclass. Despite the rightward shift of Sinn Fein and the ethnonational framework of the GFA, there have been (admittedly limited) progressive, class-based developments. Sinn Fein and the PUP have cooperated inside and outside the assembly in forging a tentative form of cross-community, class-oriented politics. The two parties have produced a 'rainbow' class politics by attempting to end selection in education, which disadvantaged a large proportion of the working class. They have also opposed university tuition fees and supported substantial increases in health spending. Sinn Fein's control of the Health and Education Ministries in the executive provided impetus. Yet the 1998 and 2003 Assembly elections confirmed that Sinn Fein and PUP voters do not provide each other's candidates with lower preference transfer votes.

The fragmentation of unionism has assisted the growth of class politics. Critical of what it perceives as the 'dinosaur' tendency among supporters of the union, the PUP has long rejected the 'sell-out' thesis propounded by the DUP in respect of the GFA, arguing that non-constitutional politics ought now to flourish. A large majority (87.5 per cent) of PUP members voted 'yes' in the May 1998 referendum and almost two thirds of PUP members think that the union between the United Kingdom and Northern Ireland is 'as strong as ever' (McAuley and Tonge, 2003). The PUP has offered a decisive break with traditional 'no surrender' politics. Central to the PUP's development are the reconstruction of political relationships, not only with other unionists but also with other political representatives of the working class, including the 'traditional enemy', Sinn Fein. This is particularly important in terms of the development of a new politics in Northern Ireland. It goes further than the limited form of civic unionism developed by the pro-GFA wing of the UUP in seeking loyalist cooperation with the strident representatives of northern nationalism and the promotion of radical politics from below. Civic unionism acknowledges the identity of the other (Porter, 1996). New loyalism indeed accepts the Irishness of the other community, but it also seeks the promotion of cross-community class identity.

Support for the PUP grew as some working-class loyalists, mainly in Belfast, were prepared to transfer their allegiance from the DUP or UUP. Under the influence of its current leadership, the PUP has grown from a single branch of around 30 members in Belfast to a structured party with a membership of around 600, organized into 11 branches. The PUP has been relatively successful in drawing support from a section of the community that hitherto has not engaged in politics. Fewer than 10 per cent of PUP members have previously been members of any political party (McAuley and Tonge, 2003).

Previously, many in the Protestant working class refused to believe that it was possible to seek any political accommodation with nationalists, and left-of-centre articulations of social and economic issues were often seen as direct challenges to unionist control of the state. The PUP's injection of working-class politics was aimed at getting people to rally around social and economic issues. As David Ervine, one of the two PUP members elected to the Assembly in 1998, put it:

> The only vehicle which will I think destroy the budding cultivated flower of sectarianism is class politics and we've got to replace that sectarianism [and] at some future date actually create real alignment in politics on economic and social issues, as opposed to the divisive religious and constitutional. (quoted in McAuley and Tonge, 2003, p. 183)

For the PUP, the development of a new politics is predicated not merely on the promotion of a less fearful loyalism, but also on the promotion of a socialist agenda to advance the interests of its working-class base. The PUP's policy agenda includes redistributive taxation, nationalization, greater economic planning, enhanced spending on public services, support for comprehensive education and the withdrawal of state control over moral issues such as abortion. In emphasizing forms of politics that have never flourished in Northern Ireland (although the old Northern Ireland Labour Party had some success), the PUP has provided a focal point for social, economic and political challenges to unionism. Women comprise almost half of the PUP executive committee, the party is the only unionist organization to support gay and lesbian rights, and it is openly pro-choice on the abortion issue. This makes the party more radical than Sinn Fein, whose *ard chomhairle* has traditionally been male dominated and whose abortion policy is equivocal, although its support for gay and lesbian rights is explicit. When the PUP entered the Assembly it promoted the idea of shared responsibility between the two traditions as the basis for a solution, with the possibility of a politics of realignment between the Protestant working class and the Catholic working class.

Sinn Fein's leftward turn in the late 1970s resulted in the party moving in a much more radical direction, accelerated temporarily during the early years of the capture of the party by the northern leadership in the early 1980s. Since the late 1980s the party has moved away from its leftist agenda, although it remains left of centre. In the Irish Republic, this approach has been promoted via community politics, advocacy of decentralization and stress on Irish neutrality. An emphasis on community politics is also apparent in the north. Sinn Fein's radicalism is distinct from that of the PUP in that it is normally expressed in the form of an equality agenda for nationalists, based on enhanced human rights, parity of esteem and increased state spending on public services. Although the two parties share broadly similar non-constitutional agendas, particularly in respect of public sector expansion, there are barriers to the advancement of class-based com- monalities. For both parties, reference to the working class often means their working class, namely the loyalist or republican working class, not the class as an entirety (Finlayson, 1999). Contentiously, one author has claimed that the basis of sympathy for the PUP is not its political philosophy but its links with the UVF, which helps reassure the loyalist working class of the tough unionist credentials of its members and associates (Bruce, 1994). There is also a growing elec- toral barrier. Having secured its working-class base, Sinn Fein is beginning to capture the middle-class Catholic vote of the SDLP, whereas the PUP has still to secure a solid foothold among a Prot- estant working class that became less enamoured with the GFA as it was operationalized. Because of this, Sinn Fein's interest in promoting class politics may be more limited than that of the PUP.

The PUP's cooperative approach to Sinn Fein has brought criticism from the DUP. As Price (1995) notes, the two are fishing in the same electoral waters in urban areas. The willingness of the PUP to work with Sinn Fein was also a contributory factor in the loyalist feud with the UDA/UFF in 2000, as cited in the disparaging literature circulated by the UDA at that time. The PUP is vulnerable to the criticism that it is supporting a deal based on the 'greening' of Northern Ireland – thus threatening the loyalist identity and rendering a transfer of sovereignty more likely – through a concealed process of unification. Although the PUP feels secure enough to reject this criticism, it remains uncer- tain about how to treat vibrant nationalism. Many PUP members, however, reject the equality agenda projected by Sinn Fein and the notion of discrimination against Catholics. PUP members are almost equally divided on whether Catholics and Protestants are treated equally today, with almost half believing that employers are more likely to give jobs to Catholics in contemporary Northern Ireland. The attitude towards the notion that Catholics remain second-class citizens can be clearly seen in the following statement by a PUP executive member:

> I think that the second class citizenry that Sinn Fein would argue about is that of attitude, because the structures in society are definitively not sectarian ... the issue of equality I don't think is anywhere near as high or should be anywhere near as high on Sinn Fein's agenda. (quoted in McAuley and Tonge, 2003, p. 188)

The extent of hostility towards Sinn Fein is also indicated in the voting preferences of PUP members, in that none list Sinn Fein among their leading seven vote transfer possibilities. Despite the existence of two solidly working-class parties, the communal divide remains stark.

Are Catholics still disadvantaged?

Although sectarianism clearly still exists, what of sectarian discrimination? The old nationalist complaints about electoral discrimination and political exclusion were addressed years ago. Careful monitoring of workforce recruitment has made it almost impossible for large organizations to pursue sectarian politics, even in the unlikely event that they are desired. The growth of a sizeable Catholic middle class appears to undermine any sense of the community being second class. Whilst occupational structures have changed in Britain and Ireland, the extent of the movement of Catholics into professional positions has exceeded that which might have been expected, although they are still underrepresented in such occupations (Bew *et al.*, 1997). Catholics have taken advantage of Northern Ireland's state-dominated education system and a marginally higher percentage of Catholics now graduate from university (ibid.).

Discrimination in recruitment was outlawed by the Fair Employment Act of 1976, which established the Fair Employment Agency to monitor and investigate allegations of discrimination. External pressure was also applied via the MacBride Principles, which originated in the Irish-American community and attempted to make US investment in Northern Ireland conditional on a religiously balanced workforce. Whilst improving Catholic representation in the public sector, the

1976 Act was relatively ineffective in the private sphere (Ruane and Todd, 1998, p. 179). Cases were difficult to prove and ending the endemic, if unsystematic, private sector discrimination proved difficult amid political violence. The private sector was largely allowed to be self-regulatory, with employers merely having to sign a 'Declaration of Principle and Intent' to qualify as equal opportunity employers (Cunningham, 2001).

Legislation was toughened via a second Fair Employment Act in 1989, which created a tribunal system to assess cases of alleged discrimination and required all but the smallest firms to register with the Fair Employment Commission, with rigid monitoring of larger employers. By then, however, most of the large firms and certainly the multinational ones were uninterested in discrimination, which served no purpose. The nature of Northern Ireland industry, insofar as it still existed, had changed vastly. Although a few bastions of alleged discrimination remained – such as Harland and Wolffe shipbuilders, where Catholics were underrepresented and 'non-sectarian' trade unions had turned a blind eye to sectarianism – the Orange clientelism of pre-1970s Northern Ireland had long disappeared. There were, however, two weaknesses in the 1989 Act. First, it lacked the affirmative action desired by the Labour opposition in Westminster, meaning that the onus was still on individuals to bring cases, which might or might not be pursued (ibid.). Second, the Act ignored small firms, where sectarian practices could continue due to discrimination or localized recruitment in largely single-religion areas. In recognition of this, the size-of-workforce threshold at which the stringencies of the Act were applied was later reduced from 25 to 10. The workings of the Fair Employment Commission elicited unionist criticism that it was a 'Catholic employment agency' (ibid., p. 145). The 1998 GFA introduced an Equality Commission, which absorbed the Fair Employment and Equal Opportunities Commissions. An Equality Directorate was established within the office of the first and deputy first minister to provide a cooperative approach to antidiscrimination and equality laws within a devolved political framework. Public employers were required to submit equality schemes to the Equality Commission.

One stubborn differential persists: the rate of unemployment among Catholics is over twice that among Protestants. Traditionally high, unemployment in Northern Ireland fell sharply from 17.1 per cent in 1986 to below 6 per cent in 2003, lower than in four other UK regions, including London (Department of Enterprise, Trade and

Investment, 25 April 2003) and below the EU average. However the Protestant–Catholic gap has not altered, and pockets of hostility to the employment of members of the other religion remain. Although three-quarters of the population claim to prefer a mixed-religion workplace, one in five Protestants would prefer a single-religion work environment, as would one in seven Catholics (Northern Ireland Life and Times Survey, 2001).

Mercifully, explanations of the Protestant–Catholic unemployment differential have become rather more sophisticated than the stereo-typical assertion that Protestants are better equipped to cope with work, a presumption that co-existed with blaming the inadequacies of Catholic schools and their lack of focus on science and mathematics (Wilson, 1955, 1989). Such explanations are also located in the wider thesis that nationalists contributed towards their own problems by declining to support the institutions of Northern Ireland. In more rational, economic analyses there are two broad schools of explanation (Bew *et al.*, 1997). The first suggests that the higher Catholic unemployment rate is accidental, being the product of locational or qualification problems (Compton, 1991), or the rapidity of the Catholic influx into the labour market and higher rate of leaving (Gudgin and Breen, 1994). The second school, whilst not suggesting that discrimination against Catholics is the dominant explanatory variable, nonetheless suggests that continued discrimination is at least a partial explanation (Smith and Chambers, 1990; Murphy and Armstrong, 1994; McGarry and O'Leary, 1995). Part of the problem has been the reluctance of Catholics, particularly those from the working class who are vulnerable to unemployment, to apply for certain state-sector jobs, notably in policing. Post-Patten, 50–50 Catholic–Protestant recruitment may remove one of these areas of Catholic reluctance. There are two caveats, however. Recruitment will be to a shrunken force, and working-class Catholics may remain somewhat hostile even to a reconstituted police service.

Representing civil society? The Civic Forum

The GFA made a very limited attempt to accommodate civil society within the new political structures, with the Civic Forum being the main representational vehicle. The idea was promoted by the Northern Ireland Women's Coalition (NIWC) as part of its effort to make the

Table 9.2   *Sectoral representation in the Civic Forum (number of members)*

Voluntary	18
Business	7
Trade union	7
First minister and deputy first minister	6
Churches	5
Culture	4
Arts and sport	4
Agriculture and fisheries	3
Community relations	2
Education	2
Victims	2

GFA as inclusive as possible. Not all the other parties that backed the idea did so primarily because they believed in its merits. For example Sinn Fein gave its support because the NIWC had been 'supportive elsewhere in negotiations, in, for example, backing prisoner releases' (Adams, 1998). Launched in October 2000, the Civic Forum comprised 60 members, plus a chair, appointed by the first minister and deputy first minister. The members were appointed for three-year terms and represent various sectors (Table 9.2).

Parties that favoured the establishment of the forum saw it as the GFA institution with the greatest potential to foster the development of cross-community consensus. However they were disappointed with its construction, arguing that it had been formulated as a middle-class 'talking shop'. The GFA said little about the role of the forum, declaring merely that it would be consultative. The agreement allowed the first minister and deputy first minister to establish guidelines for the selection of the Forum's members. In common with the PUP, Sinn Fein believed that forum representatives from the voluntary sector would include representatives of cross-community former prisoners' groups. Sinn Fein was particularly critical of the extent of business representation (interview with Mary Nelis, Sinn Fein MLA, 28 June 2000). Some republicans argued for a devolved model, with forums being based in each constituency, an idea that attracted some sympathy from the PUP. Sinn Fein MLAs believed that cross-party and cross-community class alliances would form, covering a wide range of issues, including gender. Nelis asserted that she could 'do business' more easily with Billy Hutchinson (PUP) on gender issues than with the 'middle-class professionals of the Northern Ireland Women's Coalition' (interview, 28 June 2000).

All sectors were required to provide a set of nominees who were representative of age, gender and community background and drawn from the whole of Northern Ireland. The largest organization in civil society, the Orange Order, was denied representation, to the chagrin of the DUP, which tended to be hostile to initiatives emanating from the NIWC. The Order's exclusion contradicted the claim that the forum would represent all interests in Northern Ireland. Clearly some interests were more acceptable than others, and the filtering process excluded an organization that contained one quarter of the Protestant males in Northern Ireland. Certainly the presence of the Orange Order would have been divisive, and its proposals in respect of community relations, integrated education and, above all, parades may have prevented any sense of unity in the forum. Equally, however, the forum was supposed to be a vehicle of inclusion rather than a gathering of societal 'worthies'. It is unclear why it was necessary for the first minister and deputy first minister to provide their own nominees (three each) and appoint the chair. The GFA's lack of prescription on the mechanics of forum establishment created a void that was readily filled by these ministers. Nonetheless the ministers agreed that no Assembly matter should be 'off-limits' for dissection by the forum.

Devoid of legislative powers, the forum was established as a consultative body that would meet in plenary format approximately six times a year. Under a revived agreement, the forum could be bolstered by a more formal scrutiny role, or even by being permitted to initiate legislation for Assembly approval. However the forum held none of the democratic legitimacy of the Assembly, and any elevation of its role could be construed as an undemocratic means of bolstering the interests of minority parties and sectional interest groups, at the expense of those who were obliged to seek electoral mandates. It also risked being a collection of the unelected and unelectable, devising alternative forms of non-communal, inclusive politics which failed to address the reality that electors in Northern Ireland endorsed communal division. Moreover it could be seen by critics as a means of reviving a political centre rejected by voters.

A more positive approach would have been to develop the forum's bridging role, amid politics that remained sectarian in terms of parties and voters. Equally it would allow institutionalized access to decision makers under devolved government and could promote a pluralistic, consensual form of politics. In the event the forum was not assigned delaying, revision or even scrutiny powers over Assembly legislation. However it was able to make written submissions and comments on the executive's programme for government, and on health, education, employment and community relations. In developing a proactive approach, the forum also consulted interested parties on lifelong education and learning, poverty and sustainable development (McQuade and Fagan, 2002). The forum was designed to provide advice to the Assembly, to promote equality, human rights and diversity, to innovate and to serve civic society, but it is unclear how these lofty aims were to be fulfilled. Thus far the forum has acquired the reputation of being an expansive, somewhat expensive, filtered gathering of special interests.

Cultural pluralism

The downgrading of ideological contestation by mainstream republicans in Sinn Fein has meant an increased focus on identity politics (Gilligan, 2002), so the demand for British withdrawal from Northern Ireland and politics centred on the right to national sovereignty has been less prominent in recent years. Although the constitutional question has not been entirely resolved, it has been put on hold as part of a broader attempt to depoliticize the issue. Contests of sovereignty have been largely displaced by a cultural pluralism that embraces respect for cultural identities. The GFA legitimizes and encourages the celebration of two equal cultures. At its most benign, this fosters the development of, for example, linguistic tradition. Alternatively the celebration of difference can accentuate existing divisions. It also risks equating cultural equality and the assertion of group rights with political equality. Thus nationalists have been accorded equality and human rights under the GFA, and the (island-wide) aspiration for reunification has been put on hold.

One problem with societal reconciliation is determining the limits of pluralism. Undiluted celebration of religious and political pluralism necessarily leads to support for the right of Catholics to educate their children in denominational schools (segregated education) and the right of the Orange Order (anti-Catholic Church) to hold parades, although not necessarily to march through nationalist areas (arguably this would constitute true pluralism, with nationalists 'celebrating' a rival culture). Either of the above decisions could be seen as sectarian, yet both are defendable, based on a cultural-pluralist, celebration-of-diversity approach. A pluralist approach might also mean celebration of rival historical narratives, in which the bold deeds and errant actions of the British Army and the IRA are presented on equal terms to students.

A less divisive pluralism might involve acceptance of the waiving of rights associated with the legitimation of diversity. Under this, the right of Catholics to educate their children in faith schools would be acknowledged, but waived as these children would instead be sent to integrated schools. The right of the Orange Order to march wherever it chose could also be acknowledged, given the importance of freedom of assembly, but the Order could decide not to exercise that right. Alternatively the right of the Order to march could be tempered by the rights of local residents' groups. The advantage of this approach is that it would encourage settlements 'from below', empowering local citizens. A local solution for marching rights at Drumcree, a matter that caused great unrest during the mid and late 1990s, could not be brokered. Forty-two per cent of Protestants support unfettered marching rights; only six per cent of Catholics support such rights (Irwin, 2002, p. 128). Thus far the upholding of rights and civil liberties in respect of parades has been left to the unelected Parades Commission, a body whose lowest-common-denominator decisions appear to be based more on threats of violence than a clear concept of individual or collective rights.

A pluralist approach based on parity of esteem has been played out with wrangling between unionist and nationalist parties over the flying of flags on public buildings, with Protestants arguing that the Union flag should be flown and Catholics calling for the flying of a new neutral flag, or none at all (Brown and MacGinty, 2003). The post-GFA dispensation has seen the emphasis switch to symbols of sovereignty, rather than contests over its actuality. The cultural-pluralist approach has another practical difficulty, in that it does not encourage cross-community contact at the grassroots level. It acknowledges difference rather than attempts integration. Within a cultural-pluralist framework, cross-community initiatives can of course exist and there is a wide range of local groups working towards reconciliation across the community divide. The overall situation, however, is one of mutual respect for difference, rather than integration or assimilation. Institutions associated with sectarian division, such as the Orange Order and the Ancient Order of Hibernians (although both would deny the charge), have been repackaged as benign cultural traditions, as part of what has been described as balanced sectarianism (Butler, 1991; Bell, 1998). Indeed the DUP has suggested that the Northern Ireland marching season be packaged by the Northern Ireland tourist industry. The promotion of cultural traditions leads to the emergence of countercultures; witness the strident insistence by many unionists for recognition of the Ulster-Scots language, which prior to the 1990s had attracted even less interest than the Irish language, promoted so heavily by republicans.

The emphasis on cultural pluralism, parity of esteem and equality risks the depoliticization of Northern Ireland society; which, of course may be the aim of those concerned. Under the discourse of rights, tradition and heritage, political questions on topics such as sovereignty, self-determination, colonialism and unification are downgraded. Among republicans, requests for the Irish language to be funded by the British government have displaced the call for Irish independence. For example in Ardoyne, the area in which republicans suffered the greatest losses in the political struggle, there is a mural containing the following slogan: 'Gaelic games: part of our heritage'. This is true, but arguably no more so than soccer or horseracing and is indicative of how the contest for political independence has slackened in the more benign space of cultural autonomy. Whilst cultural resistance is of importance, it is scarcely a second front to a political contest. Similarly political challenges posed to the unionist community are countered by the development of unionism within the parameters of a community relations discourse, through new efforts at attaining cultural legitimacy (O'Reilly, 2002).

Yet the new(ish) discourse of identity and legitimacy cannot be divorced from the political environment, however much policy makers hope that the GFA will eventually settle the constitutional question that is Northern Ireland. The Orange Order, for example, is not merely a cultural tradition but has also been described as a 'pseudo religious political Order in defence of the Protestant and Reformed faith, but with a belief that it cannot survive without the prop of the union. It wraps the Bible in the Union flag' (quoted in Storey, 2002, p. 38). As stated in a detailed study of the Orange Order, there 'has always been a tension between the "religious" and "political" aspects of the Order' (Bryan, 2000, p. 94). Although the Order's political influence has clearly waned in recent decades, its rituals and public roles cannot simply be dismissed as quaint cultural traditions. The Order plays an important part in the maintenance of cultural unionism as a political form (Porter, 1996). The Order's traditions enable expression of its political role. For example its speeches on 12 July, the climax of the marching season, have a religious and political content, the latter once supportive of the *status quo* but now increasingly emphasizing the perceived marginalization of the Order and the form of Protestant unionism it represents.

The cultural-pluralist approach does not dwell on the original reasons for societal division. In a withering indictment of existing writing on Northern Ireland, Miller (1998) asks why colonial explanations of the problem have slipped from view. Instead of serious political analyses of why the province has been a repository of sectarian conflict since the day of its inception, academics have acted as cheerleaders for their own causes, their writing thinly cloaked in academic objectivity. The neutrality of community-relations approaches should also be questioned. The problem is reduced to one of two communities that are unable to coexist peacefully, and there is no reference to the political approaches and denial of political rights that sustain division.

Are intercommunity relations getting better?

Normalization of society in Northern Ireland was expected to accompany the dismantling of security arrangements, post-ceasefire. There are various components of the evaluation of intercommunity relations, incorporating sociological and spatial factors. During the immediate pre- and post-GFA periods there were highly visible sectarian problems. Controversy over the routes of Orange Order parades in Portadown was not new, having flared in the mid 1980s (Bryan, 2002). In the mid 1990s the controversy took a vicious form, as until 1997 the Orange Order was allowed to proceed along its traditional route through a nationalist area. The decisions in 1995 and 1996 to allow the parade to go ahead were taken in the wake of loyalist rioting, but produced nationalist violence in response. From 1997 to 2000, the restriction upon the Order's march led to loyalist rioting and blockades.

As Sinn Fein's political agenda shifted from armed overthrow of the state to cultural forms of resistance the controversy over Orange parades increased. This was fostered by residents' groups in nationalist areas supportive of Sinn Fein, and then spread to the wider nationalist community. The outcome was that the idea of Orange parades became unacceptable in most nationalist areas, whilst the violence associated with the disputes further distanced the Order from Northern Ireland's political and business classes. The days when the 12 July processions could be described as 'rituals of state' had long disappeared (ibid., p. 97).

Whilst the parades issue festered, albeit without the grandstanding of the 1990s, there appeared to be a diminution of sectarianism in the sporting arena. A concerted campaign to rid sport of sectarianism was evident from the mid-1990s onwards. The 'Rule 21' ban on membership of the Gaelic Athletic Association (GAA) by British security forces was lifted. Previously, the ban was portrayed by supporters as representing the 'purity of gaelic games' (Cronin, 1996, p. 16). The sardonic references to the Armagh versus Tyrone GAA all-Ireland final in 2003 as the first 'all-British final' illuminated the limits of identity politics. A majority in those counties (and Fermanagh could safely be added) would not see themselves as British, owe no allegiance to Westminster, and are denied the normal political rights accruing to national identity.

There was also a thawing of tension among Irish League soccer supporters, to such an extent that in 1998, the Catholic-supported Cliftonville team in North Belfast was allowed to stage home matches against Protestant-supported Linfield for the first time since the 1970s. Sinn Fein leaders joined unionist politicians and the chief constable of the RUC at Lansdowne Road, Dublin, to support Ulster in the Rugby Union European Cup final. Support for English premiership soccer teams continues to transcend the sectarian divide. However sporting divisions according to religious persuasion remain. Widespread allegiance to Celtic (Catholic-supported) or Rangers (Protestant-supported) is an example of this. The Northern Ireland soccer team does not command the loyalty of many Catholics, whose team allegiances lie predominantly in the Republic of Ireland. The Northern Ireland soccer captain, Neil Lennon, quit the team after being jeered at by the team's Protestant supporters and later received a death threat, a consequence of Lennon being a Lurgan Catholic playing for Celtic.

Societal sectarianism remains a difficult problem to address. Institutional antisectarian measures may have a trickle-down effect, but this effect is uncertain. Educational divisions and increased residential segregation limit opportunities to meet members of the other community and the development of meaningful contacts is difficult. Moreover mixed marriages are stigmatized. Asked whether it would matter if one of their close relatives were to marry someone of a different religion, only 40 per cent said they would not mind, compared with 54 per cent who said it would matter, either a lot (21 per cent) or a little (33 per cent). Nearly twice as many Protestants said it would matter a lot (Northern Ireland Life and Times Survey, 2001).

The evidence on whether sectarianism has increased or diminished is mixed. The measurements of whether intercommunity relations are improving take a number of forms. Electoral evidence, as discussed in earlier chapters, shows that, despite a brief flurry of optimism about cross-community pro-GFA voting in the 1998 Assembly election, communal voting patterns remain largely intact. Other measurements, discussed below, cover the extent of residential segregation and the proliferation of peace and conflict-resolution organizations. The starting point, though, is people's perception of whether sectarianism has diminished or flourished since the GFA.

The Provisional IRA and loyalist paramilitary ceasefires of 1994 prompted a surge of optimism about intercommunity relations. In 1995 over 60 per cent of the population believed that relations between Protestants and Catholics were better than five years earlier and almost 80 per cent believed that intercommunity relations would be better in five years' time (Hughes *et al.*, 2002). This enthusiasm subsided to the point where the impact of the GFA on intercommunity relations was seen as broadly neutral, although some remained optimistic. By 2001 only one third of the population believed that relations between Protestants and Catholics would be better in five years' time, although only 10 per cent feared a worsening (Northern Ireland Life and Times Survey, 2001, www.ark.ac.uk/nilt/2001/Community_ Relations). The largest percentage (45 per cent) felt that relations had remained about the same. There was little difference between Protestants and Catholics in this regard, although Protestants (at 15 per cent) were more pessimistic than Catholics (a mere 5 per cent) (ibid.). Retrospective views followed similar patterns, with almost half of Protestants and Catholics believing that intercommunity relations had not changed over the last five years. Among the remainder, Protestants were split almost equally between 'got better' and 'got worse' verdicts, whereas more Catholics detected an improvement in relations (33 per cent) than a worsening (13 per cent) (ibid.).

The differences between Protestant and Catholic perceptions of the GFA, although not huge, were marked and perhaps reflected the early impact of the deal. In 2001, although almost half of Protestants felt they were being treated the same as five years earlier (and 8 per cent felt they were being treated better), 39 per cent said they were being treated worse (ibid.). Changes to policing, the release of (mainly republican) prisoners, restrictions on Orange Order parades and the arrival of nationalist-demanded human rights and equality commissions made a section of the Protestant community feel beleaguered and this neutralized the impact of the unionist constitutional victory. As Hughes *et al.* (2002, p. 10, emphasis in original) note, 'Protestants seem to see a skewed rather than a *pluralist* agenda at work'. The legacy of the conflict also polarized attitudes. One third of Northern Ireland's population claimed to be, in some form or other, a victim of the conflict (Cairns *et al.*, 2003). Protestants tended to be less favourably disposed than Catholics to the idea of intergroup forgiveness, but in general those living in areas of high violence tended to be the most unforgiving (ibid.).

The spatial division of the population appears to have increased in parts of Northern Ireland. Nonetheless the expansion of religiously mixed middle-class areas, increased mobility between areas and the sharing of space in city centres, particularly in Belfast, serve to rebut any one-dimensional picture of Northern Ireland as a region dominated by territorial division. Shared spaces and similar leisure patterns, irrespective of religious background, are now apparent. However the consolidation of territorial division that followed the widespread removal of people to single-religion areas, particularly in the early years of the Troubles, has yet to be reversed. In 2001, 8 per cent of the population said that intimidation had forced them to relocate, and 23 per cent claimed that a family member or close friend had had to move for the same reason (ibid.). The considerable population displacements that occurred during the conflict might not be permanent. Two thirds of the population would prefer to live in a mixed-religion neighbourhood, although one-quarter of Catholics and almost one third of Protestants would prefer to live in a neighbourhood comprising only people of their religion (Northern Ireland Life and Times Survey, 2001, www.ark.ac.uk/nilt/2001/Community_Relations).

The development of a shared, rejuvenated Belfast city centre has been juxtaposed with a seeming growth of sectarianism in interface areas, as evidenced by the increase in the number (to 22) and size of 'peace walls', which physically separate some Protestant and Catholic areas. Shirlow (2003) highlights a discourse stressing the permanence of intercommunity hostilities in such areas, exacerbated by intra-community disapproval of those who breach the 'normal' pattern of segregation. The peace walls reflect and maintain sectarian opposition. Their construction took place during a conflict in which 70 per cent of deaths occurred within 500 metres of an interface (ibid.). A radical approach would be to adopt the 'coercive freedom' idea and remove the walls, thus forcing the oppositional communities to live side by side without barriers. This idea was once advocated by the former Conservative Party's shadow Northern Ireland secretary, Quentin Davies. Another measure, already adopted in some areas, would be to remove murals depicting exclusivity or tribalism. The argument is that with the ideological and physical conflict over, peace walls no longer serve a purpose. Indeed residential segregation, peace walls and murals could be described as good for tourism, but bad for society.

The main purpose of the walls was to hinder the escape of attackers, but the isolation of communities behind walls can now increase their vulnerability, providing an easy mode of identification and targeting by rival communities. Instead of providing security, the walls per-petuate an oppositional stance in respect of the other community and inhibit the process of accommodation. Enclaving also reinforces people's sense of difference from the other community, whatever the extent of socioeconomic similarity. Shirlow (2003) notes that almost half of men aged 35–65 in Ardoyne, the most notorious interface area, are former Republican prisoners. However there is scant prospect of the vast majority of these former Provisional IRA members ever returning to war. Even during the conflict the walls were of limited value in preventing attacks on rival areas, as shown by the attempt to wipe out the leadership of the UFF on the Shankill in 1993, an operation in which nine civilians died.

The walls do assist the policing of areas by the security forces, but their main purpose appears to be psychological, providing a sense of security. As such the residents of interface areas such as Short Strand and Ardoyne would resist removal of the walls. Shirlow's (2003) study found that 86 per cent of respondents would not enter an area dominated by a rival sectarian group, a decision that, whilst understandable, reinforced the idea of victimhood and distorted normal consumption and mobility expectations. Only those of pensionable age were likely to engage in normal relations with the other community, whilst those of working age tended to be hostile to the people of the rival area and suspicious of cross-community initiatives.

Contrary to expectations, the removal of the walls became more difficult in the years immediately after the signing of the Good Friday Agreement, as violence increased and changed in nature. After 1998, the violence in interface areas was largely sectarian, rather than armed struggle against crown forces or suspected republicans. By 2002 the violence appeared to be waning, but the previous four years had seen a steady rise in the number of bombings and shootings, most of which were sectarian. The majority of incidents were loyalist attacks on or protests against nationalists in interface areas. Undoubtedly the most publicized of these incidents was the Holy Cross School dispute in 2001, when loyalists protested against parents taking their children to a Catholic school in a loyalist area of Upper Ardoyne. Of course the normalization of the security situation and the concomitant relaxation of tension may permeate even interface areas, including those which are most sectarian in tone, such as Ardoyne.

Cross-community groups work against a backdrop of static or even increased residential segregation. A majority of Catholics and Protestants identify their community as either mainly or exclusively single religion (Northern Ireland Life and Times Survey, 2001; Brown and MacGinty, 2003). Territory is often marked by flags, painted kerbstones and murals. However, only a minority of the other community find this intimidating and such displays 'have become enmeshed in the local tourist industry' (Brown and MacGinty, 2003, p. 96). The peace process produced a softening of the subjects of murals, with a move, initiated in nationalist areas, away from paramilitary displays and towards political and cultural messages. Murals in nationalist areas reflect the 'parity of esteem', cultural equality and rights-based approaches of the GFA. There are celebrations of Gaelic culture and language, and demands for rights and justice. There are few political murals demanding British withdrawal from Northern Ireland. Instead most political murals are commemorative, celebrating, for example, the hunger strikes of the early 1980s. Vannais (2001) suggests that modern murals in nationalist areas reflect republicans' complacency about political progress. A demand for equality and respect for Sinn Fein's political mandate has replaced the demand for reunification. Loyalist murals reflect fears of cultural and political swamping, but are arguably less sectarian than the old-style 'King Billy' murals, which are rare nowadays.

Civil society and conflict amelioration

There is no shortage of collective voluntary groups in Northern Ireland. In 2001 the number of such organizations was estimated at 5500 (Knox, 2001), 11 times higher than the estimated number of community groups and associations in existence in 1975 (Burrell and Murie, 1980). The increased stress on identity as a means of healing Northern Ireland's problems has spawned a plethora of central bodies designed to improve community relations. Amid the mass of acronyms an entire industry has developed, with the voluntary reconciliation efforts by those at the bottom being consolidated by full-time coordinating bodies at the centre (often staffed by recruits from the middle classes). The Central Community Relations Unit (CCRU) was established in 1987 as part of the Northern Ireland Civil Service (NICS) Central Secretariat. Since 1990 the CCRU has funded the Community Relations Council (CRC), which deals with the voluntary sector's peace and conflict resolution groups. The CRC's aims are to assist understanding of diversity, promote equality and encourage cross-community contact. It has been aided in the celebration of diversity by the Cultural Traditions Group, which was also established in 1990 and is designed to promote cross-community discussion and acceptance by one community of the activities of the other. During the early 1990s the CRC developed its programmes in partnership with local councils; Sinn Fein, as the representative of an unacceptable tradition of violent anticolonialism, was excluded from participation. If Sinn Fein was unimpressed by the CRC, so too was a future first minister of Northern Ireland, who, whilst acknowledging the valuable work being done on community relations, invited a Northern Ireland minister to 'agree with me that we must not fall into the trap of thinking that community relations programmes can solve the problems in Northern Ireland', adding that 'the best thing that can be done to improve community relations is to defeat terrorism' (David Trimble, House of Commons, oral question on community relations, 11 July 1991, quoted in Knox and Hughes, 1995, pp. 51–2).

The community relations industry mushroomed elsewhere in the United Kingdom, although not at the same rate. During the late 1960s the Labour government began to look closely at how to improve race relations via new institutional mechanisms. In Northern Ireland, reconciliation groups have existed since 1964. Often initially grounded in ecumenical projects, groups sometimes arose after particular atrocities and developed around a range of causes, before their placement under the broad CRC umbrella during the 1990s. Whilst the Civic Forum was designed to bring together representatives of civil society in a more formal institutional setting, voluntary organizations had for some years previously attempted to ameliorate the conflict. The development of peace groups and conflict resolution organizations has been a feature of peace processes elsewhere, including South Africa and the Middle East. In Northern Ireland, many of these organizations comprise former members of paramilitary groups and some have emerged from paramilitary organizations (Cochrane, 2001). This brings advantages that such groups are likely to carry sections of the working class, and that participants understand the rawness (and likely futility) of conflict.

As 'normal' politics have never existed in Northern Ireland it is natural that community organizations have formed on the basis of self-help. There have been two main problems with sustaining conflict resolution groups. The first is a practical one: developing sufficient cross-community contacts to make the group appear non-sectarian and afford it a genuine prospect of ameliorating the conflict from below. The second problem is ideological, in that certain groups tend to overlook the reasons behind the conflict and instead address the symptoms of the problem. Hence they tend to approach political violence as something to be treated, rather than dealing with the broader issues that underpin the problem, which admittedly are much more difficult to tackle. During the 1970s the Peace People enjoyed considerable support across the political divide, but the movement subsequently faded away because, for fear of being divisive, it offered no long-term remedy for the conflict, beyond a general call for peace.

Cochrane (2001) distinguishes between peace groups conditioned by behavioural analysis, which attempt to break down division and misunderstanding by facilitating cross-community contact, and structural groups, which accept that there is a conflict of national identity and seek to diminish that conflict. Conflict resolution groups informed by behavioural analysis assume that misunderstanding is the basis for conflict, despite the fact that paramilitaries are often highly knowledgeable about the other side. The outlook of such groups has been described by the former chairman of the Cultural Traditions Group, Maurice Hayes (quoted in O'Reilly, 2002, p. 172): 'Underlying most of these conflicts is a failure of communication, a lack of empathy and understanding which results in stereotyping and scapegoating, and a basic lack of trust without which no social, political or other contract is conceivable.'

There are flaws in this argument First, if the conflict had been about a 'failure of communication' between communities it would have taken on much more of the character of a civil war. Whilst the conflict occasionally moved towards this, for example in 1975 and 1993, it mainly involved the IRA taking on crown forces, rather than being republican versus unionist or Catholic versus Protestant. Secondly, stereotyping of the other community existed but this was not the main basis of conflict. For example, republicans had a jaundiced view of Orangemen as deluded Irishmen or slaves of British imperial masters, but if Orangemen were attacked it was because they were members of the security services, not because they were members of the Order. For the IRA the conflict was nothing to do with a 'failure of communication', but was based on a reading of history that, simply expressed, insisted that Ireland had been colonized, partitioned against the expressed will of the majority of the Irish people and, with the remaining British section being held by force of arms, denied Irish national sovereignty. Similarly loyalist violence occurred not because of a lack of understanding of the other community, but because it wanted to deter that community from supporting the IRA.

Throughout the conflict republicans and loyalists were aware of the history of the other side, but wished to impose their constitutional setting as the framework within which cultural diversity (guaranteed in the policy documents and public utterances of republicans and loyalists) could be accommodated. Yet as Gilligan (2002, p. 9) puts it, the 'diagnosis found in community relations policy is that there is communal antagonism in Northern Ireland because its citizens suffer from a cultural deficit'. The diversion of the political contest into the cultural sphere is part of a broader diminution of human agency, in which it has become more difficult for individuals to act outside conditioning ideological or social structures. Conflict resolution groups are confronted with the problem of coalition building across communities with different identities and different interpretations of the conflict. In particular shared prison experiences have helped to develop mutual understanding, if not outright acceptance, of rival viewpoints, an important factor in managing conflict and diverting it into peaceful alternatives.

Conflict resolution from below is the preferred approach of those who see social transformation, rather than elite-level consociation, as the way forward for Northern Ireland. Yet as Cochrane (2001) notes, actors engaged in social transformation via informal conflict resolution networks and groups support the consociational deal that is the Good Friday Agreement. Although the GFA was brokered by political elites, the wide remit of the voluntary sector in Northern Ireland, already evident pre-GFA, meant that policy makers had for some years taken account of its ideas to an unusual extent (Acheson and Williamson, 1995).

Social transformationists and consociationists share the assumption that societal transformation must occur within existing territorial borders, rather than encouraging the transformative possibilities of the erosion of borders (although consociationists might highlight the 'withering of the border' element of the GFA). Both groups can reasonably point to the manner in which Northern Ireland has changed in recent years as indicative that Northern Ireland is reformable. Transformation is confined to the social sphere; in constitutional terms, transformationists and consociationists are prepared to accept the constitutional *status quo*. Conflict resolution groups are more concerned with the immediacies of conflict reduction and peaceful coexistence than with wider political questions of national sovereignty and self-determination.

Conclusion

Stress on identity and cultural pluralism has been a key component of the peace and political processes. Rival British and Irish identities were acknowledged in the GFA, although the former have received preferential treatment in terms of the political manifestation of that identity by being in a polity under near-exclusive British jurisdiction. Hence equality of identity cannot be fully achieved as political parity has not been achieved. Parity of esteem is possible, such an outcome relying on the diversion of political and ideological contests of sovereignty into the spheres of culture, identity and reconciliation.

Whilst sectarian discrimination has been largely eradicated in Northern Ireland, sectarianism continues to reflect and maintain divisions in civil society. The claim that consociational political systems heighten sectarianism is superficially appealing but ultimately unconvincing, given the pre-existence of sectarianism under, variously, unionist hegemony, failed power sharing, intergovernmentalism and direct rule. The claim that sectarianism has increased is also unconvincing in aggregate terms. It is true that residential segregation has increased, although shared territory, such as Belfast city centre, has also grown. It is also true that purely sectarian, as opposed to political, violence increased after the paramilitary ceasefires, although the number of killings has been substantially lower than in the 1970s and 1980s, if one regards loyalist killings during that era as sectarian (given the random killing of Catholics, this would be justified). Furthermore the sense of there being a community divide is still strong, as indicated by the low rate of mixed marriages. However other indicators suggest that society is less sectarian. Catholics are no longer barred from most workplaces, enter university in large numbers, have moved into the middle classes, live in desirable parts of Northern Ireland, are more likely to meet or be educated with non-Catholics and often enjoy cordial relations with Protestants. This does not merely reflect the formal abolition of sectarian discrimination; it also suggests that sectarianism is waning.

The reasons why sectarianism persists can be divided into two broad groups; one behavioural, the other structural. The first emphasizes the value of communal belonging, the associated sense of identity and fear of the other. The second concerns political alignments, with an obvious link between the political divide and religious affiliation. Social transformationists argue that consolidation of this divide via consociationalism is undermining attempts at the local level by conflict resolution groups to improve intercommunity relations. Consociationists argue that political structures reflect a pre-existing political divide that requires careful management. Amid the dialogue of the deaf, the monument to the maintenance of division – a territorial border based on ethno-majoritarianism – remains largely uncriticized.

10

A New Policing Service?

The changes to policing in Northern Ireland were amongst the most contentious issues arising from the Good Friday Agreement. The agreement established an Independent Commission on Policing, chaired by the former Conservative Party chairman and governor of Hong Kong, Chris Patten. After taking exhaustive soundings across the community, the commission recommended a radical reform of policing (Independent Commission on Policing, 1999). The Patten Report led to the replacement of the Royal Ulster Constabulary by the Police Service of Northern Ireland (PSNI), plus changes to the accountability, composition, culture and ethos of policing in Northern Ireland.

Communal divisions on policing

Policing had long been a factor in communal division. Many nationalists perceived the RUC as illegitimate, and although criticism of the RUC was often scorned by the force's supporters as republican propaganda, disquiet was also evident in the nationalist community. Unionists remained supportive of the RUC and deemed that the changes to policing, many of which were recommended in the Patten Report, were unnecessary. Whilst partisan unionists saw the RUC as their police, other unionists regarded the RUC as a police service for all (McGarry and O'Leary, 1999).

Nationalists appeared to have good reason for concern; indeed disquiet over the actions of the RUC was evident within the British Government (*Guardian*, 1 January 2000). Discrimination against Catholics and partisan policing was a primary element of the conflict. The allegation that the RUC had ill-treated suspects during the 1970s had been confirmed by the European Court of Human Rights. Nationalists had been alienated in the 1980s when it was alleged that a 'shoot to kill' policy had been adopted for suspected republican paramilitaries. The investigating officer seconded from the Greater Manchester Police, John Stalker, was removed from the inquiry into these allegations without explanation. The Stevens Enquiry (www.met.police.uk/commissioner/MP.Stevens-Enquiry3) made clear the extent of collusion between the RUC and loyalist paramilitaries. It acknowledged the existence of state-sponsored killings, mainly by the British Army and agents handled by the police, the army's operations being conducted through its Force Research Unit. The Stevens Report highlighted the involvement of agents of the security forces in killings, the withholding of intelligence and evidence, obstruction of his enquiry team, the absence of accountability and a failure to keep records. As a consequence innocent people had been murdered or seriously injured and a government minister [Douglas Hogg] was compromised in the House of Commons by an RUC briefing suggesting that solicitors were unduly sympathetic to the IRA. The ministerial claim was followed by the murder of the Belfast solicitor Pat Finucane in 1989, a killing that, along with the murder of Brian Lambert, was a product of collusion and left the killers seemingly immune from prosecution. Similar allegations were made in respect of the killing of Catholic solicitor Rosemary Nelson in 2000 (*Sunday Independent*, 20 January 2002).

Details of the names and addresses of suspected IRA members were passed by the RUC and British Army to loyalist paramilitaries. Until 2002 the US government banned the RUC from training alongside FBI officers because of the human rights record of the Northern Ireland force. Despite this catalogue of accusations, no RUC officer served a jail sentence for political violence during the conflict. In evidence to the Opsahl Commission during the 1990s, it was pointed out that of 1019 citizens' allegations of assault by the RUC between 1988 and 1991, none were upheld, a 'nil rate of substantiation [which] frankly beggars belief', according to the future Northern Ireland human rights commissioner, Brice Dickson (Pollak, 1993). Given that the investigation of such matters was undertaken by the police themselves, it is doubtful that the acquittal rate beggared belief among a sceptical Catholic community (Hamilton and Moore, 1995). Even modest criticism from otherwise supportive sources was ignored. When two members of the Police Authority objected in 1996 to the flying of the Union flag on RUC stations on unionist holidays and criticized the swearing of an oath of allegiance to the queen, they were removed from the authority (McGarry and O'Leary, 1999).

The International Crime Victimization Survey (established under the terms of the Good Friday Agreement) found that fewer than one quarter of the population were dissatisfied with the RUC. However there was a large difference between Protestants and Catholics on this question: over 80 per cent of Protestants were satisfied, compared with fewer than 50 per cent of nationalists. Many unionists claimed that opposition to the RUC was primarily the result of republican terrorist intimidation. The Northern Ireland Affairs Select Committee argued that 'the major reason preventing young Roman Catholics coming forward to join the RUC is the fear of violence which would be offered towards them and to members of their family' (Northern Ireland Affairs Committee, 1998, para. 35).

Clearly the issue of policing remained divisive. The SDLP called for reforms, illustrating that moderate nationalists as well as staunch republicans were dissatisfied with the situation. Nationalists believed that drastic changes would be needed to create an accountable police service. Whilst 94 per cent of SDLP members called for radical reform of the RUC, Sinn Fein demanded complete disbandment. Sinn Fein viewed the RUC as sectarian, a partisan police force that was instrumental in maintaining unionist domination and a colonial tool of British rule in Ireland.

The RUC's under-recruitment of Catholics was blamed on intimidation by the IRA, although given that the IRA had often lain dormant since the foundation of Northern Ireland, the argument was unpersuasive. Catholic resistance to joining the RUC pre-1970 was essentially voluntary, except perhaps in 1956–62, although IRA activity undoubtedly acted as a deterrent from then onwards. This deterrence has declined and in the first year of the Provisional IRA ceasefire in the mid 1990s, 16.5 per cent of new recruits were Catholic. This was a substantial increase, although still less than half the percentage who would have been recruited if the proportion of Catholic applicants had been in line with the population balance (Bew and Gillespie, 1996). In 1998 Catholics amounted to a mere 8.3 per cent of the force, which was 88.3 per cent Protestant (Independent Commission on Policing, 1999, p. 82).

Defenders of the RUC argued that normal liberal policing techniques were not suitable for combating a guerrilla war. Unionists also argued that the demand for reform was simply an attempt to demoralize the RUC before resumption of the republican military campaign. The UUP leader, David Trimble, pointed to the findings of the House of Commons Select Committee on Northern Ireland Affairs, which stated that 'there is no clear reason to make a special case of the RUC by changing its name' (Tonge, 2002, p. 88; see also *The Times*, 27 August 1999). Members of the DUP claimed that any attempt to reform the RUC would be an insult to the 303 police officers who had died as a result of violence during the previous 30 years.

Sinn Fein mobilized its supporters behind the 'Disband the RUC' slogan, the call for disbandment being exemplified by the comment by one of its assembly members, Barry McElduff: 'I look forward to the RUC being consigned to the dustbin of history, just like the B Specials before them' (*Irish News*, 6 September 1999). Conversely the 'Friends of the RUC' placed full-page advertisements in sympathetic newspapers, headed: 'Their Service. Their Sacrifice. Our Duty-Save the RUC'. This campaign found sympathy among British Conservatives and the *Daily Telegraph* ran a strong campaign in defence of the force, including photographs of all officers who had lost their lives.

The Patten proposals

The Patten Commission had as its primary aim the establishment of a police force that would win the support of the entire community. It recognized that there was a clear difference in attitude towards the RUC between nationalists and unionists, and that 'perceptions and experience of policing can differ greatly between the two communities' (Independent Commission on Policing, 1999, p. 13). It also recognized the lack of accountability, stating that this had not been achieved in terms of community legitimacy, support or authority (ibid., p. 22). Past arrangements and structures had not held the police sufficiently accountable and had created a defensive and cautious atmosphere. The RUC was not responsible to the local community and the forums of local liaison, the Community and Police Liaison Committees, had serious weaknesses, with only 29 per cent of the population being aware of their existence (ibid., p. 34). The RUC was 'overwhelmingly Protestant and male' but the gender issue was common to all police forces and therefore, unlike the religious imbalance, would not be the subject of affirmative action (ibid., pp. 81–2). Change would be governed by fairness and pragmatism: a new police force needed to 'include appropriately large numbers of nationalists, including republicans, if it is to be fully effective' (ibid., p. 81). Meanwhile the size of the force would be cut in line with the reduced security threat.

To bring about redress, a wide variety of changes were recommended. The force should be renamed, and the newly constituted force should not be overly associated with symbols of Britishness; for example it should fly its own flag above its buildings, rather than the Union flag. Accountability could be improved by establishing a new Policing Board to replace the toothless Police Authority, and by replacing the Police Liaison Committees by District Policing Partnership Boards. The force should be reduced in size from 13 000 to 7 500, and should strive to reflect the religious balance in the community by recruiting on a 50–50 Catholic–Protestant basis. Special branch, the most controversial element of the RUC, should be integrated into the mainstream service, rather than existing as a 'force within a force'. An oath of commitment to human rights should be sworn by members of the force and membership of organizations such as the Orange Order should be declared.

The highlighting of the RUC's lack of accountability was one of the core features of the Patten Report. It argued for transformation of the closed, defensive force into an open and transparent organization. It suggested that the Policing Board should oversee a change in ethos and monitor recruitment, training, performance and satisfaction levels. The board, comprising ten representatives of the parties in the Northern Ireland Executive (but not holders of ministerial offices) and nine members of other organizations should hold the chief constable and the police service publicly to account. All information should be available to the public at any time, unless it was in the public interest (rather than as previously alleged, the police interest) to withhold certain information. Nationalists had boycotted the Police Authority and Police Liaison Committees, which were perceived as pro-unionist and pro-RUC, whereas Patten aimed to create impartial mechanisms of accountability.

The proposed District Policing Partnership Boards (DPPBs) would be local guarantors of accountability. The majority of members would be drawn from district councils, with the remaining members being selected by the council, with the agreement of the Policing Board. The DPPBs would act as consultative forums, allowing greater explanation of police activities. They would represent the consumer, voice concerns and monitor the performance of the police service at the local level. However unionists feared that the boards would give too much influence to Sinn Fein representatives in nationalist areas dominated by the party. Because of the size of the city council, four DPPBs would be established in Belfast. Clearly Sinn Fein would have considerable representation on the West Belfast DPPB. This might explain Patten's caution when recommending that there should be only a slight majority of elected representatives on the boards and his insistence that the Policing Board should 'vet' the council's other nominations for membership. The report went on to recommend the introduction of community policing of a rather different kind than that undertaken, by paramilitaries as a consequence of the rejection of the RUC in working-class areas. Officers should patrol on foot where appropriate and should serve at least three years in the same neighbourhood. Police stations should be made more accessible and the army's role continually reduced.

The Police Ombudsman, created prior to the report but strongly backed by Patten, should coordinate relations between the Policing Board and the police. Independent scrutiny should also be conducted by a commissioner for covert law enforcement. This should be a senior judicial figure, who should be given the power to inspect the police and their agencies. Patten also proposed that measures be taken to change the bureaucratic style of management in the RUC. Civilians should be employed for jobs that did not require specialist police knowledge, and district commanders should be given greater authority. Nationalists should be able to identify with the name and symbols of the police service. The RUC should be renamed the Police Service of Northern Ireland (originally Patten suggested the Northern Ireland Police Service, but the acronym was unfortunate). The changes to the symbols should include a politically neutral emblem, for example the St Patrick's Cross surrounded by the scales of justice, a harp, a torch, a laurel leaf, a shamrock and a crown. This emblem would appear on the cap badge and the police flag, the only standard to be flown on a police building in Northern Ireland. The chair of the Policing Board, Desmond Rea, described the proposed emblem as 'respectful of diversity, inclusiveness and parity' (*Daily Telegraph*, 6 April 2002).

The reduction in size of the RUC was scheduled to take place amid a more peaceful backdrop, and the full-time reserve, comprising 2900 members, should be disbanded. The problem with this proposal was that normal crime was likely to increase substantially as the war subsided. The punishment beatings and shootings meted out by paramilitary groups were widely condemned by human rights groups, but far less so by the victims of crime in certain communities, where there was a perception among some that such activities were brutal but functional. As Patten stated: 'Non-terrorist crime in Northern Ireland is at relatively low levels compared with the rest of the United Kingdom. Many people have expressed to us the fear that crime levels may increase in the future – a perverse sort of "peace dividend" ' (Independent Commission on Policing, 1999, p. 76). Indeed crime did rise by 28 per cent in the first year after the GFA (Royal Ulster Constabulary 1999). The growth in criminality, which would affect a greater proportion of society, would inhibit the plan to reduce the size of the force as political violence subsided. There were sardonic mutterings among those newly afflicted by crime about the 'price of peace', with crime soaring to levels elsewhere in the United Kingdom.

Responses to the Patten Report

Prime Minister Blair called the report a 'good piece of work' and accepted its findings. However, as anticipated, it was strongly condemned by many unionists, and instead of a consensual new start to policing the report and its proposals became part of a post-GFA bargaining process between the UUP and Sinn Fein. The UUP leader described the Patten Commission's work as 'the shoddiest official committee report ... seen in thirty years of study of such reports' (UUP, 1999, p. 2). Trimble argued that there were 'proposals in the report which if implemented in Northern Ireland would lead to corruption of policing and a corruption of the legal system' (*Irish News*, 6 September 1999). As the UUP emphasized, all parties accepted as legitimate Northern Ireland's place in the United Kingdom under the Good Friday Agreement. This acceptance of British sovereignty meant that it would be 'normal and reasonable' for the police force to display symbols that expressed the legitimacy of this arrangement. After all, the new police force would still be under British authority. Unionists objected to what they saw as a lack of sensitivity to RUC victims of the conflict and were hostile to the proposed changes to the force's name and badge. The UUP argued that the RUC's badge of crown and harp already recognized both traditions. The party also objected to the proposal to cease flying the

Union flag on police buildings, given Northern Ireland's constitutional position in the UK, and to what it saw as the discrimination of affirmative action, in which better qualified candidates of the 'wrong' denomination would be rejected in order to maintain 50 per cent Catholic recruitment. Patten, the party insisted, had overlooked the main reason (intimidation) why Catholics had not applied to join the police.

The UUP feared there would be a politicization of policing through the majority presence of elected politicians on policing boards. It also claimed that the obligation to make public an aspect of religious belief (Orange Order membership) infringed the GFA's Human Rights Act, in that the Act implied the freedom to hold private such memberships and beliefs. The Independent Commission on Policing (1999, p. 89) found that less than 1 per cent of police officers were members of the Orange Order, although an analysis of RUC victims of the conflict provides some evidence that the percentage may have been higher (McKittrick *et al.*, 1999). Eight per cent of the force declared themselves to be masons (Independent Commission on Policing, 1999, p. 89). The UUP also queried Patten's failure to recognize the success of Catholic officers in the RUC, who filled 16 per cent of senior posts. Finally the party feared the involvement of paramilitary groups in policing, under DPPBs controlled by Sinn Fein.

The Northern Ireland Assembly rejected the Patten proposals by 50 votes to 42, a futile vote of opposition given that policing remained under the control of the secretary of state. In 2000 the UUP was instructed by the Ulster Unionist Council not to re-enter the Northern Ireland Executive unless the new force retained the title RUC. Even many in the pro-GFA wing of the party were alarmed by the proposals. The award of a George Cross to the RUC did little to assuage unionists, who concentrated on the supposed unworkability of the Patten proposals. Fewer than one in five members of the Ulster Unionist Council backed the implementation of the Patten proposals. Speaking for the DUP, Ian Paisley Junior described the proposed changes as 'the mother of all concessions to the Republican movement. Its reverberations go right to the heart of sensible management and organisation of the state. They will shatter it' (quoted in *The Guardian*, 24 August 1999). The DUP was later critical that the commissioner of the *Garda Siochana*, Pat Byrne, made a speech at the ceremony launching the PSNI in April 2002.

The proposals for reform divided even the non-sectarian Alliance Party, which was officially in favour of the Patten proposals but not that for recruitment quotas on denomination. Seventy-eight per cent of its Catholic members demanded full implementation of the proposals, but only a bare majority (51 per cent) of Protestant members were in favour of the reforms (Tonge and Evans, 2001b, 113). In an appeal to critics of the plans for change, the Police Authority chairman, Pat Armstrong, called for objective consideration of the kind of police service that society in Northern Ireland needed. He stated that a fitting tribute to those police officers killed in the troubles was best achieved by putting aside politics and considering the best way forward (*Irish News*, 7 September 1999). With the GFA yet to embed, however, it was always likely that the Patten proposals would become part of the negotiating process accompanying implementation.

Amid the polemic, the SDLP welcomed the Patten Report as an integral part of the reconstitution of Northern Ireland. Ellison and Smyth (1999) argue that unionist concern about changing the name and badge of the RUC was part of a wider inability to face up to the necessity for far-reaching and fundamental change to the governance of Northern Ireland. Meanwhile Sinn Fein was prepared not only to accept the northern state but also to back a reconstituted northern police force. Whilst still calling for the disbandment of the RUC, the party elaborated plans for transitional arrangements. These included withdrawal of the RUC from nationalist areas and the establishment of an independent monitoring agency to oversee new policing responsibilities (Sinn Fein, 1998). Having once demanded an all-Ireland police force, by 2001 Sinn Fein indicated that the Patten proposals, if fully implemented, 'may be a basis for a new policing service ... in these circumstances we would not be found wanting' (Gerry Kelly, speech to the Sinn Fein *ard fheis*, September 2001.) The inference was clear: Sinn Fein would join the Policing Board after full implementation of the Patten proposals. At the party's 2003 *ard fheis*, Gerry Adams made clear that he envisaged his party joining the Police Service of Northern Ireland (PSNI), provided that implementation of the proposals proceeded. Such a decision would be ratified by a special *ard fheis*. Sinn Fein thereby confirmed the new reformist approach by a party that would formerly have supported only plans that involved the *Garda Siochana* assuming policing duties in the north. Sinn Fein's opposition to taking seats on the Policing Board had highlighted the

Table 10.1　*Public views on whether reform of the police in Northern Ireland had gone far enough, by religious denomination*

	Protestant	RC	Total
Gone too far	59	3	31
Not gone far enough	4	44	21
About right	27	38	33
Don't know/other	12	16	15

Source: Adapted from Northern Ireland Life and Times Survey (2001).

abnormality of Northern Ireland politics, with serving government ministers declining to back the state's police force.

In 2001 the SDLP decided to join the Policing Board and recommended that Catholics join the PSNI after the government indicated that a new policing bill would be introduced to implement more of the recommendations in the Patten Report (Northern Ireland Office, 2001). John Hume asked: 'How can any democrat be opposed to a police service whose governing body is drawn from the whole of the community?', whilst the deputy leader, Seamus Mallon, described the new policing proposals as a 'unique opportunity for a permanent settlement' (*The Times*, 21 August 2001). For the first time since partition a nationalist party had given its support to a police service, and as such the SDLP's move deserved the label 'historic' (*Belfast Telegraph*, 21 August 2001). The SDLP justified making this move prior to full implementation of the Patten proposals by arguing that the report had suggested that many implementation details would be undertaken by the Policing Board, so it was therefore essential to have representation on the board (Mark Durkan, leadership address to the SDLP annual conference, 2 November 2002).

It was soon clear that the changed political climate and huge reduction in violence were having an impact on Catholics' attitude towards joining the police. In 2002, 38 per cent of the 5000 applicants to the newly constituted service were Catholics, although Sinn Fein claimed that few working-class republicans were applying (*Irish News*, 2 March 2002). With the SDLP signed up to the new policing arrangements, Sinn Fein was coming under pressure from a variety of sources. For example its nationalist electoral rival was using the policing issue as a new 'respectability' demarcation line, and the Catholic Church was advocating support for the newly constituted force. Many in the

Table 10.2 *Views of the members of the main pro-GFA parties on the Patten recommendations for police reforms (per cent)*[1]

	Support changes	*Oppose changes*	*Neither*
SDLP[2]	93.6	1.1	5.3
Alliance	58.9	33.1	8.0
UUP	18.7	71.8	9.5

Notes:
[1] Figures for Sinn Fein are not available.
[2] The proposition put to the SDLP members was that the RUC should be 'radically reformed'.

nationalist electorate appeared to be prepared to back the PSNI, based on the evidence of increased Catholic applications. On Sinn Fein's other flank, republican ultras denounced the fact that fellow republicans seemed set to take a supervisory role in a six-county police service. For such republicans, the conflict had never been about getting more Catholics into the Northern Ireland police force. Any reconstituted police force would necessarily defend the statelet that republicans were supposed to challenge. In June 2002 the dissidents launched their first bomb attack on a (Catholic) member of the PSNI, and the following year targeted members of District Policing Partnerships, forcing three resignations.

Some Sinn Fein members had memories of being imprisoned by the old RUC and were hardly happy about the thought of the party joining the Policing Board. Despite the numerous policy reversals approved by Sinn Fein members over the previous decade, policing remained a sensitive issue and the PSNI raid on Sinn Fein's office at Stormont in October 2002 hardly endeared it to the party.The Jim Lochrie *cumann* in Newry, one of the few remaining hardline branches, tabled an (unsuccessful) motion at the 2003 *ard fheis* that 'no Sinn Fein representative can sit on any Policing Board or similar body while Britain has jurisdiction over the Six Counties'.

Predictably, public responses to the implementation of the recommendations in the Patten Report were divided along communal lines, as Table 10.1 shows. Even among pro-GFA parties there was considerable division over the proposed reforms (Table 10.2).

Following the creation of the PSNI there were clear signs that the public's perception of the police had improved from the old RUC days, as Table 10.3 shows. There was a rise in the percentage of people

Table 10.3   *Perceptions of the treatment of Protestants and Catholics by the RUC/PSNI (per cent)*

	1997 (RUC)			2001 (PSNI)		
	Protestant	*RC*	*Total*	*Protestant*	*RC*	*Total*
Catholics treated better	8	0	5	13	1	8
Both treated equally	69	26	51	71	55	63
Protestants treated better	15	64	35	4	35	60
Don't know/refused to answer	8	9	9	8	12	12

Sources: Adapted from Northern Ireland Life and Times Survey (2001); Police Authority for Northern Ireland (1997), p. 39.

who believed that the police treated the members of both communities equally, the figure being boosted by a substantial increase in the percentage of Catholics who took that view.

However, with over one third of Catholics still believing that the police service treated Protestants better and nearly half considering that the reforms had not gone far enough, there was still some way to go before the PSNI emerged as a normal police force. As Sinn Fein edged towards joining the Policing Board, it seemed likely that Catholic dissatisfaction would diminish. A majority of Protestants were disgruntled by the extent of policing changes, and in 2000 only a minority said they would be willing to encourage a relative to join the newly constituted police service (*Belfast Telegraph*, 2 April 2001; Dowds, 2001). In the same year less than one quarter of Catholics said they would discourage a close relative from joining, compared with one third a year earlier, a change that reflected the improved security situation and substantial reforms of policing.

Implementing the reforms: dilution and resurrection

Following talks with political parties in summer 2001 at Weston Park, the British Labour government offered a new implementation plan for the Patten proposals, which resulted in the Police (Northern Ireland) Act 2003. That a new implementation plan was deemed necessary was a tacit criticism of the manner in which the original proposals had been diluted by the then secretary of state for Northern Ireland, Peter

Mandelson, in the Police Act 2000. Sinn Fein had not been alone in arguing that the proposals had been watered down in the ensuing legislation, as even the SDLP had criticized the minimalism of the 2000 Act and one member of the Patten Commission, Clifford Shearing, had accused Mandelson of 'gutting' the recommendations (*Guardian*, 14 November 2000). The government's case had been strengthened, however, by backing from Patten for the original legislative proposals (*Belfast Telegraph*, 28 November 2000). O'Leary (2001) attributes the watering down of the Patten proposals to the involvement of Northern Ireland Office officials in drafting the legislation, assisted by a compliant secretary of state. Even by his previously high standards, the secretary of state's implementation plan of June 2000 had been a masterpiece of Mandelsonian spin (Northern Ireland Office, 2000). The plan had claimed that virtually all of Patten's recommendations had been 'accepted', 'accepted in principle', or 'accepted with amendments'. This blithely overlooked the manner in which the amendments had altered the tone of the proposals.

Aware that the Patten Report could not be sidelined in its entirety, the UUP had advocated cherry-picking from the outset, a process in which the Northern Ireland Office had been compliant (UUP, 1999). The DPPBs would have the word 'Board' omitted from their title and their function would be purely consultative rather than executive (ibid., p. 14). This had fundamentally downgraded their role as effective scrutineers of policing. Mandelson had rejected Patten's proposal to allow district police partnerships to buy additional policing services as this could lead to paramilitary organizations becoming involved. The Northern Ireland secretary had also planned to review the recruitment process every three years, although initially it would remain on a 50–50 Catholic–Protestant basis.

The revised implementation plan issued by the British government in August 2001 promised to 'reflect more fully the Patten recommendations' and led to a new Police Act (www.irl-news.com., 2 August 2001). It dealt with issues that could have been addressed the first time round, such as plans to disband the full-time and part-time police reserve forces, replace the Gough interrogation centre with normal police station custody suites and abolish the use of plastic bullets, save for exceptional circumstances. To assuage unionists the British government promised that a police fund would be established to assist the families of RUC officers killed in the conflict, and it offered to create an RUC George Cross Foundation to commemorate the sacrifices and achievements of the old force. New investigations into allegations of collusion in specific killings, including cooperation between the Provisional IRA and members of the *Garda Siochana*, were also promised, to be chaired by a judge from outside Britain and Ireland. Even the revised implementation plan, though it was enough to satisfy the SDLP, left the new police service somewhat short of Patten's vision. The main changes are outlined in Table 10.4.

The many changes to the police service were strengthened by the 2003 Act. New accountability procedures were introduced. The Special Branch and Crime Branch were amalgamated into a single Crime Department, headed by an assistant chief constable. The Policing Board commissioned a study of the relationship between the Special Branch and the Crime Branch. Although there was fear that the 'Son of Special Branch' would function as a distinct unit within the police,

Table 10.4   *An implementation deficit? The Patten Report and implementation of its proposals, 1999–2001*

Proposal	Implementation via the 2000 Police Act and 2001 Implementation Plan
New oath to be sworn by all officers	Oath sworn only by new recruits
Policing Board to oversee policing	Secretary of state and chief constable invested with the power to override recommendations
District Policing Boards to oversee local policing	District commanders only partially accountable; convicted former paramilitaries ineligible for places on boards; chief constable to determine number and territorial size of bodies; partnerships not boards
Ombudsman to have power of enquiry	Scope for retrospective investigations limited
Police officers to wear name badges	Not applicable during riots
Equal recruitment of Protestants/ Others and Catholics	For three years in the first instance, secretary of state to decide thereafter
Register of society memberships to be held by police service and ombudsman	Chief Constable to hold files, with no role for the ombudsman
Change of name of police force	RUC retained in title deeds

unlike its predecessor it did not become a 'force within a force' and the perception of it being the 'political police' was at least diminished. The aim was to bring intelligence processes in Northern Ireland into line with the national intelligence model. Recruitment on a 50–50 Protestant–Catholic basis continued, despite a legal challenge.

Given that the Patten Report contained 175 recommendations and most of these had been implemented by 2002, the pace of change could be said to be rapid. Reduction of the size of the force began, despite an overt campaign by senior police officers against this move. The assistant chief constable, Colin Cramphorn, cited sectarian rioting in 2002 to insist that reduction of the policing level should remain an 'unfulfilled aspiration … as the benign environment envisaged by Patten has never materialised' (*The Times*, 23 August 2002). Between August 2001 and July 2002, 731 officers were injured in sectarian violence (ibid.).

Sectarian violence did increase markedly between 1998 and 2002, before declining again in 2003. The violence was perpetrated mainly by loyalists who were determined to coax the Provisional IRA back into action. However the violent activities were highly localized and, compared with the early years of the conflict, on a relatively small scale. Police overtime hours nonetheless averaged 14 451 hours in 2002, nearly double the target and peaking at the traditional time of heightened tension: the marching season in July (Police Service of Northern Ireland, 2002).

Radicalism and conservatism: the extent and limits of reform

Overall the Patten Report was a mixture of radicalism and conservatism. It was radical in terms of the new structures of accountability, which, along with the changed composition and activities of the Special Branch, were the most unacceptable reforms for nationalists. The Policing Board and District Policing Partnerships (DPPs) offered the prospect of much greater local control of policing activities, although the downgrading of the latter from boards to partnerships meant that they acquired a watchdog rather than an executive role. Moreover the new recruitment ratio would end the policing of one community by the other. By 2003, 673 applicants had been accepted by the PSNI, recruited on a 50–50 basis. Finally, sections of the force would no longer be able to write their own (non) rules.

In other respects the report was less than radical. Disarming the police had been recommended in the Hunt Report (1969) 30 years earlier, but this was not among Patten's recommendations. As with so much else emanating from the GFA, the all-island dimension was limited. For example the Patten proposals for PSNI–*Garda Siochana* cooperation were confined purely to pragmatic and operational matters. Understandably Patten had remained strictly within his brief, which meant that the dubious legal framework within which the police operated remained untouched. Scores of republican and loyalist 'dissidents' were processed through juryless courts in the years after the Patten Report, their convictions unsafe and illustrative of the abnormality of Northern Ireland's legal processes (although a similar situation was evident in the Irish Republic's treatment of suspected republican dissidents). Whether citizen redress against police actions had been fully developed was open to question. Of the 381 complaints against the police that were investigated in 2002–3, only 2 per cent were upheld (Police Service of Northern Ireland, 2002). Such a figure would previously have invited derision, but now complaints were at least referred to the ombudsman rather than investigated solely by the police.

The British government anticipated the eventual devolution of broader aspects of justice to a revived Northern Ireland Executive. This would be feasible under the 1998 Northern Ireland Act, provided there was cross-community support for such a move in the Assembly. New legislation would also be required to increase the number of ministerial portfolios at Stormont, if, as was likely, a dedicated Ministry of Justice was established. This would trigger a new run of the d'Hondt selection procedure for ministries. It was also possible that policing and justice could be separated, requiring the establishment of two ministries. The criminal justice review initiated by the government envisioned a single justice department, presided over by a single minister, with a deputy from the other camp, or headed by two ministers, one unionist, one nationalist.

In their 2003 Joint Implementation Plan the British and Irish governments raised the spectre of an all-island dimension to policing and justice, declaring that it would 'be possible for them to be brought within the scope of the North/South Ministerial Council, in accordance with Strand Two of the Agreement' (www.irl-news.com, 1 May 2003). This was mere kite-flying, outside the existing strand two of the agreement. Although such a move would constitute a substantial gain for republicans, there was no prospect of unionist support for an all-Ireland implementation body. Hence policing and justice issues may remain within the intergovernmental sphere for some time, unless the British government rewrites the GFA to place such issues formally within an all-island domain. This would alter the balance of the GFA, which is presently dominated by strand one.

Conclusion

The police force was arguably the last major institution of the old unionist regime in Northern Ireland, associated by detractors with sectarianism and illegality but defended by supporters as a force operating ably in exceptionally difficult circumstances. Reform was inevitable, once it became clear that the Provisional IRA ceasefire was permanent and that Sinn Fein would accept policing changes in a six-county context. The RUC was unbalanced in terms of denomina-tional composition (although this was not entirely its fault) and was largely unaccountable, with citizen redress being almost impossible. The critique offered by the Patten Report on these issues was cogent. What emerged from the report was a police force much less associated with the symbols of queen and (one) country, one that would never again do business with loyalist paramilitaries, and one that began to reflect mirrored the religious balance of the population.

The British and Irish governments' Joint Implementation Plan, announced in April 2003, envisioned a 'normalized' security situation (although the situation in Northern Ireland had never been normal) in which militarized policing – incorporating fortified police stations, armoured Land Rover patrols and army support – would be replaced by a community police service. The plan offered a specific timetable for the defortification of police stations and the removal of army personnel and bases.

That the policing changes were emotionally difficult for unionists to accept is unsurprising. The RUC was still seen as 'their' force; it had suffered more than any other local organization in the conflict and the Patten Report had not dwelt on the sacrifices made by the force. In this context, the implementation of Patten's proposals became part of the post-GFA negotiating process. Yet it could have been much worse for unionists. The proposals did not include the principle of local autonomy, under which nationalist areas could have become self-policing. Membership of the Orange Order or the Masons re-mained permissible for members of the PSNI. The proposals were also light on all-island policing linkages, with none of the potential political connections planned under the Sunningdale Agreement's proposal for an all-island police authority a quarter of a century earlier. The report recommended 'commonsense' links only, based on coordi-nated energy planning, plus some personnel, training and information technology exchanges, but these would merely build on existing co-operative relationships and would have scant political implication. The report said nothing about all-island policing oversight by politicians, and the British secretary of state would approve all significant policing appointments. Ironically it was the British and Irish governments that revived the prospect of an all-island policing body (as contained in the Sunningdale Agreement) in their 2003 Joint Implementation Plan to revive the GFA. Such a move could, belatedly, give the all-island aspect of the new political dispensation some teeth.

Of course change would never go far enough for those republicans who viewed the claim of the British government to Northern Ireland as colonial. The PSNI would press against those pursuing violent approaches to the eradication of that colonial relationship and con-tinue to defend the state of Northern Ireland. The co-option of former republican paramilitaries to the police would merely be part of a historical cyclical process in which republicans have moved against former comrades. Even to mainstream republicans, however, the sight of the PSNI raiding Sinn Fein's Stormont offices in October 2002 was, at best, unedifying and reminiscent of the political policing of earlier decades. Despite this episode, Sinn Fein's gradual move towards acceptance of the new service is likely to result in the party making an input to policing, a process that will accelerate if the devolution of security responsibilities to a viable Northern Ireland Assembly and executive takes place in the future. Whilst this could lead to some local squabbling between elected politicians over aspects of policing, the role of the Policing Board would remain unchanged. As such devolution would mitigate the neocolonial status of the police and position the PSNI as a local force, in keeping with its revised image and symbols.

11
The International Context

During the peace process a strong international dimension emerged in conflict resolution in Northern Ireland. External referents were important, and the actors in the peace process were influenced by methods of conflict resolution elsewhere. Sinn Fein and the IRA, in particular, as primary movers of the process, were influenced by the peace and reconciliation efforts of conflict participants in other countries, although a core argument of this chapter is that this influence was used to allow the republican movement at least to claim a creditable draw, whatever the evidence to the contrary. As such it can be reasonably argued that endogenous factors were more important than exogenous ones.

In broad order of importance the endogenous factors can be summarized, as follows: the changes within Sinn Fein and the IRA; the ending of the cold war between Britain and Ireland with the removal of Ireland's territorial claim, which strengthened bilateral and confederal approaches to Northern Ireland; a more realistic, inclusive approach by the British government in negotiations; the accelerated pace of reforms in Northern Ireland; and the reconfiguration of the United Kingdom by the post-1997 Labour government through asymmetrical devolution. These changes were accompanied by a growing internationalization of the Northern Ireland problem, accelerating and consolidating political developments. The influence of the EU, with its reordering of old questions of sovereignty and its pragmatic financial aid, is covered in an earlier chapter. This chapter will therefore consider the importance of other external agents.

The argument that the primary forces in the peace process were endogenous does not invalidate the value of external referents in understanding why peace and political processes developed. Indeed a comparative approach is necessary when analysing the Northern Ireland problem. The management of ethnic division, the emergence from the legacy of colonialism and consociational efforts at conflict management all invite global comparison. In these respects the claim that Northern Ireland is entirely a 'place apart' is simplistic, even allowing for the distinctive aspects of its problems. A comparative approach can also be used, however, to highlight these distinctions.

It is often assumed that the definition of endogenous in this regard includes Britain and the Republic of Ireland, rather than just Northern Ireland. Such a definition is problematic. Unionists in particular might regard the involvement of the Irish Republic as an exogenous factor. For decades, whatever its rhetoric on the evils of partition, the real position of the Irish government, having acquired its freedom, was more akin to 'I'm alright Jack' than concern about the troublesome, destabilizing minority in the north. The Fine Gael administration of Garret FitzGerald appeared to believe, however outlandishly, that the Provisional IRA, despite its Catholic nationalist origins, was capable and desirous of turning Ireland into an offshore Cuba (FitzGerald, 1992). This view was replicated among some in academia, with one writer claiming, without evidence, that 'the collapse of the Soviet Union marked the disappearance of the guerrillas' most important external ally', whilst also linking earlier militant republicans to 'ecclesiastical allies', despite the fact that neither link had ever been substantiated (Garvin, 1998, pp. 144–55). The portrayal of the Provisional IRA as Marxist revolutionaries failed, not least because it was untrue and ignored the origins of the movement. Such depictions were often part of a wider denunciation of militant republicans and their engagement in what they saw as an anticolonial struggle. This critique is a recurring theme, and Miller (1998) argues that much writing on Northern Ireland has been polemic masquerading as academic enquiry. Accordingly most accounts dispute any colonial basis to the conflict, assume that the British left most of Ireland voluntarily, believe that all-Ireland election results could safely be ignored (except, presumably, in 1998), consider that the unionist regime of 1921–72 disbanded itself, and suggest that the fundamental changes in Northern Ireland during recent decades can be attributed to mere force of argument.

It is necessary to divide the exogenous factors in two broad categories, the first of which covers the impact of other national governments on British and Irish policy towards Northern Ireland, a process of cross-government policy learning. The second category covers the impact of external agents on paramilitary groups and political parties. The basic arguments here are that the US government was a key player in category one, whilst the second category can be divided into two phases: external paramilitary support and cheerleading until 1987, followed by external encouragement for conflict resolution through the 1990s and beyond.

The involvement of the United States

The most important external influence on the conflict was the United States. Until the mid 1990s this influence was filtered through the US State Department, which took a non-interventionist approach but by default was pro-British in that the *status quo* was not being challenged. US diplomats tended to deny that the State Department had any particular line, other than neutrality (Dempsey, 1999), but political hostility to militant republicanism and financial support for the Anglo-Irish Agreement undermine this assertion. There was considerable debate in Congress and among Irish-Americans on US policy towards Northern Ireland, but this did not greatly affect policy. The outbreak of the Troubles in 1969 reignited the hostility of some Irish-Americans to Britain. Initially the main beneficiary of this was the Provisional IRA. However the claims of Irish-Americans were set against a strong US–British intergovernmental relationship. Whatever romantic associations existed, the US government considered Ireland a provincial backwater and saw Northern Ireland as a domestic concern of Britain. Although the 1972 Bloody Sunday atrocity was followed by a Congressional inquiry into the event and witnesses from Ireland gave evidence, it was not until the Carter presidency in 1977 that the US policy of non-intervention in Northern Ireland ended.

For a short period after Bloody Sunday elite Irish-Americans took an anti-British position. Prominent figures such as Ted Kennedy called for withdrawal of the British Army, the end of internment and the eventual reunification of Ireland (White, 1984). He argued that Protestants 'who could not accept a united Ireland should be given a decent opportunity to go back to Britain' (*Irish Times*, 6 September 1979). He admitted contributing to the Irish Northern Aid Committee (NORAID), the fundraising body established in 1970 for dependants of Irish Republican prisoners, until studying developments in Northern Ireland in greater depth (White, 1984, p. 188). Soon afterwards, however, the influence of the SDLP's John Hume began to have an impact. Hume made a determined effort to remedy what he regarded as the naïve perceptions of Irish-Americans on Northern Ireland and converted Kennedy to his view (Murray, 1998).

The first significant public demonstration that the Northern Ireland conflict was not considered by the US to be simply a British problem came on St Patrick's Day 1976, when the *taoiseach*, Liam Cosgrave, addressed Congress and issued a joint communiqué with President Ford, calling on Americans to renounce 'organisations engaged in violence' (White, 1984, p. 193). During the following year, opposition to the IRA's armed struggle was reinforced when Kennedy and three fellow Irish-American democrats – Tip O'Neill (speaker of the House), Senator Daniel Moynihan and Governor Hugh Carey of New York, collectively known as the 'Four Horsemen' – urged Irish-Americans not to support or encourage violence, a message reinforced by President Jimmy Carter, who hinted at US financial support for a political settlement. Despite Hume's efforts, however, some in Congress remained critical of Britain's approach to Northern Ireland and in 1979 the export of arms to the RUC was banned. During this period the US judiciary proved reluctant to take firm action against IRA suspects, accepting the defence that their actions were political. However the US government introduced a new extradition treaty in 1986, which effectively ruled out the political defence.

The hostility towards the IRA by the US administration might have left the Provisional IRA isolated, but Irish-Americans continued to raise questions about the nature of British rule in Ireland. As SDLP leader, Hume opposed the MacBride Principles as a potential barrier to investment. The nine MacBride principles (antidiscrimination measures strongly supported by Sinn Fein) were similar to the Sullivan Principles, which promoted equal opportunities for black workers in South Africa. The Irish National Caucus (INC), an umbrella group formed in 1974 and claiming to represent Irish-Americans, succeeded in having the principles adopted by 16 states by 1994 (Elliott and Flackes, 1999). The INC was instrumental in establishing an Ad Hoc Committee on Irish Affairs in the House of Representatives, with Mario Biaggi, a republican sympathizer, as its chairman. The organization harried the US and Irish governments over Northern Ireland, and even called for the recall of the Irish ambassador, Sean Donlon, on the ground of his anti-republicanism. The group was ahead of its time in condemning IRA violence whilst insisting that paramilitary groups had to be involved in the solution. The portrayal of Irish-Americans as ignorant of the pro-British majority in the north was wide of the mark as the INC had begun talks with loyalists as early as 1978 (ibid.).

During the early 1980s the Friends of Ireland (FoI) group was formed to offer an alternative to the militant republicanism of NORAID and the vigorous nationalism of the INC. The FoI insisted Irish unity could only come about through consent and the group did not engage in the campaigns of the INC. Its position as a representative of Irish-Americans was consolidated by the support of the US administration for the Anglo-Irish Agreement in 1985. Congress approved aid of $50 million for the first year of the agreement, as part of a rolling programme of assistance (Finnegan, 2002, p. 104). The agreement was supported on the basis that it had the potential to address the strong sense of minority alienation in Northern Ireland. Another moderate Irish-American group emerged, Americans for a New Irish Agenda, which encouraged further US government intervention in the Northern Ireland problem, thus increasing the isolation of NORAID.

The involvement of the US government became considerably more marked after Bill Clinton was elected president in 1992 (O'Clery, 1996). According to the account of one participant, during the 1990s US policy did not venture beyond a desire for amelioration of the conflict; 'what changed in 1994 was not the attitude in Washington, but the situation on the ground in Northern Ireland' (Dempsey, 1999, p. 107). This was broadly true, reinforcing the claim that endogenous change in Northern Ireland was more important than exogenous factors. Clinton's use of the National Security Council nonetheless meant that residual pro-British elements in the US State Department could be bypassed. Clinton's main US policy adviser, Nancy Soderberg, suggested that Clinton intervened because the constellation of forces in Northern Ireland offered a 'historic opportunity' that required pragmatism rather than the politics of purity and a self-imposed ban on talking to terrorists (Wilson, 1997, p. 31).

Clinton had used his 1992 presidential election campaign to criticize RUC-related aspects of security policy in Northern Ireland. Despite the campaign support he had received from Irish-Americans, during the early period of his term of office Clinton twice refused a visa to Gerry Adams. However he changed course in 1994 after being satisfied of the IRA's move away from violence. US aims converged with those of the Irish and British governments for most of the peace process. Even the supposed tension between the US and Britain over the granting of a US entry visa to Adams was largely manufactured for political purposes, the British government having to be seen to oppose such a move (Dixon, 2001). The only substantial difference between the two governments was over the decommissioning of paramilitary weapons. Whilst Britain regarded decommissioning as an essential part of the peace process, not because of its tangible value but as a confidence-building measure for unionists, the US view was that 'a prolonged state of non-war, however edgy, will cause the combat effectiveness of a non-active IRA to simply atrophy (as it had in the 1960s)' (Dempsey, 1999, p. 114).

The US administration facilitated the Good Friday Agreement in several ways. First, Clinton adopted a more relaxed approach towards Sinn Fein, epitomized by the granting of a visa to Adams and the maintenance of contact with him even when he was outflanked by hardliners, resulting in a temporary breakdown of the IRA ceasefire in 1996. Second, Clinton's visit to Northern Ireland, including a brief meeting with Gerry Adams, in late November 1995 was the first such visit by an incumbent US president and emphasized the US commit-ment to the peace process. The visit was of symbolic rather than actual importance, given that the IRA had already decided in principle to return to violence (Holland, 1996). It nonetheless helped orchestrate a mood that was subsequently reflected in large peace demonstrations when the IRA briefly halted its ceasefire. Third, the appointment of Senator George Mitchell, first as special adviser, then as chair of the negotiations that culminated in the GFA and finally as chair of a review of the agreement, signified a clear US brokerage role. Fourth, Clinton preferred to utilize his own national security advisers in deal-ing with Northern Ireland, perhaps less committed to a pro-British outlook on Northern Ireland. Finally, with unionists divided over whether to accept a deal, given its ambiguity on the decommissioning of weapons, Clinton intervened personally to reassure the UUP leader-ship. He encouraged the British prime minister to write a letter (outside the terms of the agreement and a harbinger of later problems) stating that decommissioning was a requirement of the deal, not merely an expectation. The part played by the US was thus evident, although subsequently there was some disagreement between the British and US administrations over where the credit lay for the GFA, with some in the Labour government arguing that the extent of Clinton's role had been exaggerated (Riddell, 2003).

It is commonly claimed that the Bush administration has shown less interest in Northern Ireland and this may well be true, although inevitable given that the peace deal has been brokered and the Provisional IRA ceasefire is permanent. Notwithstanding the problems of embedding the GFA, the focus has returned to security and terrorism, particularly since 11 September 2001, with the US government moving quickly to register the Real and Continuity IRAs as terrorist groups (although their cause and *modus operandi* place them very low on the US hierarchy of concerns) and banning their associates from entering the US. Although President Bush has appointed special advisers on Northern Ireland, with the grandstanding of the GFA complete and Northern Ireland eclipsed by other regions as a site of terrorism, US interest has diminished, despite the failure to complete the political process.

Examinations of US involvement in the peace process have tended to concentrate on the political facilitation role played by the US government. It engaged in what Arthur (2000) calls soft diplomacy, in which facilitation, management and personal contact, rather than the aggressive pursuit of self-interest, were key factors. There was also direct US involvement in security aspects of the conflict, in addition to the proscribing of republican ultras and, in 2001, the outlawing of aid to dependants of republican prisoners. The FBI played a large part in securing the conviction of the Real IRA leader, Michael McKevitt, in 2003, having run the main witness, David Rupert, as an agent for several years. At times even the *Garda Siochana* was reportedly 'out of the loop' in terms of FBI activity (*Sunday Independent*, 10 August 2003). Such an approach had the advantage of being subject to less scrutiny than normal techniques.

The end of the Cold War has been seen as a primary factor in the willingness of the US administration to aid the peace process in Northern Ireland (Cox, 1998; Cox *et al.*, 2001). The demise of the East–West political polarity allowed the US and other national governments to focus more on national conflicts and the accommodation of diversity elsewhere. The discrediting of Soviet-type regimes accelerated the IRA's move from left-wing politics, and Northern Ireland's lack of strategic value in the changed world order allowed the British government to insist it was neutral on Northern Ireland's future. Far from Northern Ireland being a crucial Atlantic base for the United Kingdom or NATO, in the 1993 Downing Street Declaration the

British government formally claimed it had no 'selfish strategic or economic interest' in the region.

However there are strong arguments against the assertion that the end of the Cold War was a primary factor in the progress made in the peace process. As Moloney's (2002) account of the IRA makes clear, Gerry Adams' private peace initiatives predated these events and the peace process would probably have proceeded anyway. Nonetheless the ending of the Cold War provided a convenient framework to develop the process and allowed the ditching of ideological baggage. Britain could begin to refute the charge of it being a colonial aggressor; republicans could tacitly, though not publicly, accept this; and the US could act as an honest broker. The other effect of the end of the Cold War was to heighten demands for secession and self-determination in Eastern Europe, based on local ethnic majoritarianism. As Guelke (1998, p. 208) argues, the result is that 'Northern Ireland's conditional status appears less anomalous', as local self-determination, rather than territory, shapes new states.

International influences

International influences on the republican movement can be placed in two categories: those which armed the movement, physically or morally; and those which shifted its strategy towards peace. The first category comprises an eclectic bunch: Hibernian and Fenian movements in the United States, the Libyan regime from 1974–87, and Basque nationalists. The second category includes the Afrcian National Congress (ANC) and, to a lesser extent, the Palestine Liberation Organization (PLO).

Despite receiving propaganda gifts from the British security forces during the early 1970s, the inward-looking nature of Irish republicanism meant it was slow to internationalize its cause. Republicans were largely concerned with the import of weapons. Most of the arms shipments to republicans during the early 1970s came from the US, often from Irish-born republicans still committed to a united and fully independent Ireland (English, 2003). NORAID enjoyed early fund-raising success by capitalizing on the propaganda value of the unsavoury, neocolonial aspects of British rule, such as internment, the events of Bloody Sunday and the verdict by the European Commission of Human Rights that the interrogation of internees by the British Army constituted inhuman treatment. Whilst Irish-Americans in Congress adopted Hume's view of the need to reconcile the two competing traditions in Ireland, NORAID continued to emphasize British occupation, a stance that attracted much sympathy in the 1970s when the security forces were seen to be breaching human rights. In the 1980s NORAID highlighted such aspects of British colonial rule as juryless courts, the broadcasting ban on Sinn Fein in 1988 and the use of supergrasses in trials. This campaign was less dramatic than its 1970s predecessor, was countered by the moderation and opposition to violence of most of Irish America and was dulled by the fact that related legislation in the Irish Republic had become even more severe than that in the United Kingdom in some respects (such as the broadcasting ban), so NORAID found it more difficult to get its message across.

After years of providing assistance to republicans, NORAID eventually split over Sinn Fein's peace strategy, with the Friends of Irish Freedom group being formed in 1989 to maintain support for republican prisoners and their families (Elliott and Flackes, 1999, p. 301). By the late 1990s NORAID was in meltdown, as supporters had ceased fundraising altogether, or joined more moderate organizations. Having been marginalized by most US politicians, NORAID's role as republican financier had already been in decline by the late 1980s, with donations falling from $1 million a year in the early 1980s to less than $200 000 by the 1990s (*Financial Times*, 30 May 1994). Provisional Sinn Fein was later backed by the Friends of Sinn Fein, led by Chuck Feeney and supported by 'respectable' Irish-American businessmen. Many had previously supported the 'Americans for a New Irish Agenda' organization and strongly backed the peace process. Rita O'Hare, Sinn Fein's chief US fundraiser, acknowledged the 'loss of good people' but this was compensated by the larger sums that came from the Friends of Irish Freedom (interview by the author, 9 April 2000). Republican ultras offered withering criticism of the '$500-a-head dinners in five star New York hotels' associated with Friends of Sinn Fein (*Sovereign Nation*, June–July 2001, p. 5).

During the 1980s, when Sinn Fein developed as an electoral force, the IRA landed four large shipments of arms from Libya, whose leader, Colonel Qaddafi, had long offered succour to republicans. The fifth and largest arms delivery was intercepted, probably due to a tip-off from an IRA informer (Moloney, 2002). This rendered the IRA incapable of launching a planned all-out offensive. This had been designed to prompt an aggressive response by the security forces that would anger the nationalist community and lead to enhanced support for the IRA. After 1987 Libya ceased to supply arms and was not replaced by a similarly significant source.

The leftward shift of republicans after 1977 facilitated the forging of solidarity links with a range of other organizations, although the far left and anarchists were ignored. Links were developed with the Palestine Liberation Organization (PLO) although there were few tangible benefits. Similarly supportive links were developed with Herri Batasuna, the political representatives of the Basque separatist armed group ETA (see below). Relationships were also formed with Breton, Corsican and Kurdish political prisoners.

The loyalist paramilitary groups were virtually friendless, although their campaign relied far less on bomb-making equipment and its supply than did the offensives of the Provisional IRA. Some armaments were shipped to loyalist paramilitaries by the white South Africa regime of the late 1980s, apparently linked to its wish to acquire missiles from the firm Short Brothers in Northern Ireland (Guelke, 1998).

Unionist politicians have drawn parallels between unionists and the Turks in the north of Cyprus, one of only ten islands in the world over which sovereignty is contested (Guelke, 2001). Indeed the situation in Cyprus is probably the closest of any country to that in Northern Ireland, although there are substantial differences. When Cyprus was under British colonial rule the majority Greek population expressed a desire for British withdrawal, preferring union with Greece, an aspiration that led to violence in the 1950s. However the minority Turkish population (one-fifth of the island's population) remained pro-British, or at least opposed to British withdrawal, as they feared union with Greece. When Britain awarded independence to Cyprus it prohibited union with Greece or Turkey. In this respect the parallel with the unionists' position in Northern Ireland is far from close. A consociational attempt to reconcile Greek and Turkish Cypriots failed; indeed consociation has not had a particularly successful global record in terms of conflict resolution (Horowitz, 2001). In the case of Cyprus its failure was predictable as there was a general lack of loyalty to the newly independent island state. Greece took control of the island in 1974, followed swiftly by a Turkish invasion, and the island remains partitioned into the northern Turkish sector, amounting to 37 per cent of the land, and the southern Greek sector (Guelke, 2001). The unionist parallel is the viability of a small northern statelet in a divided island. In 2004, however, the Turkish-Cypriots voted *for* a united island, a move *rejected* by the Greek majority.

Basque nationalists: Sinn Fein's erstwhile allies

The links between the IRA and other armed groups should not be over-stated. The most authoritative of the recent studies of the organization do not even mention such links, and instead stress the importance of arms imports from rogue states (Moloney, 2002; English, 2003). The PLO spent much of the 1980s denying links with the IRA. Although Irish republicans maintained contact with a variety of nationalist movements, including Corsicans and Bretons, the most sophisticated and enduring ties were developed with Basque separatists, represented politically by Herri Batasuna and militarily by ETA. Superficially it might appear odd that Irish republicans seeking territorial unity should back a group seeking political separation. Nonetheless Sinn Fein backs the secession of the seven provinces that comprise the historical Basque country. The largely autonomous Basque government presides over a polity in which native Basques are favoured over the minority 'immigrant' community in terms of employment, but full independence is still demanded. Thus although there are similarities and shared policies between Basques and Irish republicans, there are also many differences or paradoxes.

Secession has become more politically acceptable since the fragmentation and reconfiguration of parts of East and Central Europe in the 1990s, but Spain, whilst granting considerable autonomy to the Basque region, refuses to contemplate its withdrawal from the state. The same refusal is applied by the French government to Corsican nationalists and by the Canadian government to Québecois secessionists. Keating (2001, p. 183) argues that the Basque and Irish nationalisms, 'like nearly all such movements, are "inventions", relying on a tendentious account of history' as their countries were only ever united under Spanish and British rule respectively. This is true of course, although a colonial history need not be fiction, nor undermine a contemporary claim to self-determination. Whilst Irish republicans follow the French revolutionary tradition of liberty, equality and fraternity, Basque nationalism has its origins in ethnic exclusivity, based on notions of homeland and language. Its claim is essentially political – self-determination for the Basque country – but it is fuelled by ethnic exclusivism.

Unlike Basques, Irish nationalists can at least claim a historical democratic mandate, rather than myth or invention, as the basis for withdrawal of the parent state. Despite the contortions of revisionists, Sinn Fein's electoral victory in 1918 showed the desire of the majority of Irish people for a united, independent Ireland under the normal practice of democracy – that is, a party that wins a majority of votes and seats is entitled to form a government and exercise its mandate in the territory in which the election took place. Irish unity remains an overwhelming aspiration of the Irish people (Hayes and McAllister, 1996), but the violent politics of the first *Dail* have found less favour in recent decades. The Irish electorate voted to downgrade the territorial claim to Northern Ireland in 1998, and in the north Sinn Fein only overtook the SDLP as the majority representative of nationalism in 2001, four years after the renewal of the Provisional IRA ceasefire.

In the Basque country, whilst the award of autonomy to the Basque region received widespread approval, the violent actions of ETA have been condemned by an ever increasing proportion of the people of the region (Liera, 1994). Whereas backing for Sinn Fein has expanded beyond its urban bases, support for Herri Batasuna, ETA's political wing, is largely confined to native, often young, Basque-speaking militants in parts of Guipuzcoa, Vizcaya and Navarre (Keating, 2001). The moderate Basque nationalist party, the Partido Nacionalista Vasco (PNV), enjoys more working-class backing than the SDLP. Both are middle-class-oriented parties, but the SDLP is more so because of Sinn Fein's command of working-class support. Herri Batasuna has endured a weakening of support due to association with ETA's violence. Herri Batasuna, unlike Sinn Fein, has not yet moved away from condoning armed struggle. The Spanish government can justifiably claim, given survey evidence, that the majority of people residing in the Basque provinces do not want secession, a move that would also have to be endorsed by the French government, which presides over Basque provinces where the demand for independence is weak. The unspoken fear of the Spanish government is that acquiescence would be followed by a similar demand by Catalonia, although the Catalan struggle for greater autonomy has not included violence.

By 1998 Sinn Fein had distanced itself from the militant Basque nationalists and no longer shared Herri Batasuna's unequivocal support for ETA's campaign of violence, which offered a reminder of how Sinn Fein candidates had been mandated in the early 1980s to serve as cheerleaders for the IRA. With the leaders of Herri Batasuna in prison, ETA called a ceasefire in 1998, but returned to violence in 1999. The format that produced ETA's 1998 ceasefire bore similarities to that in Northern Ireland and was influenced by Sinn Fein's new approach. It was also preceded by state-sponsored terrorism, with the Spanish government using its own version of 'loyalist death squads' to assassinate ETA supporters and members. The PNV and a smaller similar party, Eusko Alkartasuna, agreed a programme of self-government and, reminiscent of the pan-nationalism of the Irish peace process, a formula for Basque self-determination. The commonalities between the Basque and Northern Irish situations were apparent. The PNV, the Basque equivalent of the SDLP, had become increasingly nationalist in outlook, in a similar manner to that in which the SDLP had been 'greened'. Like the SDLP it was strongly anti-violence, and it displayed political altruism by assuming a pivotal role in the pan-Basque alliance, pointing out to Herri Batasuna that electoral marginalization could result from continued absolutism and support for political violence.

The tendency to compromise, for so long evident in Irish republicanism, had not yet developed in ETA, an organization only founded in 1959. However, ETA was confronted with similar problems to those of the IRA: a ceiling on political support, insufficient backing for its 'war' and the inability to impose military defeat on its opponent. It also risked a split if it compromised without preparing its base. As demands for regional autonomy gained credence across Europe, the cross-national secessionist demand of the militant Basque nationalists, or even the staging of a referendum to determine the legitimacy of this demand, was rejected by the Spanish and French governments. Having none of Sinn Fein's historical mandate and less of its political strength, Herri Batasuna has been less willing to compromise. Hence whilst the peace processes in the Basque region and Northern Ireland have been similar in terms of construction, the responses of combatants in the Basque case, allied to the absence of external peace facilitators, have marked the terrain as less fertile for accommodation.

Although the parallel is far from exact, Sinn Fein appears to have moved closer to Catalan-style nationalism, as illustrated by its desire for formal recognition of identity, legitimacy of culture and lack of immediate pressure for full Irish autonomy. Meanwhile aspects of Catalan autonomy are under pressure. The Catalan language is in decline, a majority of young Catalans preferring to speak Castilian after being educated in both tongues. As ETA rejected the peace process and continued its violent activities, despite intense public hostility in all but a few areas, its campaign and the ensuing tough security responses mirrored, on a much larger scale, the situation with republican ultras in Northern Ireland. Sinn Fein continued to support 'democracy, equality and self-determination for the Basque people' and backed an 'independent Basque state (motions 175 and 176, Sinn Fein *ard fheis*, 2003). Thus old links died hard, but it was notable that, by 2003, Sinn Fein *ard fheis* motions were studiously avoiding reference either to ETA or to Herri Batusana, although the latter's representatives still attended Sinn Fein conferences.

The failed Basque peace process was illustrative of how peace processes in general are not guaranteed to succeed. There have been attempts to bring about peace in Sri Lanka, where the Tamil Tigers have fought to create an independent homeland within the island, but the bloody conflict has persisted. However the Provisional IRA's option of returning to violence has long been closed. Its paramilitary expertise has been noted, however, by FARC guerrillas in Columbia, and it has continued to recruit and train. Nonetheless the 1997 IRA decision to place decommissioning in the hands of its Army Council, dominated by moderates, ensured that Adams' vision of an Ireland without the (Provisional) IRA would eventually be realized. That this might take time should come as no surprise: the 'Official' IRA, on ceasefire since 1972, was reportedly still in existence in the 1990s.

The impact of peace processes in South Africa and the Middle East

Peace processes elsewhere have had some impact on the situation in Northern Ireland. The South African process has had an effect in terms of the negotiating techniques of parties. In 1997 the African National Congress (ANC) invited all parties from Northern Ireland to a symposium on modes of conflict resolution. Perhaps surprisingly, all attended, although proximity talks, rather than cross-table dialogue, indicated the limits of cooperation at that stage. The talks covered a variety of aspects of conflict resolution, including transition, prisoner releases, peace and reconciliation. Unsurprisingly the favoured comparison of Sinn Fein with external peace processes was the South

African model, even if there was one rather important difference: the ANC won its struggle and went on to form a democratically elected government. White minority rule was ended and the structures of apartheid dismantled. Nationalists in Northern Ireland had not endured the degree of discrimination and deprivation suffered by the black majority in South Africa, although the unionist government did have the option of utilizing draconian measures under the Special Powers Act.

The value of the South African model lay in its negotiating techniques and compromises. At the conclusion of the 1997 symposium in South Africa the representatives of all Northern Ireland parties expressed a positive view of the proceedings and most recognized that negotiation would be an essential part of the peace process at home (O'Malley, 2001). However their positivity could not be sustained: some of those who had praised the negotiating ideal either stayed away from the GFA negotiations or walked out as the negotiations reached a climax. For republicans, negotiating meant dealing not only with the obstacle to Irish unity, the British government, but also with the representatives of the 900 000 unionists who would not be coerced into a unitary Irish state. Republicans had long shown a willingness to talk to unionists; however there was clearly a conceptual difference between talking to and negotiating with unionists. The new South African constitution, which emerged at the end of the negotiations between the ANC and the white government, was a model of clarity compared with certain sections of the GFA, notably the one on decommissioning. O'Malley (ibid.) argues that an important difference between the situations in South Africa and Northern Ireland was that the IRA was not fighting a just war, unlike the ANC, which had broad black support even though some of its actions were more ruthless than those undertaken by the IRA. For example some ANC members conducted 'necklace killings', in which a tyre was placed around a victim's neck and set alight. The extent of support is one criterion of what constitutes a just war, although any definition of a just war is inevitably subjective.

In 2001 Gerry Adams spoke of the internationalization of the Northern Ireland problem and the extent of support for Sinn Fein: 'from South Africa to North America there are commitments and promises to support our efforts' (quoted in Arthur, 2002, p. 84). This was true, although the commitments and methods of republicans had changed, as had the North American support base. Comparison to the ANC helped maintain a feeling of momentum and made it easier to sell the peace process to grassroots republicans. Earlier criticism of

British policy in Northern Ireland by Nelson Mandela had been useful propaganda: the ANC appeared to view Sinn Fein's struggle as anti-colonial. Recent Sinn Fein *ard fheisanna*, including the crucial 1998 event at which the GFA was accepted, had been marked by speeches by ANC representatives urging acceptance of peace as a means of moving towards the achievement of historical goals. The ANC also gave advice to Sinn Fein on maintaining the unity of the movement which was notorious for splits.

An ANC visitor to a Sinn Fein gathering in 1998 was lauded as a person 'who had journeyed from guerrilla fighter to politician and stayed a revolutionary' whilst enduring 'painful compromises' ('Change is a Permanent Condition', *An Phoblact/Republican News*, 30 April 1998, p. 9). Shortly before the reconvening of the 1998 *ard fheis*, which backed the GFA, ANC delegates visited republican prisoners to outline their view of peace processes and transition. However the ANC delegates and Sinn Fein representatives acknowledged that there were 'major differences between the two situations', and the delegates felt that it would be 'inappropriate to refer to the detail of the [Good Friday] Agreement' (*An Phoblacht/Republican News*, 30 April 1998). After all, in its own peace process the ANC had not been asked to disarm, nor had it failed to achieve its basic objective.

In general the Middle East has offered less than ideal examples of peace processes. However there is the encouraging example of Lebanon and the 1989 Ta'if Accord, which resulted in the decommissioning and disbandment of paramilitary groups. In contrast the 1993 Oslo Agreement between Israel and the neighbouring Arab states proved fragile and was an example of a contentious partitionist settlement, with 'incompatible nationalisms claiming the same territory' (Tessler, 1994; Smooha, 2001, p. 312). One positive aspect of the agreement, or at least for unionists, was that it enshrined partition. Jews had long accepted the principle of partition, but it had been rejected by the Palestine Liberation Organization (PLO) until 1988. The agreement recognized Israel's right to exist, confirmed the legitimacy of the PLO as the representative of the Palestinian people and offered the eventual prospect of Israel withdrawing from the areas it had occupied in the 1967 Arab–Israeli war. Palestinians within Israel supported a permanent settlement along those lines as they believed it would mean they would no longer be seen as internal enemies (Smooha, 2001).

However the extent and depth of Arab extremism dwarfed that in Northern Ireland. Suicide bombings never occurred in Northern

Ireland and the activities of republican ultras, Omagh apart, were on nothing like the scale of those of Hammas. In this regard the claim by Prime Minister Blair during his overseas tours in 2001 that the GFA indicated that peace could be brokered in the Middle East, overlooked the greater depth of the problem in that region. There were some similarities between Sinn Fein and the PLO, notably in the manner in which the latter had inched its way from terrorist status to becoming an organization with which governments could do business. For a period after the signing of the GFA, Israeli flags were flown in some loyalist areas of Belfast, for a combination of reasons (although these may overstate the local knowledge of the situation in the Middle East). The flags were flown in response to the flying of PLO flags in republican areas, as an expression of support for the right of a state to exist under a partitionist settlement and as a mark of belief in a chosen people.

Conclusion

The parochialism that characterized the Northern Ireland conflict has been replaced by external referents. Whilst it was patronizing and profoundly mistaken for commentators to dismiss the struggle for national sovereignty and self-determination as retarded and anachronistic (particularly when anticolonial struggles elsewhere were looked at in a positive light), the global context of transnationalism and pooled sovereignty came to weigh heavily on the republican movement, forcing political change. The movement was anxious to avoid political isolation, as electoral politics and the achievement of power became dominant concerns, at the expense of ideological purity. Sinn Fein pointed to examples of peace processes elsewhere to justify change, but the South African model, despite providing lessons in negotiating, was far from an exact parallel, given the different outcomes of the respective processes.

A comparative approach is necessary when studying the utility of partitionist and consociational settlements elsewhere, but it should not lead to false external comparisons, as each peace process has involved distinct ways of resolving particular historical and contemporary problems. Sinn Fein and the IRA were moving towards a compromise before the end of the Cold War. A lack of British selfish interest was evident in Northern Ireland since 1920. EU influences have arguably been more important in ameliorating the conflict, but have had scant impact on national identity. In their continued commitment to an Irish nation state, republicans have harnessed the process of European integration to their 'inevitability' thesis in respect of Irish unity. The vernacular of the South African peace process has been utilized, including words and phrases such as transition, permanent revolution and historic compromise, even though Sinn Fein has been participating in a peace process shaped largely by the demands of the British and Irish governments.

The interdependence of states and the binational approach to the GFA made republican demands for exclusive national sovereignty appear dated. Ethno-nationalism was far from redundant elsewhere, however, as the secessionist demands in Central and Eastern Europe in the 1990s made clear. Such demands challenged existing territorial boundaries and the United Nations, whilst keen to reinforce the existing boundaries, was obliged to become far more amenable to reconfiguration. The situation in Northern Ireland has not been directly akin to that in any other region in Europe or elsewhere. This of course does not invalidate a comparative approach, nor does it diminish the extent of policy learning from other countries or from international developments. The SDLP's political approach has long been influenced by the interdependence of states and the pooling of sovereignty in the EU context. Meanwhile Sinn Fein has adopted the negotiating styles of other actors in different conflicts. Ultimately, theories of colonialism, adapted to a modern setting, are as useful as theories of European integration and global interdependence for explaining the status of Northern Ireland. Keating's (2001, p. 205) description of the British government as a 'colonial trustee' seems particularly apposite. Offering a benign rule, devoid of economic interest, the British government acts as a ringmaster, maintaining sovereignty, legitimizing its rule and determining the type, form and even dates of electoral contests.

Conclusion

Despite its lack of support among unionists, the Good Friday Agreement helped create a new Northern Irish politics after 1998. The conflict subsided and constitutional politics developed rapidly among those republicans who had formerly rejected Northern Ireland as a gerrymandered, illegal political entity. The idea of devolved power sharing remained popular and the GFA enjoyed substantial support (Irwin, 2002). However the mechanics of the agreement were seen by some unionists as unacceptable, and limited continuation of paramilitary acts undermined the deal. Paradoxically, a section of unionism appeared incapable of celebrating a constitutional victory, while many in the republican movement found considerable consolation in the electoral gains that followed their (unacknowledged) constitutional defeat. Moreover the nationalist architect of the three-stranded agreement, the SDLP, rapidly lost support among its electorate, and the party that had secured the union, the UUP, also saw its electoral support dwindle.

The requirement for consolidated new politics: societal transformation, consociation or neither?

The Good Friday Agreement's consociational mechanics offended those who saw the deal as cementing the divisions in Northern Ireland. Although not necessarily opposed to the GFA, social transformationists take what they regard as a more optimistic view of human nature, in which humans, as individuals, are able to 'think outside' their ascribed ethnic bloc. Identities are not primordial, and individuals can free themselves from the shackles of bloc designation, the development of integrated education and cross-community workplace initiatives being examples of this (Taylor, 2001). Social transformationists argue that bottom-up, cross-community initiatives can eradicate the fault line between communities. It is questionable whether the development of integrated schools can be called bottom up, being primarily confined to the middle classes, but this does not negate the transformationist argument. Societal reconciliation ensures the gradual erosion of division, rather than the permanent compartmentalization of ethno-nationalisms under consocation. Societal transformationists reject the elitism of consocation, in which the members of a small political class divide up the political spoils according to their ability to mobilize an ethnic vote.

The strongest argument of societal transformationists is that consociationists are vague about how the dismantling of ethnic bloc structures will eventually occur. The rigidity of bloc identification, rights of veto and community autonomy inhibit the eventual dissolution of such structures in the event of a more hospitable political climate. As such, 'consociationalism is a means of regulating conflict, not transforming it' (ibid., p. 37). In the Northern Ireland context, transformationists may be correct in criticizing the manner in which unionist and nationalist identities are given greater importance than other identities. The requirement for cross-community support means that if a majority of unionists and nationalists support a measure it could be passed even if other groups are opposed to it. Of course few voters in Northern Ireland support the other groups, so the proviso hardly constitutes a negation of democracy. Nonetheless the rule diminishes these groups and may make it even more difficult for them to persuade voters that they are worthy of support.

There are, however, several weaknesses with the social transformation argument. For example there is no coherent explanation of how ethnic divisions arose. The optimistic view of human nature inherent in the transformationist approach fails to accept the possibility that ethnic divisions exist because humans develop a sense of identity they wish to retain. Political rivalries arising from ethnic division or personal persuasion are implicitly viewed as unhealthy and pernicious. Ultimately the transformationist approach can also depoliticize and de-ideologize in a similar manner to the way in which the stress on identity politics under consociationism depoliticizes. There is no persuasive evidence that bottom-up eradication of societal division can produce a transformation of society in the short to medium term. Even proponents of this view acknowledge that 'sectarianism is what makes people tick' (Bew, 2002). Residential segregation, most clearly illustrated by the existence of 'peace walls', has increased. The vote share of unionist and nationalist parties has grown at the expense of the political centre, a trend that preceded the consociationism of the GFA.

Within these blocs, the more militant parties have enjoyed greater electoral success since the agreement.

The stiffening of the unionist and nationalist blocs should not be conflated with greater political extremism. Rather the nationalist bloc has undergone a significant internal political change, as illustrated by the new moderation exhibited by Sinn Fein. Herein lies another weakness of the transformationist argument. It assumes a rigidity of politics within a designated ethnic bloc, in which political views are polarized and unchanging. This ignores the possibility of change among political elites and the degree to which such elites can be the instigators of reform. Again the classic example here is Sinn Fein. It was the elite in that party who helped to develop the peace process, sometimes to the chagrin of party sceptics. Had such developments been left to the republican grassroots, it is entirely possible that the conflict would have endured. Certainly there was little grassroots republican momentum for Provisional IRA ceasefires and the dramatic political change seen afterwards. In its origins and formulation, republican political change was leadership driven, albeit abetted and hastened by structural changes, in particular the development of a Catholic middle class, which limited Sinn Fein's electoral growth. Attempts at societal trans-formation have also been made by political elites within the bloc system, an example being the antisectarianism initiatives by the Sinn Fein Mayor of Belfast, Alex Maskey, during his term of office in 2002, amid widespread scepticism.

More fundamentally, transformationists appear to think that holding an identity and a concomitant political position is somehow retarded and should be overcome. Most problematically, however, transformationists wish to eradicate sectarian structures in a province whose formation and maintenance have been based on sectarian headcounting. The ultimate fulcrum of the societal transformationist position ought to be the withering of the most prominent divider of peoples, the border. The unionist majority in just two counties, Down and Antrim, is effectively the current basis for the continuing division of Ireland, despite the survey evidence cited earlier in this book that the aspiration for Irish unity is as strong as ever (Hayes and McAllister, 1996). Transformationists concentrate on the eradication of ethnic division without demonstrating a proper historical understanding of the basis of that division and its consolidation by territorial boundaries. Their plea for societal integration is accompanied by acceptance of territorial division.

In accepting the constitutional *status quo* and its entrenchment of division, 'transformationists' and consociationists prioritize the territorial claim by one section of the population over the broader aspirations of the majority. It allows partisan ethnic appeals to be maintained by political parties, with the long-term constitutional future of Northern Ireland remaining unresolved. It allows Sinn Fein to maintain a different definition of transformation, one that depicts the cross-border aspects of the GFA as a move towards Irish unification. In reality, the binational aspects of the agreement were woefully thin, or Faulknerite 'necessary nonsense', based (EU programmes apart) on the banal issues of inland waterways and food safety, when it could have covered issues such education and health, over which Sinn Fein ministers held sway in the north.

Rearranging deckchairs? Proposals for institutional and voting reform

Transformationists and consociationists offer prescriptions for institutional reform and societal change, although consociationists tend to be quieter on the latter. They offer reform proposals for a reconstituted Northern Ireland Assembly and executive. Broadly, consociationists view the communal registration of party MLAs as a necessary evil, even though such designations may be at odds with pure consociation. Transformationists wish to redesign the institutional apparatus created under the GFA, and see civic society as the arena that offers the best prospect of substantive change. Integrationists reject the 'either/or' constitutional choices in the agreement. They also oppose the single transferable vote (STV) electoral system, communal registration for MLAs and use of the D'Hondt mechanism for government formation (Wilson and Wilford, 2003). The STV voting system allows candidates in multimember constituencies to be elected despite winning only a minority of votes. In elections to the Assembly, six members are elected from each of Northern Ireland's 18 constituencies. This means that candidates need only secure 14 per cent of the vote to be elected. The result, claim critics, is the pursuit of communal votes, with no requirement for candidates to secure votes from the other community. Although this may understate the extent to which lower-placed candidates (from first preference votes) require cross-community votes in order to be elected, the broad point is true. The solution they offer is the alternative vote, which would require a candidate to win an overall majority to be elected.

Wilson and Wilford (ibid., p. 8) assume that 'more conciliatory' electoral messages may emerge to secure this majority. In predominantly nationalist or unionist constituencies, however, candidates who offer a strong ethnic message could still win a seat and there might be no representation for unionist or nationalist minorities. In more moderate constituencies, STV could act as a means of moderating the agenda of a party. Sinn Fein's pitch for SDLP votes is a clear example of this. Finally, the assumption of critics of STV is one that infects the societal transformation approach in its entirety: that nationalism and unionism are suspect ideologies to be overcome. Societal transformationists and integrationists prefer depoliticization to contestation.

The criticism of communal registration in the Assembly carries the same implicit assumption about the illegitimacy of nationalism and unionism. If there is to be a permanent Assembly, there is a case for abolishing communal designations in favour of weighted majority voting. A requirement for 65 per cent majority support for a measure in the Assembly would still require a unionist-drafted measure to receive some support from nationalists, and *vice versa*. The problem with the numerical weighted majority, as opposed to joint communal majorities, is that a majority of nationalists or unionists could oppose a measure passed by the Assembly.

The application of the D'Hondt mechanism to executive selection is unusual and this mode of government formation was not particularly successful in Northern Ireland in 2000–2. Although there were useful individual performances, there was a lack of cohesive government, although this owed as much to party attitude as to the means of government formation. The use of the D'Hondt mechanism led to government by the 'big four' parties, to the exclusion of the centrist Alliance Party, although it is questionable whether its inclusion would have dramatically reshaped the executive and steered it towards collective responsibility. Wilson and Wilford (2003) suggest that Assembly support ought to be a requirement for constituting the executive, an extension of the cross-community Assembly ratification of the choice of first minister and deputy first minister. Nominations would emerge from interparty agreement, which is a possibility, if a rather sanguine take on Sinn Fein–DUP cooperation. Assembly support would require a threshold if the DUP (and possibly others) were to be prevented from exercising a veto on Sinn Fein's presence in government. Moreover this change in the means of constituting a government would not address another criticism of the GFA: the absence of a system of government and opposition.

Whatever the drawbacks of the D'Hondt mechanism, the executive was at least inclusive in that each of the four parties that were entitled to a presence took their seats and could not be excluded purely at the whim of other parties (despite the best efforts of the UUP and DUP). However there was no mechanism to prevent the neocolonialism displayed by Secretaries of State Mandelson and Reid in suspending the political institutions, nor the colonial governance exhibited by the British prime minister in avoiding an election in May 2003 for fear of the 'wrong' result, which merely postponed the inevitable until November that year.

The weakness of the transformationist (and in some cases, consociationist) arguments lies in the belief in technical solutions to what are fragile core assumptions. The condemning of 'either/or' constitutional choices under the GFA ignores electoral evidence that suggests these are precisely the choices favoured by the electorate. Locating Northern Ireland in the context of a 'variable geometry' of international relationships does not allow escape from the essential question of whether Northern Ireland should have its own border, elected assembly and associated institutions. Either a border should exist, or it should not. Integrationists appear to take the existence of Northern Ireland as given and condemn sectarianism within it, ignoring the possibility that the mere existence of the UK province and its concomitant border is the cause and symbol of sectarianism. A province with undemocratic origins is founded on ethnic majoritarianism and perpetuated on a crude sectarian headcount, despite the eradication of most of its sectarian institutions since 1972. The question begged is why antisectarian initiatives in Northern Ireland can (or deserve) to work when the North's existence rests on the unwillingness of a significant number of its citizens to share political structures with the Irish Republic. The modernized Irish Republic is instead derided as the 'pathetic, mono-cultural, sectarian state to our South' (Trimble, 2002). The 'two traditions' of Northern Ireland are expected to live together peacefully and harmoniously, yet a border remains in place to divide the people of the island of Ireland, cutting one tradition from its parent state. Unless placed in an overarching federal or confederal context, a reconstituted Northern Ireland Assembly and its attendant institutions would do little to alter this problem.

Old Northern Irish politics: Britain's sovereign claim

For the Provisional IRA the struggle in Northern Ireland ended in defeat, if defeat is measured by whether an organization's objectives are attained (and there seems to be no viable alternative measure). The scale of that defeat, the IRA having brought about neither an end of British rule nor the establishment of joint authority, is apparent in the private discourse of republicans and the public utterances of British and Irish political leaders. In a speech to the Irish Association in 1995, prior to becoming *taoiseach*, Bertie Ahern insisted that:

> Irish Nationalism has changed. Irredentism is dead. I know of almost no one who believes it is feasible or desirable to attempt to incorporate Northern Ireland into the Irish Republic or into a united Ireland against the will of a majority there, either by force or coercion. Ireland is, in the view of the vast majority of us, one nation, which is divided, because its two traditions have by and large chosen up till now to live under two different jurisdictions. In my view, we have to leave behind us the territorial claims. (quoted in Bew *et al.*, 1997, p. 228)

The statement about people's choice is questionable, given that the majority of Irish people had never chosen to live under different jurisdictions and a majority had persistently expressed their desire for Ireland to be united under a single jurisdiction. Indeed later in the speech Ahern remarked that the nationalists in the north had been 'absorbed against their will'. Despite this, Ahern cautioned against the idea that limited binationalism in any future agreement would have wider constitutional implications:

> North–South institutions with executive powers are a fundamentally different concept from joint authority. Joint authority, which Fianna Fail have never advocated or regarded as a realistic possibility, is essentially joint rule over Northern Ireland by the Irish and British governments. North–South institutions relate not just to the North, but to North and South equally ... Even if Government institutions in the North were to break down, there is no question of resorting to joint authority. (ibid., p. 229)

Of course Ahern occasionally relapsed into more traditional republican rhetoric, outlandishly claiming in 1999 that the GFA had created an 'irresistible dynamic' for a united Ireland (Elliott and Flackes, 1999, p. 154). Unfortunately for Ahern the British prime minister, Tony Blair, appeared to be unaware of any dynamic for unity, insisting in his first speech in Northern Ireland after his election that there would not be a united Ireland in his or anyone's lifetime (Tonge, 2002). Britain's sovereign claim to Northern Ireland remained intact, conditional on the will of the people of the territorial unit created by the British government in 1920 and regardless of the aspiration of the majority of Irish people, although many were indifferent to unity. This conditionality was evident in the Sunningdale Agreement, the Anglo–Irish Agreement and the Good Friday Agreement. Blair went on to declare in his speech that 'those who wish to see a united Ireland without coercion can argue for it, not least in the talks. If they succeeded we would certainly respect that' (quoted in *Belfast Telegraph*, 16 May 1997). It was not quite clear how they could succeed, given that – despite the rhetoric of self-determination – such an option was never going to be laid before the people of Ireland.

New politics and the end of republicanism

The Good Friday Agreement marked another phase in Irish republicanism's willingness to compromise (see, for example Ryan, 1994; Arthur, 2002), to the chagrin of a small number of republican critics but the satisfaction of the majority. Sinn Fein's new nationalism amounted to a breach of traditional Irish republican principles, while the abandonment of the constitutional claim to Northern Ireland by the Irish Republic ended the 'illegitimate' status of the province. When Sinn Fein entered government in Northern Ireland, the question was not whether a united Ireland could be achieved, but whether republicanism had finally expired. Republicans had long known that IRA violence would not drive the British into the sea. Combined with Articles 2 and 3 of the Republic's constitution, the purpose of such violence had been to undermine the legitimacy of Britain's claim to Northern Ireland and prevent the province bedding down into the United Kingdom, in the hope of eventually creating an Irish Republic through slow British withdrawal.

The new Northern Irish politics saw Sinn Fein managing the country it had done so much to undermine. The clearest acknowledgement of this somersault came from one of Sinn Fein's senior figures, Francie

Molloy, in 1999: 'We are prepared to work an Executive. We are really prepared to administer British rule in Ireland for the foreseeable future. The very principle of partition is accepted and if the Unionists had that in 1920 they would have been laughing' (*The Sunday Times*, 28 March 2003).

Those republicans who had broken away in 1970 over recognition of a northern parliament, but had later come to run just such an institution, were perhaps the most upset about its suspension in 2002. Participation in institutions both north and south had provided Sinn Fein with tangible rewards. The biggest fear of Adams and his cohorts was that the struggle would end with nothing, as had previous republican campaigns. The all-island structure of Sinn Fein put it at greater advantage than all others on the island, enabling possible places in government north and south and giving the impression of momentum in respect of republican objectives. Political violence ceased to have utility for Sinn Fein as electoralism came to dominate the republican movement. The new politics raised uncomfortable questions for the few republicans who cared to dwell on the past. An obvious question was the purpose of the IRA's war after the Sunningdale Agreement. In response republicans could (legitimately) claim that they had gained equality for nationalists through the 'cutting edge' of the IRA; on its own the SDLP could not have achieved such sweeping reforms in Northern Ireland. The pursuit of equality was, after all, a fundamental republican aim. Few in the movement, however, had been aware that they were engaged in a war solely to reform Northern Ireland.

For adherents to traditional forms of republicanism, mandates and consent are unimportant, subordinate to the vanguardism of 1916, 1956–62 and 1970–97. Yet with support for armed struggle apparently at its lowest for decades, will the tradition of physical force disappear? There is some very tentative evidence that it has just enough support to survive. In autumn 2002, when admittedly there was considerable dissatisfaction with the outworking of the GFA, 1.5 per cent of the population of Northern Ireland thought that Republican Sinn Fein, linked to the Continuity IRA, best represented their views and a further 1.3 per cent supported the 32 County Sovereignty Committee, linked to the Real IRA (BBC Northern Ireland Hearts and Minds Poll, 12 November 2002, www.news.bbb.co.uk/1/hi/northern_ireland). The combined figure of 2.8 per cent appears tiny, but it is larger than the percentages that gave the Women's Coalition and the Progressive Unionist Party representation in the Assembly after the 1998 election. Moreover nationalist support for republican ultras amounted to 7.1 per cent, a surprisingly high figure considering it was only four years since the carnage of the Omagh bombing. Given people's tendency to give socially acceptable answers to survey questions the total might be considered strikingly large; other 'sneaking regarders' might be added. Nonetheless the figure is way below the third of the nationalist vote acquired by Sinn Fein when it entered electoral politics in 1982. Sinn Fein's claim that such micro groups have no mandate is of course true, if amounting to cant by overlooking the absence of a mandate for armed republicans from 1970–98, when the SDLP dominated the nationalist vote.

Successful implementation of the GFA would probably extinguish the very limited support for republican ultras, but a political vacuum could ensure that fundamental republicanism is kept alive. The ultras' military campaign, insofar as it has been maintained since the Omagh bombing, appears to be in disarray, amid infiltration, dissent and imprisonment. The jailing of the former Real IRA leader Michael McKevitt in August 2003 was just one of a series of setbacks. Republican ultras are incapable of launching a sustained insurrection campaign against British rule in Ireland. This, however, perhaps misses the point that, since the mid 1970s, the purpose of political violence has been to stop the 'state' of Northern Ireland embedding, an obvious risk for republicans given Sinn Fein's co-option into the structures of governance. The ultras hope that violence will highlight the abnormality of the state and perpetuate the perception of Northern Ireland as a failed political entity. However they are pitted against the most formidable range of forces ever assembled against the physical force tradition, devoid of the succour that came from the Irish Republic's constitutional claim to the north, abandoned (again) by erstwhile colleagues, infiltrated by the security forces and internally divided.

The failure of republicans to end partition during the twentieth century has shown little sign of being reversed under the new Northern Irish politics of the twenty-first century. For nationalists too, the GFA, whilst clearly popular in giving nationalists a genuine part in the running of Northern Ireland, contained little in terms of an all-island dimension. Strand two of the deal could have been much stronger, but instead the cross-border dimension was constrained and minimal. If a section of unionism remains reluctant to accept a palpable constitutional victory, failure to implement the agreement could usefully be followed by a period of more determined binationalism. Although unlikely, this would more accurately reflect the long-term aspirations of the people of the island, beyond the limited exercise of the 1998 GFA referendum. Joint British–Irish authority over the north – in which the Irishness of the growing nationalist population (a majority in substantial parts of the province) would be properly reflected by dynamic all-island bodies, rather than superficial 'identity politics' – might offer a really new Northern Irish politics.

Bibliography

Acheson, N. and A. Williamson (eds) (1995) *Voluntary Action and Social Policy in Northern Ireland* (Avebury: Aldershot).

Adams, G. (1995) *Free Ireland. Towards a Lasting Peace* (Dingle: Brandon).

Adams, G. (1998) Presidential address to Sinn Fein *Ard Fheis*, RDS Dublin, April.

Adams, G. (2001) Speech to Conference of Dublin Sinn Fein members, March.

Adamson, I. (1974) *Cruithin: The Ancient Kindred* (Newtownards: Nosmada).

Alcock, A. (2001) 'From Conflict to Agreement in Northern Ireland: Lessons from Europe', in J. McGarry (ed.), *Northern Ireland in a Divided World* (Oxford: Oxford University Press), pp. 159–80.

Alliance Party of Northern Ireland (2000) *Centre Forward: Alliance Leading the Way* (Belfast: APNI).

Alliance Party (2004) *Agenda for Democracy: Alliance Party Proposals for the Review of the Agreement* (Belfast: Alliance Party).

Anderson, J. (1998) 'Rethinking National Problems in a Transnational Context', in D. Miller (ed.), *Rethinking Northern Ireland* (London: Longman), pp. 125–45.

Arthur, P. (2000) *Special Relationships: Britain, Ireland and the Northern Ireland Problem* (Blackstaff: Belfast).

Arthur, P. (1992) 'The Brooke Initiative', *Irish Political Studies*, vol. 7, pp. 111–15.

Arthur, P. (2002) 'The transformation of republicanism', in J. Coakley (ed.), *Changing Shades of Orange and Green* (Dublin: UCD Press), pp. 84–94.

Arthur, P. and K. Jeffrey (1996) *Northern Ireland since 1968* (Oxford: Blackwell).

Aughey, A. (1989) *Under Siege: Ulster Unionism and the Anglo-Irish Agreement* (London: Hurst).

Aughey, A. (1997) 'The Character of Unionism', in P. Shirlow and M. McGovern (eds), *Who are 'The People'? Unionism, Protestantism and Loyalism in Northern Ireland* (London: Pluto), pp. 16–33.

Barnett, J. (2001) Speech to House of Lords, *Hansard*, cols 225–29, 7 November.

Bean, K. (1995) 'The New Departure? Recent Developments in Republican Strategy and Ideology', *Irish Studies Review*, vol. 10, pp. 2–6.

Bean, K. and M. Hayes, (eds) (2001) *Republican Voices* (Monaghan: Seesyu).

Bell, D. (1998) 'Modernising History. The Realpolitik of Heritage and Cultural Tradition in Northern Ireland', in D. Miller (ed.), *Rethinking Northern Ireland* (Harlow: Longman).

Best, M. (2001) *The Capabilities and Innovation Perspective: The Way Ahead in Northern Ireland* (Belfast: Northern Ireland Economic Council).

Bew, P. (2002) 'The State of the Peace Process', lecture to Salford University tour, Queen's University, Belfast, 30 November.

Bew, P., P. Gibbon and H. Patterson (1996) *Northern Ireland 1921–1996: Political Forces and Social Classes* (London: Serif).

Bew, P. and G. Gillespie (1996) *The Northern Ireland Peace Process 1993–1996: A Chronology* (London: Serif).

Bew, P., H. Patterson and P. Teague, (1997) *Between War and Peace. The Political Future of Northern Ireland* (London: Lawrence and Wishart).

Birnie, E. and D. Hitchens (2001) 'Chasing the Wind? Half a Century of Economic Strategy Documents in Northern Ireland', *Irish Political Studies*, vol. 16, pp. 1–29.

Bishop, P. and E. Mallie (1988) *The Provisional IRA* (London: Corgi).

Boyce, D. G. (1991) *Nationalism in Ireland* (London: Routledge).

Bradley, J. and J. Birnie (2001) *Can the Celtic Tiger Cross the Irish Border?* (Cork: Cork University Press).

Breen, S. (2001) 'Fast Operators', *Fortnight*, April p. 7.

Brown, K. and R. MacGinty (2003) 'Public Attitudes toward Partisan and Neutral Symbols in Post-Agreement Northern Ireland', *Global Studies in Culture and Power*, vol. 10, pp. 83–108.

Bruce, S. (1986) *God Save Ulster! The Religion and Politics of Paisleyism* (Oxford: Oxford University Press).

Bruce, S. (1994) *At the Edge of the Union* (Oxford: Oxford University Press).

Bruce, S. (2000) 'The DUP and the Peace Process', paper presented to the New Northern Irish Politics Seminar, University of Salford, November.

Bryan, D. (2000) *Orange Parades* (London: Pluto).

Bryan, D. (2001) 'Security, Justice and Equality', in R. Wilson (ed.), *Agreeing to Disagree? A Guide to the Northern Ireland Assembly* (London: HMSO).

Bryan, D. (2002) 'Drumcree. Marching towards Peace in Northern Ireland', in J. Neuheisser and S. Wolff (eds), *Peace at Last? The Impact of the Good Friday Agreement on Northern Ireland* (London: Berghahn), pp. 94–110.

Buckland, P. (1981) *A History of Northern Ireland* (Dublin: Gill and Macmillan).

Burns Report (2001) *Education for the 21st Century* (Belfast: HMSO).

Burrell, D. and A. Murie (1980) *Policy and Government in Northern Ireland: Lessons of Devolution* (Dublin: Gill and Macmillan).

Butler, D. (1991) 'Ulster unionism and British broadcasting journalism, 1924–89', in B. Rolston (ed.), *The Media and Northern Ireland: Covering the Troubles* (London: Macmillan).

Cairns, E. and J. Mallet, with C. Lewis and R. Wilson (2003) *Who are the Victims? Self-assessed Victimhood and the Northern Irish Conflict* (Belfast: Northern Ireland Statistics and Research Agency).

Carmichael, P. and C. Knox (2003) *Democracy Beyond the Northern Ireland Assembly, Devolution Policy Papers* (Birmingham: ESRC).

Coakley, J. (2001) 'The Belfast Agreement and the Republic of Ireland', in R. Wilford (ed.), *Aspects of the Belfast Agreement* (Oxford: Oxford University Press), pp. 223–44.

Coakley, J. (ed.) (2002) *Changing Shades of Orange and Green* (Dublin: UCD) pp. 84–94.

Coates, J. (2004) 'Reunification or the end of Republicanism? An electoral analysis of Sinn Fein's peace strategy in Ireland', unpublished MA thesis, University of Salford.

Cochrane, F. (1994) 'Any Takers? The Isolation of Northern Ireland', *Political Studies*, vol. 42, no. 3, pp. 378–95.

Cochrane, F. (1995) 'The Isolation of Northern Ireland', *Political Studies*, vol. 43, no. 3, pp. 497–505.

Cochrane, F. (2001) 'Unsung Heroes? The Role of Peace and Conflict Resolution Organizations in the Northern Ireland Conflict', in J. McGarry (ed.), *Northern Ireland and the Divided World* (Oxford: Oxford University Press), pp. 137–58.

Compton, P. (1991) 'Employment Differentials in Northern Ireland and Jobs Discrimination. A Critique', in P. Roche and B. Barton (eds), *The Northern Ireland Question. Myth and Reality* (Aldershot: Avebury).

Coogan, T. P. (1995) *The Troubles: Ireland's Ordeal 1966–1995 and the Search for Peace* (London: Hutchinson).

Coulter, C. (1997) 'The Culture of Contentment', in P. Shirlow and M. McGovern (eds), *Who are 'The People'? Unionism, Protestantism and Loyalism in Northern Ireland* (London: Pluto), pp. 114–39.

Coulter, C. (1999a) *Contemporary Northern Irish Society* (London: Pluto).

Coulter, C. (1999b) 'The Absence of Class Politics in Northern Ireland', *Capital and Class*, vol. 69, pp. 77–100.

Cox, M. (1998) 'Northern Ireland: the war that came in from the cold', *Irish Studies in International Affairs*, vol. 9, pp. 73–84.

Cox, M., A. Guelke and F. Stephen (eds) (2001) *A Farewell to Arms? From 'Long War' to 'Long Peace' in Northern Ireland* (Manchester: Manchester University Press).

Cox, W. Harvey (1985) 'Who wants a united Ireland?', *Government and Opposition*, vol. 20, pp. 29–47.

Criminal Justice Review Group (2000) *Review of the Criminal Justice System in Northern Ireland* (Belfast: HMSO).

Cronin, M. (1996) 'Defenders of the Nation? The Gaelic Athletic Association and Irish nationalist identity', *Irish Political Studies*, vol. 11, pp. 1–19.

Cronin, M. (2001) *A History of Ireland* (Basingstoke: Palgrave).

Cunningham, M. (2001) *British Government Policy in Northern Ireland* (Manchester: Manchester University Press).

Curtice, J. and L. Dowds (1999) 'Has Northern Ireland Really Changed?', paper presented to the Elections, Parties and Opinion Polls Specialist Group of the PSA, University College Northampton, September.

Darby, J. (1976) *Conflict in Northern Ireland* (Dublin: Gill and Macmillan).

Delanty, G. (1996) 'Habermas and Post National Identity. Theoretical Perspectives on the Conflict in Northern Ireland', *Irish Political Studies*, vol. 11, pp. 20–32.

Democratic Unionist Party (2003) *Towards a New Agreement* (Belfast: DUP).

Dempsey, G. (1999) 'The American Role in the Northern Ireland Peace Process', *Irish Political Studies*, vol. 14, pp. 104–17.

Department of Economic Development (1999) *Strategy 2010: Report by the Economic Development Strategy Review Group* (Belfast: DED).

Department of Education for Northern Ireland (2004) *The Costello Report* (Belfast: DENI).

Department of Education for Northern Ireland (2004) *Transfer Tests and New Post Primary Arrangements*, The Costello Report (Belfast: DENI).

Department of Enterprise, Trade and Investment (2003) *Labour Force Statistics* (Belfast: DETI, 25 April).

Department of Health, Social Services and Public Safety (2002) *Delivering Better Services*, White Paper, 45/02 (Belfast: HMSO).

Dixon, P. (1995) 'Internationalization and Unionist Isolation: A Response to Fergal Cochrane', *Political Studies*, vol. 43, no. 3, pp. 497–505.

Dixon, P. (2001) *Northern Ireland: the Politics of War and Peace* (Basingstoke: Palgrave).

Dixon, P. (2003) 'CONsociationalism – why the Good Friday Agreement is NOT consociational', paper presented to the American Political Science Association Annual Conference, Philadelphia, August.

Dowds, L. (2001) 'Public Attitudes and Identity: Devolution Monitoring Programme Northern Ireland Report' (London: University College London, Constitution Unit, May).

Elliott, S. (1997) 'The Northern Ireland Forum/Entry to Negotiations Election 1996', *Irish Political Studies*, vol. 12, pp. 111–22.

Elliott, S. (1999) 'The Referendum and Assembly Elections in Northern Ireland', *Irish Political Studies*, vol. 14, pp. 138–49.

Elliott, S. and W. Flackes (1999) *Northern Ireland: A Political Directory* (Belfast: Blackstaff).

Ellison, G. and J. Smyth (1999) *The Crowned Harp: Policing Northern Ireland* (London: Pluto).

English, R. (2003) *Armed Struggle* (London: Macmillan).

Evans, G. (ed.) (1999) *The End of Class Politics? Class Voting in Comparative Context* (Oxford: Oxford University Press).

Evans, G. and B. O'Leary (1999) 'Northern Irish Voters and the British–Irish Agreement: Foundations of a Stable Consociational Settlement', paper presented to the Elections, Parties and Opinion Polls Annual Conference of the PSA, University College Northampton, September.

Evans, J. and J. Tonge (2003) 'The Future of the "Radical Centre" in Northern Ireland after the Good Friday Agreement', *Political Studies*, vol. 51, no. 1, pp. 26–50.

Evans, J., J. Tonge and G. Murray (2000) 'Constitutional Nationalism and Socialism in Northern Ireland: The Greening of the Social Democratic and Labour Party', in P. Cowley, D. Denver, A. Russell and L. Harrison (eds) *British Elections and Parties Review 10* (London: Frank Cass), pp. 117–32.

Farrell, M. (1980) *Northern Ireland: the Orange State* (London: Pluto).

Farrell, M. (1983) *Arming the Protestants: The Formation of the Ulster Special Constabulary and the Royal Ulster Constabulary, 1920–7* (London: Pluto).

Farren, S. (1996) 'The View from the SDLP: A Nationalist Approach to an Agreed Peace', *Oxford International Review*, vol. 7, no. 2, pp. 41–6.

Farry, S. and S. Neeson (1999) 'Beyond the band-aid approach: an Alliance Party perspective upon the Belfast Agreement', *Fordham International Law Journal*, vol. 22, no. 4, pp. 1221–49.

Feeney, B. (2002) *Sinn Fein: A Hundred Turbulent Years* (Dublin: O'Brien).

Fianna Fail (1995) 'The Nature of the Problem and the Principles Underlying its Resolution', submission to the Irish Forum for Peace and Reconciliation (Dublin: IFPR).

Finlay, F. (1998) *Snakes and Ladders* (Dublin: New Island Books).

Finlayson, A. (1999) 'Loyalist Political Identity After the Peace', *Capital and Class*, vol. 69, pp. 47–66.

Finnegan, R. (2002) 'Irish–American relations', in W. Crotty and D. Schmitt, *Ireland on the World Stage*, (Harlow: Longman), pp. 95–110.

Fisk, R. (1975) *The Point of No Return* (London: Andre Deutsch).

FitzGerald, G. (1992) *All in a Life* (Dublin: Gill and Macmillan).

Fraser, T. (2000) *Ireland in Conflict 1922–1993* (London: Routledge).

Gallagher, M. and M. Marsh (2002) *Days of Blue Loyalty: the politics of membership of the Fine Gael Party* (Dublin: PSAI Press).

Garvin, T. (1998) 'Patriots and republicans: an Irish evolution', in W. Crotty and E. Schmitt, *Ireland and the Politics of Change* (Harlow: Longman), pp. 144–55.

Gilland, K. and F. Kennedy (2002) 'Irish Political Studies Data Yearbook', *Irish Political Studies*.

Gillespie, G. (1998) 'The Sunningdale Agreement: lost opportunity or an agreement too far? *Irish Political Studies*, vol. 13, pp. 100–14.

Gilligan, C. (1998) 'Structure and Agency in the Northern Ireland Peace Process', paper presented to the Political Studies Association of the United Kingdom Annual Conference, University of Keele, April.

Gilligan, C. (2002) 'Identity as a Concept for Understanding the Peace Process', unpublished PhD thesis, University of Salford.

Goodman, J. (1996a) 'The Northern Ireland Question and European Politics', in P. Catterall and S. Dougall, *The Northern Ireland Question in British Politics* (London: Macmillan).

Goodman, J. (1996b) *Nationalism and Transnationalism: The National Conflict in Northern Ireland and European Integration* (Aldershot: Avebury).

Greaves, S. (2002) 'Transcending the State? Nationalists and European Integration in Northern Ireland', unpublished MSc thesis, London School of Economics and Political Science.

Greer, A. (1994) 'Policy Networks and State–Farmer Relations in Northern Ireland, 1921–72', *Political Studies*, vol. 42, no. 3, pp. 396–412.

Gudgin, G. and R. Breen (1994) *Ratios of Unemployment Rates as an Indicator of Fair Employment in Northern Ireland* (Belfast: Northern Ireland Economic Research Centre).

Guelke, A. (1998) 'Northern Ireland: international and north/south issues', in W. Crotty and D. Schmitt (eds) *Ireland and the Politics of Change* (Harlow: Longman).

Guelke, A. (2001) 'Northern Ireland: international and island status', in J. McGarry (ed.), *Northern Ireland and the Divided World* (Oxford: Oxford University Press), pp. 228–52.

Hamilton, A. and L. Moore (1995) 'Policing a Divided Society', in S. Dunn (ed.), *Facets of the Conflict in Northern Ireland* (London: St Martin's).

Harnden, T. (1999) *'Bandit Country': The IRA and South Armagh* (London: Hodder and Stoughton)

Harris, C. (2002) 'The evolution of consociationalism in Northern Ireland', unpublished PhD thesis, University College Cork.

Harvey, C. (2001) 'Human rights and equality', in R. Wilson (ed.), *Agreeing to Disagree? A Guide to the Northern Ireland Assembly* (Belfast: HMSO), pp. 103–12.

Hayes, B. and I. McAllister (1995) 'Social Class, Class Awareness and Political beliefs in Northern Ireland', *Economic and Social Review*, vol. 26, no. 4, pp. 1–18.

Hayes, B. and I. McAllister (1996) 'British and Irish Public Opinion towards the Northern Ireland problem', *Irish Political Studies*, vol. 16, pp. 61–82.

Hayes, B. and McAllister, I. (2000) 'Sowing Dragons' Teeth: Political Support for Paramilitarism in Northern Ireland', paper presented to the Political Studies Association of the United Kingdom Annual Conference, London School of Economics, April.

Hayes, B. and I. McAllister (2001) 'Who Voted for Peace? Public Support for the 1998 Good Friday Agreement', *Irish Political Studies*, vol. 16, pp. 73–93.

Hazleton, W. (1994) 'A Breed Apart. Northern Ireland's MPs at Westminster', *Journal of Legislative Studies*, vol. 1, no. 4, pp. 30–53.

Hazleton, W. (2001) 'Never the Sum of the Parts? The Politics of Implementing the Good Friday Agreement', paper presented to the Annual Conference of the Political Studies Association of Ireland, NUI Galway, November.

Heald, D. (2001) *Funding the Northern Ireland Assembly: Assessing the Options* (Belfast: Northern Ireland Economic Council).

Hennessey, T. (2000) *The Northern Ireland Peace Process: Ending the Troubles?* (Dublin: Gill and Macmillan).

Hirschman, A. (1970) *Exit, Voice and Loyalty* (Cambridge, Mass.: Harvard University Press).

HM Government (1972) *The Future of Northern Ireland* (London: HMSO).

HM Government (1973) *Northern Ireland Constitutional Politics*, Cmnd. 5259 (London: HMSO).

HM Government (1995) *Frameworks for the Future* (Belfast: HMSO).

Holland, J. (1996) 'Keeping Peace at Arm's Length', *Irish Post*, 2 March.

Horgan, J. and M. Taylor (1997a) 'The Provisional Irish Republican Army: Command and Functional Structure', *Terrorism and Political Violence*, vol. 9, no. 3, pp. 1–32.

Horgan, J. and M. Taylor (1997b) 'Proceedings of the Irish Republican Army General Army Convention, December 1969', *Terrorism and Political Vioence*, vol. 9, no. 4, pp. 151–8.

Horowitz, D. (1985) *Ethnic Groups in Conflict* (Berkeley, CA: University of California Press).

Horowitz, D. (2001) 'The Northern Ireland Agreement: Clear, Consociational and Risky', in J. McGarry (ed.), *Northern Ireland and the Divided World* (Oxford: Oxford University Press).

Hughes, J., C. Donnelly, D. Robertson and L. Dowds (2002) *Community Relations in Northern Ireland: The Long View*, policy paper, ESRC Devolution and Constitutional Change Programme (Birmingham: ESRC).

Hume, D. (1996) *The Ulster Unionist Party 1972–92* (Lurgan: Ulster Society).

Hunt Report (1969) *Report of the Advisory Committee on Police in Northern Ireland*, Cmnd 535 (Belfast: HMSO).

Independent Commission on Policing (1999) *A New Beginning: Policing in Northern Ireland*, The Patten Report (London: HMSO).

Irvin, C. and S. Byrne (2002) 'Economic Aid and its Role in the Peace Process', in J. Neuheiser and S. Wolff (eds), *Peace at Last? The Impact of the Good Friday Agreement on Northern Ireland* (Oxford: Berghann), pp. 132–52.

Irwin, C. (2002) *The People's Peace Process in Northern Ireland* (Basingstoke: Palgrave).

Irwin, C. (2003) 'Devolution and the State of the Northern Ireland Peace Process', *Global Review of Ethnopolitics*, vol. 2, nos 3–4, pp. 71–91.

Jackson, A. (1999) *Ireland 1798–1998: Politics and War* (Oxford: Blackwell).

Kearney, R. (1997) *Postnationalist Ireland* (London: Routledge).

Keating, M. (2001) 'Northern Ireland and the Basque Country', in J. McGarry (ed.), *Northern Ireland and the Divided World* (Oxford: Oxford University Press), pp. 181–208.

Kelly, M. and J. Doyle (2000) 'The Good Friday Agreement and electoral behaviour – an analysis of vote transfers under PR-STV in the Northern Ireland Assembly elections of 1982 and 1998', paper presented to the Annual Conference of the Political Studies Association of Ireland, University of Cork, October.

Kennedy, D. (1994) 'The European Union and the Northern Ireland Question', in B. Barton and P. Roche (eds), *The Northern Ireland Question: Perspectives and Policies* (Aldershot: Avebury).

Kennedy-Pipe, C. (1997) *The Origins of the Present Troubles in Northern Ireland* (Harlow: Longman).

Knox, C. (2001) 'A civil service and a civil society', in R. Wilson and J. Mullin (eds), *Agreeing to Disagree? A Guide to the Northern Ireland Assembly* (London: HMSO).

Knox, C. and J. Hughes (1995) 'Local Government and Community Relations', in S. Dunn (ed.), *Facets of the Conflict in Northern Ireland* (London: Macmillan).

Kymlicka, W. (1989) *Liberalism, Community and Culture* (Oxford: Oxford University Press).

Lambkin, B. (1996) *Opposition Religions Still?* (Aldershot: Avebury).

Laffan, B. and Payne, D. (2002) 'The EU in the Domestic: Interreg III and the Good Friday Institutions', *Irish Political Studies*, vol. 17, no. 2, pp. 74–96.

Laffan, M. (1999) *The Resurrection of Ireland: The Sinn Fein Party 1916–1923* (Cambridge: Cambridge University Press).

Laver, M. (2000) 'Coalitions in Northern Ireland: Preliminary Thoughts', programme for Government Conference, Belfast, June.

Leonard, A. (1999) 'The Alliance Party of Northern Ireland and Power-Sharing in a Divided World', unpublished MA thesis, University College Dublin.

Liera, F. (1994) *Los Vascos y la politica* (Bilbao: Universidad de la Pais).

Lijphart, A. (1977) *Democracy in Plural Societies: A Comparative Exploration* (New Haven, CT: Yale University Press).

Loughlin, J. (1995) *Ulster Unionism and British Political Identity since 1985* (London: Pinter).

MacCarthaigh, M. and K. Totten (2001) 'Irish Political Data 2000', *Irish Political Studies*, vol. 16, pp. 287–352.

MacGinty, R. (2003) 'Research Update', *Northern Ireland Social and Political Archive*, vol. 18, April.

MacGinty, R. and R. Wilford (2002) 'More Knowing than Knowledgeable: Attitudes towards Devolution', in A. Gray, K. Lloyd, P. Devine, G. Robinson and D. Heenan (eds), *Social Attitudes in Northern Ireland* (London: Pluto), pp. 5–21.

MacStiofain, S. (1975) *Memoirs of a Revolutionary* (Edinburgh: Gordon Cremonesi).

Mallie, E. and D. McKittrick (1996) *The Fight for Peace. The Secret Story behind the Irish Peace Process* (London: Heinemann).

McAllister, I. (2004) 'The Armalite and the ballot box: Sinn Fein's electoral strategy in Northern Ireland', *Electoral Studies*, vol. 21, no. 1, pp. 123–42.

McAllister, I. and B. Wilson (1978) 'Bi confessionalism in a confessional party system: the Northern Ireland Alliance Party', *Economic and Social Review*, vol. 9, no. 3, pp. 207–25.

McAuley, J. (2000) 'What's New about New Loyalism?', paper presented to the Elections, Public Opinion and Parties Annual Conference of the PSA, University of Edinburgh, September.

McAuley, J. (2002) 'The emergence of new loyalism', in J. Coakley (ed.), *Changing Shades of Orange and Green* (Dublin: UCD), pp. 106–22.

McAuley, J. and J. Tonge (2003) 'Over the Rainbow? Republican and Loyalist Cooperation in Northern Ireland since the Good Friday Agreement', *Etudes Irlandaises*, vol. 28, no. 1, pp. 177–96.

McCall, C. (1999) *Identity in Northern Ireland* (London: Macmillan).

McGarry, J. (ed.) (2001) *Northern Ireland and the Divided World* (Oxford: Oxford University Press).

McGarry, J. and B. O'Leary (1995) *Explaining Northern Ireland* (Oxford: Blackwell).

McGarry, J. and B. O'Leary (1999) *Policing Northern Ireland: Proposals for a New Start* (Belfast: Blackstaff).

McGough, S. (2003) 'British Policy in Northern Ireland in the Period Between 1912 and 1985', unpublished PhD thesis, University of Birmingham.

McGovern, M. (1997) 'The SDLP and the Peace Process', in C. Gilligan and J. Tonge (eds), *Peace or War? Understanding the Peace Process in Ireland* (Aldershot: Avebury), pp. 54–71.

McGurk, T. (2002) 'Time to lay down the Armalite', *Sunday Business Post*, 27 October.

McIntyre, A. (1995) 'Modern Irish Republicanism: The Product of British State Strategies', *Irish Political Studies*, vol. 10.

McIntyre, A. (2001) 'Modern Irish Republicanism and the Belfast Agreement: Chickens Coming Home to Roost or Turkeys Celebrating Christmas?' in R. Wilford (ed.), *Aspects of the Belfast Agreement* (Oxford: Oxford University Press), pp. 202–22.

McKittrick, D. and D. McVea (2001) *Making Sense of the Troubles* (London: Penguin).

McKittrick, D., S. Kelters, S. Feeney and C. Thornton (1999) *Lost Lives* (Edinburgh: Mainstream).

McLaughlin, M. (2000) 'Sinn Fein and the Peace Process', lecture to 'The New Northern Irish Politics' seminar series, University of Salford, November.

McNamara, K. (1992) *Oranges or Lemons? Should Labour Organise in Northern Ireland?* (Westminster).

McQuade, O. and J. Fagan (eds) (2002) *The Governance of Northern Ireland* (Moira: BMF/Lagan Consulting).

McVeigh, R. (1998) 'Is sectarianism racism? Theorising the racism/sectarianism interface', in D. Miller (ed.), *Rethinking Northern Ireland* (Harlow: Longman).

Meehan, E. (2000) '*Relations with the EU*'. *Devolution Monitoring Programme Northern Ireland Report* (London: University College London, Constitution Unit, May).

Meehan, E. (2001) 'The British–Irish Council', in R. Wilson and J. Mullin (eds), *Agreeing to disagree? A guide to the Northern Ireland Assembly* (London: HMSO).

Miller, D. (1998) *Rethinking Northern Ireland* (Harlow: Longman).

Mitchell, P. (2000) 'Vote transfers in Northern Ireland', paper presented to the Annual Conference of the Political Studies Association of Ireland, University College Cork, October.

Mitchell, P., B. O'Leary and G. Evans (2002) 'The 2001 Elections in Northern Ireland: Moderating "Extremists" and the Squeezing of the Moderates', *Representation*, vol. 39, no. 1, pp. 23–36.

Mitchell, P. and R. Wilford (eds) (1999) *Politics in Northern Ireland* (Oxford: Westview).

Moffat, C. (2001) 'Burns report passes the first test', *Fortnight*, vol. 400, November, p. 14.

Moloney, E. (2002) *A Secret History of the IRA* (London: Penguin).

Moloney, E. and A. Pollok (1986) *Paisley* (Dublin: Poolbeg).

Mooney, J. and M. O'Toole (2003) *Black Operations. The Secret War Against the Real IRA* (Ashbourne: Maverick House).

Murphy, A. and D. Armstrong (1994) *A Picture of the Catholic and Protestant Male Unemployed* (Belfast: Central Community Relations Council).

Murphy, R. and K. Totten (2000) 'Irish Political Data 2000', *Irish Political Studies*, vol. 15, pp. 249–35.

Murray, G. (1998) *John Hume and the SDLP* (Dublin: Irish Academic Press).

Nelson, S. (1984) *Ulster's Uncertain Defenders* (Belfast: Appletree).

New Ulster Political Research Group (1987) *Common Sense* (Belfast: NUPRG).

Northern Ireland Affairs Committee (1998) *Third Report*, House of Commons 1997/98, para. 35.

Northern Ireland Life and Times Survey (1999, 2000, 2001) www.ark.ac.uk.

Northern Ireland Office (2000) *Report of the Independent Commission on Policing for Northern Ireland, Implementation Plan* (Belfast: NIO).

Northern Ireland Office (2001) *The Community and the Police Service* (Belfast: NIO).

Northern Ireland Women's Coalition (2003) *Common Cause. The Story of the Northern Ireland Women's Coalition* (Belfast: NIWC).

O'Clery, C. (1996) *The Greening of the White House* (Dublin: Gill and Macmillan).

O'Leary, B. (1997) 'The Conservative Stewardship of Northern Ireland 1979–97: Sound-Bottomed Contradications or Slow Learning?', *Political Studies*, vol. 45, no. 4, pp. 663–76.

O'Leary, B. (1999) 'The 1998 British–Irish Agreement: Consociation Plus', *Scottish Affairs*, vol. 26, pp. 1–22.

O'Leary, B. (2001) 'The Belfast Agreement and the Labour Government', in A. Seldon (ed.), *The Blair Effect: The Blair Government 1997–2001* (London: Little, Brown), pp. 449–88.

O'Leary, B. and G. Evans (2001) 'Northern Irish Voters and the British–Irish Agreement: Foundations of a Stable Consociational Settlement?', *Political Quarterly*, vol. 71, pp. 1–24.

O'Leary, B. and J. McGarry (1993) *The Politics of Antagonism: Understanding Northern Ireland* (London: Athlone).

O'Malley, P. (2001) 'Northern Ireland and South Africa: Hope and History at a Crossroads', in J. McGarry (ed.), *Northern Ireland and the Divided World* (Oxford: Oxford University Press).

O'Reilly, C. (2002) 'The Politics of Culture in Northern Ireland', in J. Neuheiser and S. Wolff (eds), *Peace at Last? The Impact of the Good Friday Agreement on Northern Ireland* (London: Berghann).

Patterson, H. (1997) *The Politics of Illusion. A Political History of the IRA* (London: Serif).

Pennings, P. (1999) 'The utility of party and institutional indicators of change in consociational democracies', in K. Luther and K. Deschouwer (eds), *Party Elites in Divided Societies* (London: Routledge), pp. 20–40.

Pimlott, B. (1992) *Harold Wilson* (London: HarperCollins).

Police Authority for Northern Ireland (1997) *Listening to the Community: Working with the RUC. The Work of the Police Authority 1 July 1995 to 31 March 1997* (Belfast: PANI).

Police Service of Northern Ireland (2002) *Report of Chief Constable, 2001/02* (Belfast: PSNI).

Police Service of Northern Ireland (2003) *Report of Chief Constable, 2002/3* (Belfast: PSNI).

Pollak, A. (ed.) (1993) *A Citizen's Inquiry: the Opsahl Report on Northern Ireland* (Dublin: Lilliput).

Porter, N. (1996) *Rethinking Unionism. An Alternative Vision for Northern Ireland* (Belfast: Blackstaff).

Porter, N. (2003) *The Elusive Quest. Reconciliation in Northern Ireland* (Belfast: Blackstaff).

Price, J. (1995) 'Political Change and the Protestant Working Class', *Race and Class*, vol. 31, no. 1, pp. 57–69.

Pulzer, P. (1967) *Political Representation and Elections in Britain* (London: Allen and Unwin).

Riddell, P. (2003) *Hug Them Close* (London: Politicos).

Rolston, B. (1998) 'What's wrong with multiculturalism?', in D. Miller (ed.), *Rethinking Northern Ireland* (Harlow: Longman), pp. 253–74.

Rooney, K. (1998) 'Institutionalising Division', *Fortnight*, June, pp. 21–2.

Rose, R. (1971) *Governing without Consensus: An Irish Perspective* (London: Faber).

Royal Ulster Constabulary (1999) *Report of the Chief Constable 1998/99* (Belfast: RUC).

Ruane, J. and J. Todd (1998) 'Peace Processes and Communalism in Northern Ireland', in W. Crotty and D. Schmitt, *Ireland and the Politics of Change* (London: Longman), pp. 178–94.

Ruane, J. and J. Todd (eds) (1999) *After the Good Friday Agreement: Analysing Political Change in Northern Ireland* (Dublin: UCD).

Ryan, M. (1994) *War and Peace in Ireland: Britain and the IRA in the New World Order* (London: Pluto).

Scott, R. and M. O'Reilly (1992) *Exports of Northern Ireland Manufacturing Companies* (Belfast: Northern Ireland Economic Research Centre).

Shirlow, P. (2003) 'Who Fears to Speak? Fear, mobility and ethno-sectarianism in North Belfast', paper presented to the ESRC Northern Ireland Research Group seminar, Belfast, May.

Sinn Fein (1992) *Towards a Lasting Peace in Ireland* (Dublin: Sinn Fein).

Sinn Fein (1998) *Policing in Transition: Ard Chomhairle Position Paper* (Dublin: Sinn Fein).

Sinn Fein (1999) *Sinn Fein and the European Union: Draft Policy Discussion Paper* (Dublin: Sinn Fein Ard Chomhairle).

Sinn Fein (2001) *Westminster Election Manifesto 2001* (Belfast: Sinn Fein).

Sinn Fein (2003a) *The Private Finance Initiative* (Dublin: Sinn Fein).

Sinn Fein (2003b) *'Educate that you may be free': Sinn Fein's proposals for an Irish Education System in the 21st Century* (Dublin: Sinn Fein).

Sinn Fein (2003c) *Sinn Fein and the European Union*, discussion document (Dublin: Sinn Fein Ard Chomhairle).

Sinn Fein (2004) *Ard Fheis 2004: Motions* (Dublin: Sinn Fein).

Sinnott, R. (1998) 'Centrist politics make modest but significant progress: cross-community transfers were low', *Irish Times*, 29 June.

Sinnott, R. (1999) 'Interpreting electoral mandates in Northern Ireland: the 1998 referendum', paper presented to the CREST/QUB Conference on 'Agreeing to disagree? The voters of Northern Ireland', Queen's University, Belfast, June.

Smith, D. and G. Chambers (1990) *Inequality in Northern Ireland* (Oxford: Clarendon Press).

Smooha, S. (2001) 'The Tenability of Partition as a Mode of Conflict Regulation: Comparing Israel with Palestine–Land of Israel', in J. McGarry (ed.), *Northern Ireland and the Divided World* (Oxford: Oxford University Press), pp. 309–35.

Social Democratic and Labour Party (1992) *Agreeing New Political Structures: The SDLP's Submission to the Brooke-Mayhew Talks* (Belfast: SDLP).

Storey, E. (2002) *Traditional Roots* (Dublin: Columba).

Tannam, E. (1996) 'The European Union and Business Cross-Border Cooperation: The Case of Northern Ireland and the Republic of Ireland', *Irish Political Studies*, vol. 11, pp. 103–29.

Taylor, R. (2001) 'Northern Ireland: Consociation or Social Transformation?', in J. McGarry (ed.), *Northern Ireland and the Divided World* (Oxford: Oxford University Press), pp. 36–52.

Tessler, M. (1994) *A History of the Israeli–Palestinian Conflict* (Bloomington: London).

Todd, J. (1987) 'Two Traditions in Unionist Political Culture', *Irish Political Studies*, vol. 2.

Todd, J. (1999) 'Nationalism, Republicanism and the Good Friday Agreement', in J. Todd and J. Ruane (eds), *After the Good Friday Agreement: Analysing Political Change in Northern Ireland* (Dublin: UCD).

Tonge, J. (2000) 'From Sunningdale to the Good Friday Agreement: Creating Devolved Government in Northern Ireland', *Contemporary British History*, vol. 14, no. 3, pp. 39–60.

Tonge, J. (2002) *Northern Ireland: Conflict and Change* (London: Pearson).

Tonge, J. and J. Evans (2000) 'Party Attitudes to Devolution in Northern Ireland', paper presented to the Annual Conference of the Political Studies Association of the United Kingdom, University of Manchester, April.

Tonge, J. and J. Evans (2001a) 'The Future of the Radical Centre in Northern Ireland after the Good Friday Agreement', paper presented to the Annual Conference of the Political Studies Association of Ireland, NUI Galway, November.

Tonge, J. and J. Evans (2001b) 'Northern Ireland's Third Tradition(s): The Alliance Party Surveyed', in J. Tonge, L. Bennie, D. Denver and L. Harrison (eds), *British Elections and Parties Review 11* (London: Frank Cass), pp. 104–18.

Tonge, J. and J. Evans (2001c) 'Faultlines in Unionism: Division and Dissent within the Ulster Unionist Council', *Irish Political Studies*, vol. 16, pp. 111–31.

Tonge, J. and J. Evans (2002) 'Party Members and the Good Friday Agreement', *Irish Political Studies*, vol. 17, no. 2, pp. 59–73.

Trimble, D. (2002) Leadership address to the Annual Conference of the Ulster Unionist Party, Belfast.

Ulster Unionist Party (1995) *Response to Frameworks for the Future* (Belfast: UUP).

Ulster Unionist Party (1999) *A Response to 'A New Beginning: Policing in Northern Ireland'. The Report of the Independent Commission on Policing for Northern Ireland*, The Patten Report (Belfast: UUP).

Ulster Unionist Party (2002) *'Our Children, Our Future': Response to the Report by the Post-Primary Review Body – The Burns Report* (Belfast: UUP).

Ulster Unionist Party (2003) *Manifesto 2003* (Belfast: UUP).

Urban, M. (1992) *Big Boy's Rules: the SAS and the Secret Struggle Against the IRA* (London: Faber and Faber).

Vannais, J. (2001) 'Postcards from the Edge', *Irish Political Studies*, vol. 16, pp. 133–60.

Walker, G. (2001) 'The British–Irish Council', in R. Wilford (ed.), *Aspects of the Belfast Agreement* (Oxford: Oxford University Press), pp. 129–41.

White, B. (1984) *John Hume: Statesman of the Troubles* (Belfast: Blackstaff).

Whyte, J. (1983) 'How much discrimination was there under the unionist regime 1921–68?', in T. Gallagher and J. O'Connell (eds), *Contemporary Irish Studies* (Manchester: Manchester University Press).

Wilford, R. (ed.) (2001a) *Aspects of the Good Friday Agreement* (Oxford: Oxford University Press).

Wilford, R. (2001b) *'The Assembly': Devolution Monitoring Programme Northern Ireland Report* (London: University College London, Constitution Unit, May), pp. 12–27.

Wilford, R. and S. Elliott (1999) '"Small Earthquake in Chile": The First Northern Ireland Affairs Select Committee', *Irish Political Studies*, vol. 14, pp. 23–42.

Wilson, J. (1997) 'From the Beltway to Belfast: The Clinton Administration, Sinn Fein and the Northern Ireland Peace Process', *New Hibernian Review*, vol. 1, no. 3, pp. 23–39.

Wilson, R. (2001) *'Finance': Devolution Monitoring Programme, Northern Ireland Report* (London: University College London, Constitution Unit, May).

Wilson, R. and J. Mullin (2001) (eds) *Agreeing to Disagree? A Guide to the Northern Ireland Assembly* (London: HMSO).

Wilson, R. and R. Wilford (2003) *Northern Ireland: A Route to Stability?*, ESRC Devolution and Constitutional Change Programme Paper (Birmingham: ESRC).

Wilson, T. (ed.) (1995) *Ulster under Home Rule* (Oxford: Oxford University Press).

Wilson,T (ed.) (1989) *Ulster: Conflict and Consent* (Oxford: Blackwell).

Wolff, S. (2002a) 'The Peace Process in Northern Ireland Since 1998: Success or Failure of Post-Agreement Reconstruction?', *Civil Wars*, vol. 5, no. 1, pp. 87–116.

Wolff, S. (2002b) 'Introduction: From Sunningdale to Belfast, 1973–98', in J. Neuheiser and S. Wolff (eds), *Peace at Last? The Impact of the Good Friday Agreement on Northern Ireland* (Oxford: Berghahn), pp. 1–24.

Woods, J. (2001) 'The Civic Forum', in R. Wilson and J. Mullin (eds) *Agreeing to Disagree? A Guide to the Northern Ireland Assembly* (London: HMSO), pp. 79–84.

Index

Act of Union 1800   10
Adair, Johnny   62
Adams, Gerry   20, 119, 121, 227, 241, 242, 244, 250, 251
  see also Hume–Adams Dialogue; Sinn Fein
African National Congress (ANC)   244, 250–2
Ahern, Bertie   261–2
Alliance Party of Northern Ireland (APNI)   24, 34, 40, 82–98, 100, 145, 191
  and the Assembly   85, 127, 130, 142, 143, 155
  and the GFA   86, 90, 94
  and the Patten Report   227
Ancient Order of Hibernians   193, 207
Anglo–Irish Agreement 1985   25–8, 31, 52, 103
Anglo–Irish Governmental Conference   25
Anglo–Irish Treaty 1921   12, 37, 120
Armitage, Pauline   124, 127

Barnett Formula   154
Basque Region   245–9
Beare, Nora   125
Best Report   155
Blair, Tony   225, 262
Bloody Sunday   16, 22, 239, 244
Boal, Desmond   19
British Army   16, 17, 22, 25, 206, 220, 244–5
British–Irish Council   169, 171
Brooke, Peter   28
Burns Report   157–8
Bush, George W.   243

Carey, Hugh   240
Carron, Owen   19

Catalans   249–50
Central Community Relations Unit (CCRU)   214
Civic Forum   131, 202–5, 215
Clinton, Bill   241, 242
Community Relations Council (CRC)   214, 215
consociationalism   2, 4–5, 30, 35–46, 84–86, 100–1, 188–92
Costello Report   145
Cultural Traditions Group   214, 216
Cyprus   246

De Brun, Bairbre   141, 156, 170
decommissioning   43–4, 46, 54, 116, 120, 127, 151, 153, 242, 250
Democratic Unionist Party (DUP)   2, 60, 61, 63, 137, 153, 172, 194, 199, 259
  and the Assembly   124, 126, 150, 204
  and the Assembly election 2003   42, 45, 67
  and the EU   183
  formation   14
  and the GFA   31, 37, 56–7, 62
  and the Patten Report   226
Devalera, Eammon   120
Devlin, Paddy   108–9
D'Hondt   44, 146, 151, 152, 153, 258, 259, 260
Dickson, Brice   220
District Policing Partnership Boards (DPPB)   223, 224, 228, 233
Donaldson, Jeffrey   125
Donlon, Sean   240
Downing Street Declaration   20, 30
Drumm, Jimmy   19
Durkan, Mark   152, 154, 160

Easter Rising 1916   11
Elections
   Assembly Election 1973   24
   General Election 1983   25
   Forum Election 1996   33
   Assembly Election 1998   34, 210
   Assembly Election 2003   42
Ervine, David   198
ETA   246–9
European Court of Human Rights   220
European Union   173–85

Fair Employment Acts   200–1
Farren, Sean   157
Faulkner, Brian   41
Federal Bureau of Investigations (FBI)
   243
Fianna Fail   26, 27, 261
Fine Gael   26, 27, 47, 238
Finucane, Patrick   220
Fitt, Gerry   107
Fitzgerald, Garret   26, 47, 238
Force Research Unit   220
Ford, David   34, 100, 161
Foster, Arlene   125
Framework Document   40, 60
Free Presbyterian Church   14, 62, 194
Friends of Ireland (FOI)   241
Friends of Irish Freedom Group   245
Friends of Sinn Fein   245

Gaelic Athletic Association   209
Garda Siochana   226, 227, 232
Good Friday Agreement (GFA)   30,
   31–58, 59, 82, 128–9, 130, 136, 138,
   163–4, 169, 175–6, 188–92, 206–7,
   210–11, 213, 217, 234–5, 242, 255–65
   see also Civic Forum; Northern
      Ireland Assembly and Executive;
      North–South Ministerial Council;
      Patten Report; Sectarianism
Goulding, Cathal   15
Government of Ireland Act 1920   11–12
Griffith, Arthur   120

Haas, Richard   243
Haughey, Charles   26
Hayes, Maurice   216

Herri Batastuna   247–8
Hogg, Douglas   220
Holy Cross School   213
Home Rule bills   10
Hume–Adams Dialogue   20, 28, 109
Hume, John   20, 34, 50, 104, 228, 239–40
   see also Hume–Adams Dialogue;
      SDLP
Hutchinson, Billy   131, 204

International Fund for Ireland (IFI)   176
internment   22
Irish Civil War   11
Irish National Caucus (INC)   240, 241
Irish National Liberation Army (INLA)
   17
Irish Northern Aid Committee
   (NORAID)   239, 241, 244–5
Irish People's Liberation Organization
   (IPLO)   17
Irish Republican Army (IRA)   11, 12
   ceasefires   20, 25, 112, 115, 257
   Continuity IRA   113, 118, 243, 263
   Official IRA   15, 16, 250
   operations   21, 23, 26, 115
   Provisional IRA   14, 16, 17, 21, 22,
      30, 37, 104, 115–16, 121, 126,
      150–1, 188, 191, 206, 232, 244,
      261, 263
   Real IRA   118, 119, 188, 243, 263, 264
   Stormont spy ring   59, 60, 126, 229

Joint Ministerial Committee on
   Devolution   169

Kelly, Gerry   227
Kennedy, Ted   239, 240
Kinner, Eddie   131

Lambert, Brian   220
Lennon, Neil   209

MacBride, Sean   19
MacBride Principles   200, 240
Magee, Roy   52
Major, John   52
Mallon, Seamus   23, 43, 152, 160, 228
Mandelson, Peter   43

Mason, Roy 19
Mayhew, Patrick 29
McCartney, Robert 61, 91
McLaughlin, Mitchel 51
McGuinness, Martin 131, 157–9
McKevitt, Michael 243, 264
McStiofain, Sean 15
Mitchell, George 33
Molloy, Francie 263
Molyneaux, James 27
Morrow, Maurice 159
Moynihan, Daniel 240
Murphy, Conor 139

Nelson, Rosemary 220
New Ireland Forum 26
New Ulster Political Research Group 28
Northern Ireland Assembly
    1982 25
    1998 43, 44–5, 51, 60, 123–48, 170
Northern Ireland Assembly Executive
    149–62
Northern Ireland Civil Rights Association
    (NICRA) 12–13
Northern Ireland Civil Service 214
Northern Ireland Human Rights
    Commission (NIHRC) 53–4
Northern Ireland Labour Party 103
Northern Ireland Unionist Party 61
Northern Ireland Women's Coalition
    (NIWC) 44, 91, 98–9, 127, 130,
    202–4, 263
North–South Language Body 165
North–South Ministerial Council
    (NSMC) 50, 59, 149–50, 153, 163,
    164–5, 167–9, 171, 174, 178

O'Bradaigh, Ruairi 15, 20
O'Neill, Terence 12, 13, 14
O'Neill, Tip 240
Opsahl Commission 220
Orange Order 30, 65, 70–1, 73, 113, 190,
    193, 204, 205, 207, 208–9, 226

Paisley, Rev. Ian 14, 28, 46, 66, 174, 183
    see also Democratic Unionist Party
Paisley, Ian Jr. 226

Palestinian Liberation Organization
    (PLO) 244, 252–3
Partido Nacionalista Vasco 248–9
Patten Report 147, 219, 222–35
Peace People 215
Pearse, Padraig 16
Plantation of Ulster 9
policing legislation 231, 232
Police Service of Northern Ireland
    (PSNI) 219, 227, 228, 235–6
Prior, James 25
Progressive Unionist Party (PUP) 33,
    37, 62, 64, 77, 131, 132–4, 175,
    197–200, 203–4, 263
Protestant Unionist Party 14, 61

Qadaffi, Col. Muammar 245

Reid, Fr Alec 20
Reid, John 128
Republican Sinn Fein 20, 119, 263
Royal Ulster Constabulary 17, 24,
    219–25
Rupert, David 243

Sands, Bobby 19, 119
Sands-McKevitt, Bernadette 53, 118
sectarianism 190–5, 200–2, 207, 209,
    212–14, 219
Shipley-Dalton, Duncan 130
Sinn Fein 2, 10, 11, 36, 109, 111–21, 152,
    153, 166–7, 173, 197, 198–200, 205,
    214, 259
    and the Assembly 126, 129–30, 131–4,
        142, 143, 155, 203–4
    and Basque nationalism 247–9
    and electoralism 19–20, 33, 112, 115,
        121
    and the EU 183
    and the GFA 38, 40, 46, 51, 53, 117,
        262–3
    and the hunger strikes 19
    and Irish America 244–5
    and the Orange Order 208–9
    and the Patten Report 226, 227–9
    Towards a Lasting Peace 109, 115
Smyth, Rev. Martin 67–70, 71

Social Democratic and Labour Party
    (SDLP)   2, 103–14, 152, 182, 259
  and abstentionism   24
  and the Anglo–Irish Agreement   104
  and the Assembly   129–30, 132, 142,
    155
  and the Assembly election 2003   109
  and Basque nationalism   248
  and the EU   183, 184
  formation   18, 103
  and the GFA   40, 41, 106–8, 110–11
  and Irish America   239–40
  and the Patten Report   228
Soderberg, Nancy   241
Special European Union Funding
    Programme Body (SEUPB)
    178–81
Sunningdale   23–5, 32–3, 39, 50, 52, 263
Stalker, John   220
Stevens Report   18, 220

Thirty-Two County Sovereignty
    Committee   *see* Real IRA
Tone, Wolfe   9
Trimble, David   12, 43, 68, 71, 127, 152,
    153, 160, 172, 214, 260
  see also Ulster Unionist Party

Ulster Defence Association (UDA)   18,
    28, 62

Ulster Defence Regiment   17
Ulster Democratic Party (UDP)   33, 62
Ulster Freedom Fighters   18, 62
Ulster Resistance   28
Ulster Volunteer Force (UVF)   18, 62,
    188, 191
Ulster Unionist Labour Association   65
Ulster Unionist Party (UUP)   2, 59,
    60, 64, 65, 124, 137, 145, 152, 172,
    242
  and the Assembly   130, 143
  and the Assembly election 2003   42, 67
  and the EU   182
  and the GFA   37, 40, 41, 42, 51, 60, 76,
    144
  and integrationism   78–9
  and the Orange Order   70–1, 73, 74,
    77
  and the Patten Report   225–6
  and the Ulster Unionist Council
    (UUC)   63, 65–6, 67, 124, 226
Ulsterization   25
Union First   66
United Kingdom Unionist Party
    (UKUP)   37, 61
United States State Department   239, 241

Weir, Peter   124
Whitelaw, William   22
Wilson, Harold   14, 22